Volume 5 Number 2 2010

Corpora

Corpus-based
Language Learning,
Language Processing
and Linguistics

Edinburgh University Press

Contents

Modern Diachronic Corpus-Assisted Discourse Studies (MD-CADS) on UK newspapers: an overview of the project

Alan Partington[1]

Abstract

This edition of *Corpora* contains one of the first ever collections of papers pertaining to the nascent discipline of Modern Diachronic Corpus-Assisted Discourse Studies (MD-CADS). This discipline is characterised by the novelty both of its methodology and the topics it is, consequently, in a position to treat. It employs relatively large corpora of a parallel structure and content from different moments of contemporary time (in this case the SiBol corpora, see below) in order to track changes in modern language usage but also social, cultural and political changes as reflected in language.

In this overview, I will attempt to give an idea of what both corpus-assisted discourse studies (CADS) and MD-CADS involve, to provide some information about the newspaper corpora we employ, and to outline methodologies commonly followed in this area, including those employed by the other contributors to this issue. I will also present two sets of practical analyses. The first is inductive and bottom-up, derived from a close analysis of the comparative keywords generated by comparing the lists of items from the two parallel corpora from different time periods; the aim is to uncover changes over time both in language and in what social, political and cultural issues were considered worthy of attention. The second is more intuitive and hypothesis-driven; the hypothesis is that an examination of a certain term, namely *moral panic*, can shed some light on which issues writers thought did *not* merit all the attention they were receiving. I will conclude with brief sketches of the other papers in this issue, and reflections on the relevance of MD-CADS in both language research and teaching.

[1] Dipartimento di Lingue e Lettere Straniere Moderne, University of Bologna, via Cartoleria 5, 40124 Bologna, Italy.
Correspondence to: Alan Partington,   *e-mail*: alanscott.partington@unibo.it

Corpora 2010 Vol. 5 (2): 83–108
DOI: 10.3366/E1749503210000407
© Edinburgh University Press
www.eupjournals.com/cor

1. Diachronic corpus-based studies of English language

Diachronic corpus linguistics is, of course, nothing new. Extensive use has been made of the celebrated Helsinki Diachronic Corpus of English Texts, which contains about 1.5 million words of English in the form of 400 text samples dating from the eighth to the eighteenth centuries. It is divided into three main periods, namely, Old, Middle and Early Modern English.

Other important diachronic collections are the Lampeter Corpus of early Modern English, incorporating over one million words of pamphlet literature between 1640 and 1740 and the ARCHER corpus containing texts in both British and American English from 1650 to 1990 (McEnery *et al.*, 2006: 65). Whilst it is not strictly a corpus, of course, the Oxford English Dictionary on CD-ROM, which contains many thousands of examples of authentic uses of words throughout the development of the language, is a very valuable asset in diachronic studies. Corpora of these types are employed to track developments in the evolution of language, both lexical and grammatical.

Somewhat more germane to the topic of this paper is the work of Mair *et al.* who have conducted several studies comparing the language contained in the LOB (Lancaster–Oslo–Bergen) and FLOB (Freiburg–Lancaster–Oslo–Bergen) corpora, which they constructed themselves. The first of these was compiled using texts from the early 1960s,[2] originally as a British mirror to the slightly earlier US Brown Corpus. Both of these corpora contain 500 extracts from a wide range of different written discourse types. Each extract is approximately 2,000 words long, and this means that each corpus contains about one million words in total. The FLOB Corpus was built in the early 1990s, following exactly the design of LOB, in order for precise diachronic comparisons to be made between them. Mair and his colleagues have produced a set of very interesting observations on the development of grammatical aspects of the language over the period, for instance, in the process of modalisation of the word *help* (Mair, 1995) and a greater use of nominalisation in practically all discourse types, though much more in some types than in others (Mair *et al.*, 2002). Leech and Smith in the early 2000s also used the same corpora to study recent grammatical changes in British and American English (Leech and Smith, 2006).[3]

Baker (2009) describes the construction of the BE06 Corpus, a one-million word reference corpus of general written British English from the year 2006 that was designed to be comparable to the Brown family of corpora. He conducted, *inter alia*, three studies of lexical frequency using BE06 and the Brown-type comparable corpora (LOB, FLOB and BLOB (i.e., Before-LOB, a 1930s version)). These involve a comparison of the twenty most frequent words, an examination of pronoun usage, and an investigation of keywords derived from comparing the 1991 FLOB corpus with the BE06.

---

[2] See: http://ucrel.lancs.ac.uk/history.html
[3] See: http://ucrel.lancs.ac.uk/floblob.html

Also relevant in terms of this special issue is Westin's (2002) analysis of language change in newspapers. She traces linguistic changes in English up-market newspaper editorials from the beginning of the twentieth-century to 1993 by sampling corpora from the *Guardian*, the *Telegraph* and *The Times* at ten-year intervals. Her subcorpora are relatively small – from 11,557 to 22,410 words per paper per year selected; that is an average of about 16,700 per paper per year, or about 50,100 words per year. The linguistic features she looks at are primarily those established by Biber (1988).

In the next section, I shall begin to outline some of the philosophical and technical aspects of the current research project.

2. Modern Diachronic Corpus-Assisted Discourse Studies (MD-CADS)

This set of studies employs the Siena–Bologna Modern Diachronic Corpus (the SiBol Corpus), which consists of two (sub-)corpora from different, but contemporary, periods in time; these are designed and compiled to be as similar as possible in order to eliminate any maverick variables. The first, SiBol 93, contains all the articles published by the three main UK broadsheet or so-called 'quality' newspapers, namely, *The Times* and *Sunday Times*, the *Telegraph* and *Sunday Telegraph*, and the *Guardian* in the year 1993. The second, SiBol 05, contains articles which appeared in the same three newspapers in the year 2005. The first contains about 100 million words (about twenty-seven million from the *Guardian*; thirty-four million from the *Telegraph* and *Sunday Telegraph*; and thirty-nine million from the *Times* and *Sunday Times*), and the second contains about 144 million (forty-one million from the *Guardian*; thirty-six million from the *Telegraph* and *Sunday Telegraph*; and sixty-seven million from the *Times* and *Sunday Times*). The *Guardian*'s sister paper, the *Observer*, was available in 2005, but not in 1993, and so we excluded the *Observer* from most of our comparative studies. Our very first observation, then, is that English quality newspapers have increased considerably in size over the period, particularly the *Guardian*. This is, presumably, largely the result of the introduction of new magazine and special-interest supplements.

The SiBol corpus came about partly by accident and partly by design. The 1993 corpus was compiled by me, together with John Morley, in the mid-1990s so that we could have at our disposal a large corpus of recent texts for both language research and teaching in faculties of political science (it was interesting, for instance, to compare the stances of left- and right-leaning papers on political issues). The three papers in question were included for the simple fact that, in the mists of pre-Internet time, they were the only ones for which the entire year's editions were available. The 2005 corpus was, of course, compiled for the precise purposes of providing an instrument for comparative MD-CADS research. We intend to compile additional corpora of parallel structure for future years.

The corpora were originally in raw text form, but Anna Marchi also prepared another version to allow them to be interrogated using Xaira software. The two corpora were arranged in files by month, converted into XML format[4] and marked up according to TEI guidelines.[5] The mark-up allows us to retrieve metalinguistic information about the sources (e.g., political orientation, date and specific source). This information can be used to partition the corpora and adopt one of the dimensions as a pivotal investigation parameter. The mark-up encoded here also allows access to information about the individual articles (e.g., page number and section, and type of news, when available) and to specific elements of the articles, namely, headlines and bylines.

Using their comparatively small corpora, Mair and his co-workers were able to conduct studies of changes in the behaviour of very frequent words or constructions; their studies are, therefore, largely focussed on grammar. Having at our disposal much larger corpora, studies of less frequent items, the so-called *lexical* (as opposed to *grammatical*) words also becomes possible. As Baker notes:

> My own experiences with corpus research would suggest that a million words is probably acceptable for examining usage of high frequency words (most grammatical words and a couple of hundred lexical words) but only very cautious conclusions can be made about other lexis.
>
> (Baker, 2009: 314)

Having at one's disposal very large corpora, however, opens up entirely new avenues of research in modern diachronic linguistics: we can study changes in meaning, especially of sets of lexical items in relation to both internal linguistic factors and also in response to external social influences. Being in a position to study lexical patterns and how they differ in the two corpora, we are also able to study changes in discourse processes. In the current overview, for instance, we will touch on how UK 'quality' newspapers appear to be adopting some of the language practices once thought typical of their downmarket counterparts, the tabloid papers; this topic is developed by Duguid (2010a) in the following paper in this issue.

The main tools of investigation employed here are, first of all, the WordSmith Keywords tool, one of the WordSmith Tools (version 5.0) suite of programs (Scott, 2008). This allows us to compare the *relative* frequency of items in any corpus with reference to another corpus. The analyst first prepares a list of the items in the corpus, in order of their absolute frequency, using the Wordlist tool. The same procedure is followed for the second corpus. The Keywords tool can then compare the contents of the two lists and those items whose occurrence is statistically significant (using chi-squared or log-likelihood tests) more frequently in the first list are themselves put in an

---

[4] eXtensible Mark-up Language (see: http://www.w3.org/XML/).
[5] Text Encoding Initiative (see: http://www.tei-c.org/index.xml).

ordered list. The more statistically significant an item is, the more *key* it is, and the higher it is placed on the list. This keyword list, providing an ordered series of items which are *salient* in one corpus compared to another corpus, is likely to suggest items which warrant further investigation (Baker, 2006: 125). The procedure can then be repeated but by inverting the two corpora to reveal the items which are salient in the second corpus. Following this methodology, then, we obtained two lists of keywords, one of the salient items in 2005 newspapers and the other of the key items from the 1993 set of texts. Even when setting the WordSmith Keywords significance setting at the highest level envisaged (that is by setting the *lowest p*-value available, namely $p = 10^{15}$), the two corpora being compared were so large that each list contained over 7,000 items. However, for most practical purposes we confine ourselves to analysing the first 2,500 items in each list.

Lemmatised versions of each list were also prepared (Clark, 2010). The basic wordlist function of WordSmith lists word forms discretely, which, depending on what one wishes to count, can create inaccuracies when comparing separate frequency lists. For example, *think* appears separately from *thinks*, *thought* and *thinking*, and, as a result, the true frequency of *think* as a lemma is skewed. This discrepancy was resolved by importing a language lemma list compiled by Someya (1998), which comprises 40,569 words grouped in 14,762 lemmas. This text file was used as a basis, and further lemmas were added to reflect the research aims. For example, an increase in contracted forms was found in SiBol 05 – an increase which may have gone unnoticed were it not possible to lemmatise the forms, that is, by lemmatising or grouping *I*, *I'll*, *I've* and *I'd*, and so on, the difference in frequency of *I* between the two corpora became significant. Similarly, by grouping terms of address (*Mr*, *Mrs*, *Ms*, *Miss*, etc.), a much clearer picture of the difference in honorific usage over time could be established.

The lemma function is equally useful when compiling keyword lists based on lemmatised wordlists. The order of the resulting keyword lists can alter quite significantly, which was the case in the examples *I* (including *I'm*, *I'll*, etc.) and *Mr* (including *Mrs*, *Ms*, *Miss*, etc.).

The keyword lists were then examined for items, and, especially, sets of items, which might be of interest in the context of the piece of research that is being undertaken. Different items will attract attention if the focus of interest is on changes in grammar rather than on political issues. When items are chosen they can be individually concordanced in the corpus in question. In this way, the analyst can begin to formulate hypotheses as to why particular items are more salient in a given set of texts. As implied earlier, the presence in the list of an individual item may simply be a question of happenstance or the quirk of an individual writer's style. It is when sets of similar or related items are uncovered that real evidence of changes in linguistic or discourse practice may be found.

Comparing corpora of these sizes is a relatively new endeavour within corpus linguistics, and novel challenges can breed novel methodological practices – necessity and labour-saving being the parents of invention.

Since the search for even only moderately frequent words and phrases can generate concordance lines from each SiBol corpus running into the thousands, both Taylor (2010) and Marchi (2010) in this issue have experimented with what Taylor has called 'concordance-corpora' and 'concordance-keywords'. A concordance of the search item is prepared, with a generous stretch of co-text, between, say, 400 to 600 characters, since corpus-assisted studies of discourse tend to deal in larger chunks of meaning than is typically required in standard lexical grammar analyses. These concordances can in themselves contain several million words and can be considered to constitute corpora (hence the term 'concordance-corpora') in their own right. Wordlists may then be compiled for each of the concordance-corpora which can serve as the basis for a two-way comparative keyword listing. Cluster and key-cluster lists can, of course, also be prepared using them.

3. Corpus-Assisted Discourse Studies (CADS)

3.1 What CADS does

As the name implies, MD-CADS is a sub-discipline of Corpus-Assisted Discourse Studies (CADS; for a recent overview, see Partington, 2008). The principal endeavour of Corpus-Assisted Discourse Studies can be summarised quite simply: it is the investigation and comparison of features of particular discourse types, integrating into the analysis, where appropriate, techniques and tools developed within corpus linguistics. I prefer the term *discourse type* to other labels we encounter, such as *text-type* or *genre*, since, for some, *text-type* implies work on written texts, whereas much of CADS has been carried out on spoken discourse, and *genre* is a term which is accompanied by a huge baggage in the literature. Furthermore, some of the discourse types we may wish to examine might not meet everyone's criteria of what constitutes a 'genre'. For instance, do White House briefings (Partington, 2003, 2006) or Parliamentary debates on the Iraq war (Bayley and Bevitori, 2009), both objects of recent CADS scrutiny, count as genres?

The aim of the CADS approach is to uncover, in the discourse type under investigation, what we might call *non-obvious meaning* – that is, meaning which might not be readily available to perusal by the naked eye. Much of what carries meaning in texts is not open to direct observation: 'you cannot understand the world just by looking at it' (Stubbs, 1996: 92, after Gellner, 1959). We use language 'semi-automatically', in the sense that speakers and writers make semi-conscious choices within the various complex overlapping systems of which language is composed, such as those of transitivity, modality, lexical sets, including among 'synonyms' (*freedom, liberty, emancipation* and *deliverance*), modification, and so on. Authors themselves are, famously, generally unaware of all the meanings their texts convey; (an extreme expression of this notion is the 'intentional fallacy' (Wimsatt and Beardsley, 1946)). By combining the so-called *quantitative* approach, that is, statistical overviews of large amounts of the discourse in question (more precisely, large numbers of tokens of the discourse type under study contained in a corpus) with the more *qualitative* approach typical of discourse analysis (that is, the close, detailed analysis of particular stretches of discourse – stretches whose particularly interesting nature may well have been identified by the initial overview) it may be possible to understand better the processes at play in the discourse type. It may be possible, in other words, to access such non-obvious meanings.

CADS arises from the pioneering work in particular of Hardt-Mautner (1995) and Stubbs (1996, 2001). A considerable body of research has also been conducted in Italy either by individual researchers or under the aegis of combined inter-university projects, such as Newspool (Partington *et al.*, 2004) and CorDis (Morley and Bayley, 2009). It has concentrated on political and media language, mainly because a nucleus of linguists in Italian academia work in Political Science faculties and are interested in the use of corpus techniques to conduct socio-political discourse analysis.

3.2 CADS compared with traditional corpus linguistics

Traditional corpus linguistics has, naturally, tended to privilege the quantitative approach. In the drive to produce more authentic dictionaries and grammars of a language, it has been characterised by the compilation of often very large corpora of heterogeneric discourse types. This reflects the desire to obtain an overview of the greatest quantity and variety of discourse types possible – in other words, of the chimerical but useful fiction we call the 'general language' ('general English', 'general Italian', and so on). This has led to the construction of immensely valuable research tools such as the Bank of English and the British National Corpus. Some early schools of corpus linguistics proper were frequently characterised by the treatment of the corpus as a 'black box', that is, the analyst rarely invested much time in familiarising himself or herself with particular texts within the corpus, since the characteristics of individual texts or sets of text were not of central interest to linguists who were using corpora to build dictionaries or grammars of the language 'as a whole'. The result was that, until comparatively recently, and as McEnery and Wilson (2000: 114) note, 'discourse analysis is [an] area where the "standard" corpora have been relatively little used', while, conversely, as Biber *et al.* (1998: 106) remarked, discourse studies, for their part, 'are not typically corpus-based'.

The aim of CADS is, on the other hand, radically different. Here, the whole aim of the exercise is to acquaint ourselves as much as possible with the discourse type(s) under investigation. In contrast to some earlier tendencies in mainstream corpus linguistics, CADS researchers typically engage with their corpus in a variety of ways. As well as using wordlists and concordancing, intuitions for further research can also arise from reading, watching or listening to parts of the dataset; this process can help to provide a feel for how things are done linguistically in the discourse type that is being studied. CADS work also frequently combines what can be learned from corpus analysis with other sources of information on a given topic, be this linguistic or socio-cultural. In this issue, for instance, Duguid (2010a) makes extensive use of dictionary definitions of the terms she investigates, whilst Taylor (2010) looks at websites and popular science books to compare what they have to say about attitudes to science with her corpus data.

CADS is also characterised by the compilation of ad hoc specialised corpora, since, very frequently, there is no existing collection of the discourse type that is under investigation. Typically, other corpora of various descriptions are utilised in the course of a study for purposes of comparison. These may include pre-existing corpora or they may need to be compiled by the researcher. In some sense, all work with corpora – just as all work with discourse – is properly comparative. Even when a single corpus is employed, it is used to test the data it contains against another body of data. This may consist of the researcher's introspection, or the data found in reference works such as dictionaries and grammars, or it may be statements made previously by authors in the field. Corpus-assisted studies of discourse types are, of course, and by definition, comparative: it is only possible to both uncover and evaluate the particular features of a discourse type by comparing it with others. In the case of this set of studies, the principal form of comparison will be mainly diachronic, that is, of one corpus or subsection thereof against one or more sections of its sister corpora from a different, recent period of time. However, since the three newspapers can be accessed separately, several of the studies, here, also compare how journalists view certain issues from different political stances. For example, I look at what different papers view as *moral panics* in Section 5, whilst Marchi (2010) looks at differences and similarities in what the three papers have to say on sexual morality.

4. The keyword lists

The keyword lists described in Section 2 were examined for items and, especially, sets of items, which might be of interest in the context of the particular piece of research under investigation. As already stated, different items will attract attention if the focus of interest is on changes in grammar than if it is on political issues. Here, I will simply give an overview of those sets which might offer clues about changes in either newspaper language or in the social, cultural and political issues which were filling the papers.

4.1 Grammatical items

The most striking feature of the 2005 keyword list from the grammatical perspective is the salience of first- and second-person personal pronouns. We find *you* in fourth place in the list (after three Internet-related items), closely followed by *I*, *your*, *my*, *we*, *me* and *us*. (N.B. All the word sets in this section are given in the descending order in which they appear in the respective keyword list.) We also come across *yourself* and *myself*.

Perhaps the second most apparent characteristic of the list is the very large number of verb contractions among the first one hundred salient items. These include *it's*, *I'm*, *don't*, *that's*, *he's*, *there's*, *you're*, *I've*, *didn't*, *doesn't*, *we're* and *I'd*. These are accompanied by a large variety of negative contractions. The top 500 keywords include *don't*, *didn't*, *doesn't*, *can't*, *wasn't*, *isn't*, *won't*, *couldn't*, *wouldn't*, *aren't*, *haven't*, *hasn't* and *weren't*.

We also find that a considerable number of items which can be used either as 'empty subjects' or deictically are very prominent in the 2005 list, either alone or as part of contractions, (e.g., *it's*, *that*, *that's*, *there's*, *it*).

The most salient verb is *get*, followed by *can*, *think*, *want*, *got*, *know*, *like*, *see*, *do*, *need*, *make* and *look*, all items commonly found in conversational forms of the language.[6]

Along with verb contractions and negative contractions (see above), Leech and Smith (2006) include the increased use of the progressive among their changes apparently indicative of 'a suspected trend of "colloquialization"' (Leech, 2004: 63). Among the first 1,000 items of the 2005 keywords are *going*, *getting*, *looking*, *doing*, *playing*, *drinking*, *thinking*, *watching*, *working*, *having*, *using*, *eating* and *wearing*. There are no equivalent *–ing* verb forms among the top 1,000 keywords for 1993. Leech and Smith also claim that 'questions of all kinds' are indicative of colloquialisation, and the 2005 list indeed includes *where*, *when*, *why*, *how* and *what*.

Turning to the 1993 keyword list, we come across a good number of formal terms of address or personal appellation, all of which disappear from the 2005 list. These include *Mr*, *Mrs*, *Lord*, *Dr*, *Sir*, *Lady*, *Rev*, *Herr*, *Signor* and even *President*. The UK press seems to have curtailed its use of courtesy forms.

Another significant lexico-grammatical change is in the relative frequency of the type of linkers present in the lists. In 1993 we find relatively literary items such as *therefore*, *moreover*, *nevertheless* and *indeed*. The 2005 keywords instead include *and*, *but*, *because* and *also*. In 1993 we come across *whilst*; in 2005, we find, instead, *while*.

All these sets are indications of an increase in the personalisation or familiarisation of newspaper register over the twelve years between the two

---

[6] They are to be found in the Lancaster University spoken versus written language keyword list (based on occurrences in the BNC). See http://ucrel.lancs.ac.uk/bncfreq/lists/2_2_spokenvwritten.txt and also Leech *et al.* (2001).

corpora. This finding is perhaps unsurprising: Fairclough (1995) has written on what he terms the *conversationalisation* of media discourse; others talk of *political cross-discourse* (Alvarez-Cáccamo and Prego-Vásquez, 2003). As regards newspapers in particular, McNair (2003) describes what he calls the *tabloidisation* of UK so-called quality newspapers, whilst Carter and McCarthy note two particular linguistic features used to attempt this familiarisation with the reader:

> journalists also achieve impact and get on a 'conversational' wavelength with their readers by using common spoken discourse markers and purposefully vague language in a projected conversational exchange
> (Carter and McCarthy, 2006: 238)

Duguid (2010a) goes on to study this change in newspaper discourse style in some length.

It might be objected that these sets were apparent simply due to the growth in the size of papers, given the addition over the period of magazine-style sections, whose registers might tend towards the conversational. To check this we made a list of comparative keywords from the one newspaper which had not increased in volume, namely the *Telegraph*, and these sets were still found to be very prominent.

Nevertheless, by no means all the items in the lists indicate a progressive stylistic informalisation in all newspaper sections: some must, indeed, be the product of the change in paper format and the relative growth in the magazine, non-hard news sections. For instance, the 1993 list contains *yesterday* – an item that is notoriously frequent in the first sentence of hard news stories – along with a good variety of verbs in past time reference form that are typical of hard news reporting, including *were*, *had*, *was* and *been* (*had* and *been* are also evidence of passives, one of Leech and Smith's (2006: 194) indications of non-colloquialised style).

There are a good number of modals which appear to be less popular than before: *would*, *must*, *shall*, *should* and *may* are all in the 1993 list. In recompense we find *can*, *can't*, *cannot* and *need* among the 2005 keywords.

Prepositional use, too, seems to have altered. In 1993 we find *against*, *under*, *between*, *upon*, *throughout*, *among*, *within*, *towards* and *amongst*, whilst in 2005 we come across *with*, *across*, *alongside*, *onto* and *around*. Some of the 1993 words may have fallen away because of their relatively formal air – notably *throughout* and *amongst* – but it is not easy to explain the distinct changes in popularity of most of the others.

It is interesting to compare these observations on recent grammatical changes with those of Baker (2009) who analyses the LOB family of corpora of general British English (LOB 1961, FLOB 1991 and BE06 2006) which, though much smaller than SiBol since they each consist of one million words, contain a wider variety of text types – namely, press, general prose, learned writing and fiction. He finds the same decrease in the use of the modals *shall*, *must*, *may* and *should*, and a similar increase in *need*. Likewise, the use of

	1993	*2005*
Linkers	*thus, therefore, moreover, nevertheless, in spite of, whilst, indeed*	*but, also, because, then, while*
Prepositions	*against, under, between, upon, throughout, among, within, towards, amongst*	*with, across, alongside, onto, around*
Modality	*would, must, shall, should, may*	*need, can / can't / cannot*
Function verbs, auxiliaries, etc.	*were, had, was, been*	*is, am, have, having, do, get(s), getting, got*
Personal pronouns		*you, I, your, my, we, me, us, our, she, them, him, her, yourself, myself*
Question words		*where, when, why, how, what*
Relative pronouns	*which, whose*	*that*
Determiners	*the*	*a*
Others	*its, itself, nor, not, of*	*this, here, yeah, yes*

Table 1: Grammatical keywords

contractions has risen whilst the employment of terms of address seems to be falling away across the board, in British English at least. He does not detect in the LOB-family data, however, the other developments we saw in the SiBol newspaper data, in first- and second-person pronoun use, in different patterns of linkers, of function words and of determiners; nor is there the same evidence of the wholesale increase in question words (WH-forms).

From this comparison it would seem that some forms of conversationalisation and informalisation are taking place throughout a good number of text types; for example, the preference for contractions and the abandoning of formal address terms is evidence of a general difference in the way writers attempt to align themselves with their readers, which presumably reflects changes in societal developments regarding *face* (Brown and Levinson, 1987) and social space (increased democratisation, or the decline of respect, depending on one's point of view). Many of the other changes we have identified would seem, in contrast, to be specific to the type of newspaper prose under scrutiny.

4.2 Content items

As one might expect, the list of keywords from the 2005 corpus contains a good number of items relating to the technological advances which have taken place since 1993: *www, internet, online, dvd, email, mobile,* and so on. It is equally unsurprising that it also contains a large number of proper names of people and places, reflecting those events which came into the news in 2005, but which were not there in 1993; for instance, *Bush* as opposed to *Clinton* and *Blair* as opposed to *Major.* There are so-called seasonal items (Gabrielatos and Baker, 2008) relating to current newsworthy events such as *tsunami* and *Katrina* (and *hurricane*). Inevitably, in 2005 we find several *Iraq*-related items (*Iraq, Iraqi, Shia, Sunni, Sunnis* and *insurgents*), and Afghanistan-related items (*Afghanistan, Taleban* and *Guantanamo*), whereas in 1993 we have Balkans-related terms (*Bosnia, Serbs, Sarajevo* and *Croats*).

What other news topics do the 2005 keywords suggest? We find *global* as well as *warming, climate, emissions* and *carbon,* but, when concordanced, *global* also collocates with *terrorism.*

Health and health concerns are prominent: *health, NHS, flu, healthcare, MRSA, MS* and *obesity.* Whether or not the nation's waistlines really have spread so much since 1993, the papers are certainly chewing the fat about obesity much more. But it is talked about in a strange way. Its two most frequent lexical collocates are *childhood* and *epidemic,* and one of the most frequent four-word clusters around *obesity* is *epidemic of childhood obesity* (in 1993 *epidemic* was only the forty-third most common collocate of *obesity*). Reversing the direction, in 2005 the single most frequent lexical collocate of *epidemic* is *obesity.* The second most frequent is *proportions,* and, if we concordance *epidemic proportions,* we find, indeed, still more references to obesity. This tells us much about the way newspapers use the word *epidemic.* The OED provides the following definition of the word:

> Epidemic: Of a disease: prevalent among a people or a community at a special time, and produced by some special causes not generally present in the affected locality.

A rise in rates of obesity, clearly, does not fit the second part of the definition; if anything, obesity is becoming *endemic* among the UK population. However, *epidemic* is a more dramatic scare word. Interestingly, things described as reaching *epidemic proportions* are as likely to be metaphorical as literal health and disease issues, especially in the 2005 data. They include plagiarism in academia, morbid sentimentality after the death of Princess Diana, young women binge-drinking (see Section 5 on moral panics) and groping on Tokyo trains. The 2005 keyword list contains the even more scary item *pandemic,* whose first lexical collocates are *flu* and *bird.*

In a more serious vein, we also find that suicide among young males is claimed to be reaching epidemic proportions, and *suicide* is among the 2005 keywords. This is very largely a reflection of the rise of the suicide bomber. In fact the whole tenor of the co-occurring items changes dramatically. In 1993, the most frequent four-word clusters for *suicide* include *tried to commit suicide, likely to commit suicide, a verdict of suicide, the apparent suicide of*, and the like. In 2005, instead, we find clusters like *by a suicide bomber*, *a suicide car bomber* and *in a suicide bombing*. And yet the 'normal' non-homicidal taking of one's own life was as prevalent in 2005 as 1993. This sounds a note of warning about the relationship between corpus data – indeed, about linguistic data in general – and the real world. Linguistic analysis has to be accompanied by a modicum of common sense and knowledge of the world.

Health issues feature much less in the 1993 list, but the most prominent exception to this is *Aids*.

The 2005 list includes items relating to high finance or venture capitalism, including *FTSE*, *bid*, *takeover*, *executive*, and the sadly celebrated *hedge* (funds), as well financial institutions such as *Deutsche* and *HSBC* (both banks). In contrast, in 1993 we find a few items from the sphere of high finance but far more relating to the national economy in general: economic *recession*, *recovery*, *inflation* and *economy*; to the relationship of government to the economy: *treasury*, *devaluation*, *privatisation*, *budget* and *trade union(s)*; to national economic problems, such as *unemployment*; and to industrial matters: *coal*, *chairman* and *industrial*. Commerce and trade feature prominently: *trade*, *market*, *profits* and *losses* (these are, principally, monetary, but also *job* is the sixth most common collocate), and both *export* and *exports*.

Another set of items that is very strikingly present in the 1993 list are those relating to war, to 'defence'. Among the first 500 items alone we find *UN*, *defence*, *NATO*, *military*, *troops*, *peacekeeping*, (armed) *forces*, *commander*, *artillery*, (arms) *embargo*, *convoys* and *war*. This should not imply that the world in 2005 had necessarily become more peaceful. Unsurprisingly, in 2005 there are a number of terrorism-related words: *bombing(s)*, *terrorist*, *terror*, *Qaeda* (or *Qaida*) and *Madrid*. The large quantity of formal lexis on military matters may be a reflection of the greater relative attention given to hard news reporting in 1993.

However, the single most noticeable feature of the 2005 keywords, in terms of content words was the very high proportion of top keywords relating to sport, especially to football. Of the first 100, as many as twenty-one refer to sport or sporting personalities (for instance, *Premiership*, *Chelsea* and *Beckham*), whereas in 1993, the top 100 keywords contains only three sports items (one from football, *soccer*; one from cricket, the cricketer, (Graham) *Gooch*; and the third is *chess*). Perhaps an important lesson that the quality newspapers have learnt from the tabloids, then, is that sport sells papers.

5. And what the papers (purport to) play down: the *moral panic* label

The keyword lists, then, paint a fairly detailed picture of the issues our newspapers felt deserved their attention in the periods in question. But it might also be interesting to look at what, conversely, the newspapers and their sources contended were *less* noteworthy issues. For an insight into this, we can analyse the item *moral panic(s)*. The item was concordanced in SiBol 93 and then SiBol 05 with a span of 600 characters of co-text. (Generally, CADS analysis into discourse meaning uses concordances with greater co-text than is common, say, in grammatical or lexicological study, where the focus of attention tends to be on more immediate patterns of co-occurring items.)

The term was, famously, coined in 1973 by the sociologist Stanley Cohen in his work *Folk Devils and Moral Panics*, in which he defines the phenomenon thus:

> Societies appear to be subject, every now and then, to periods of moral panic. A condition, episode, person or group of persons emerges to become defined as a threat to societal values and interests; its nature is presented in a stylized and stereotypical fashion by the mass media; the moral barricades are manned by editors, bishops, politicians and other right-thinking people.
>
> (Cohen, 2002 [1973]: 1)

However, such a definition leaves out as much as it contains. Perhaps the single most important semantic function of the term is its 'over-the-fence' function; it is invariably an outsider word used to describe the interests, concerns and preoccupations of another group – a group of which the writer does not regard himself or herself as a member. Moreover, by labelling the concern in question as a *moral panic*, writers disaffiliate themselves from whatever anxiety the group is supposedly exercising itself about: they indicate that the issue is being exaggerated and not worth the attention it is receiving. Otherwise, a term like moral *issue* (145), *concern* (11) or *problem* (21) will be chosen instead (figures in brackets indicate the number of times each of these words is preceded by *moral* in SiBol 05). Thus, for instance, women's groups will not use the term *moral panic* in relation to their concerns over domestic violence, and Jewish groups are highly unlikely to describe their own worries about rising anti-Semitism across Europe as a *moral panic*.

The item is, indeed, used with this disaffiliative function in SiBol and can thus give us some indication of what journalists were portraying as exaggerated issues. SiBol 93 contains eighty-four mentions (*Guardian* thirty-nine, *Times* thirty-two and *Telegraph* thirteen), whilst SiBol 05 contains seventy-four occurrences (*Guardian* forty-four, *Times* eighteen and *Telegraph* twelve) and in only one case is it used about a group the writer subscribes to, and even then it is ironic:

> (1) Our crime waves, **moral panics** and hand-wringing are not measures of relative depravity but of a civilised willingness to look more steadily at something that has been there all the time.
>
> (SiBol 93, *Telegraph*)

Moral panics are variously described as *manufactured, spurious, vacuous, unwarranted, mere, counter-productive* and *drug-fuelled*; they are *doom-laden* and spread by *doom-mongers*. They *afflict* or *beset* the nation. People are said to be *in the grip of* or *in danger of lapsing into* them and require a *cure* for their *fit of* moral panic. Clearly, moral panics are not a good thing.

Moral *panicking* is frequently contrasted in some way with more appropriate ways of reacting to an issue. Such as *justifiable anxiety* (from an interview with a sociologist):

(2) "The media is not simply engaging in yet another **moral panic** by highlighting 'mad murders' but reflecting justifiable anxiety about the perceived danger from mentally disordered people in the community and the apparent ineptitude of mental health services and personnel."

(SiBol 05, *Times*)

or *dispassionate objectivity*:

(3) Our duty is not to be swayed by short-run **moral panics** or claims about this trend or that trend but rather to consider the issues around broadcast as objectively and dispassionately as we can.

(SiBol 05, *Guardian*)

or *rational thinking*:

(4) [...] it could prompt a **moral panic** in which emotion plays a more important role than rational thinking in policy-making.

(SiBol 93, *Guardian*)

or *honest recognition*:

(5) That is not **moral panic**, but an honest recognition of the threads of collective responsibility that make society more than an aggregate of individuals.

(SiBol 93, *Times*)

And to underline just how the concept of moral panic is dependent on point of view, we find once or twice that journalists on the same newspaper cannot agree whether an issue is mere panic or a genuine concern. The issue most frequently flagged up by the *Guardian* in 2005 as an exaggerated moral panic is crime, especially juvenile offending, whilst another is drug use. But the paper also includes the following alarming report (an interview with a psychiatrist):

(6) "I'm not an alarmist," she says, "nor a reactionary [...] But I am really worried. What my generation smoked as cannabis and what today's kids are smoking are completely different. This isn't some cosy,

middle-class **moral panic** – we're talking about kids with knives, kids in trouble with the police, kids on lock-up wards and in psychiatric hospitals. I used to get just a trickle of cases – now I've a long waiting list of kids who have lost their way".

(SiBol 05, *Guardian*)

Similarly, one of its commentators pokes ironic fun at concern over 'binge-drinking' which, it says 'continued to be the nation's favourite moral panic in 2005'. Yet elsewhere in the same paper we read:

(7) With 33% of British teenagers now classified as binge drinkers, alcohol abuse among the young is a rising problem, often overshadowed by **moral panics** over illegal, harder but less universally harmful drugs.

(SiBol 05, *Guardian*)

One journalist's *moral panic* is another journalist's *rising problem*.

5.1 The politics of *moral panic*

It is noticeable how much more the label (or accusation) *moral panic* is employed by left-leaning *Guardian* writers (thirty-nine times in 1993 and forty-four in 2005 in the pertinent corpora sections of twenty-seven million and forty-one million words respectively – i.e., sixty-eight million words in all) than by those on the conservative *Telegraph* (thirteen and twelve in corpora sections of thirty-four and thirty-six million words respectively – i.e., seventy million words in all). Indeed, a number of academic commentators believe that moral panics are typical of, and are the preserve of, conservatives and right-wing institutions:

[...] moral panics are mounted by conservative forces as a reaction to social change and [...] their ultimate function is to shore up the existing moral order.

(Critcher, 2006: 16)

Others, such as Goode and Ben-Yehuda (2006), tend to see them as more bottom-up, volatile and folk-driven, which tend to come and go with little rhyme or reason. Be this as it may, the charge of engaging in moral panic appears to be a stick commonly used by the left with which to beat conservatives and their preoccupations – a kind of mirror to the accusation of moral *relativism* which often flies the other way (see Marchi, 2010). The *Guardian* occasionally likes to have its cake and eat it. When an issue is raised by the Conservative party, it is a moral panic, but when discussed by the newspaper it becomes a *problem* and a *concern*; in this example, the topic is immigration:

(8) [. . .] the deep well of public concern – tapped by the Conservatives in the general election campaign – could be seen as just another **moral panic** that, if ignored, would disappear of its own accord. But there are stark differences between earlier manifestations of public concern over immigration and today's problem.

(SiBol 05, *Guardian*)

However, this negative evaluation can be rather cleverly subverted and exploited by institutional figures to hit back at critics of their actions and decisions. All three papers from 2005 report the words of Sir Henry Newby:

(9) THE head of the universities' funding council wrote off concern over the closure of chemistry and physics departments as **"moral panic"** yesterday and praised new cross-curricular courses such as forensic science.

(SiBol 05, *Telegraph*)

But the accusation needs to be used cautiously. The following is by far the most sardonically ironic and unfortunate use of the term in the entire corpus:

(10) Dan McLaughlin, an economist, showed up on Eamon Dunphy's radio show last week to pour scorn on those who are concerned that our flash lifestyles are being funded by increasing debt. He accused the Central Bank of engaging in "ritualistic **moral panic**". McLaughlin believes that worrying about our profligate borrowing is unnecessary and rather silly. We should remember that McLaughlin is not any old economist, though. He is chief economist at the Bank of Ireland.

(SiBol 05, *Times*)

One suspects Mr McLaughlin lived to regret dismissing fears about profligate borrowing as a mere *moral panic*.

5.2 Who is responsible for them? Who suffers from it?

Who *stirs* or *stokes* moral panics? The media, of course, 'excites itself when dealing breathlessly with moral panics, sex and drugs' (*Guardian 05*). The *Guardian*, not surprisingly, cites 'the right-wing press', whilst the *Times* names names '[. . .] sparking moral panic stories in the *Daily Express* and *Daily Mail*'. Occasionally, politicians are responsible: '[. . .] to make lone parents scapegoats, as many politicians and commentators do [. . .]' (*Guardian*). Or politicians and the press together:

(11) Michael Howard is descending into a new kind of tabloid politics, exploiting **moral panics** stirred up by the press

(SiBol 05, *Guardian*)

and on two occasions, the police are the guilty party, as in this example, where the issue is drugs:

(12) Instead of sponsoring a moral panic, the police should realise they are engaged in an expensive but futile effort to suppress a basic demand-driven business.

(SiBol 05, *Guardian*)

However, it is most striking that, typically, neither an instigator nor a suffering group is mentioned explicitly. Moral panics are, generally, simply averred to exist; for example, typical wordings include, 'the current moral panic about', 'in the atmosphere of moral panic', 'during last year's moral panic about' and 'no wonder that, out there, there is talk of moral panic'. They are rarely traced to a source and, since the group suffering the panic is generally unspecified, cannot be measured. This all confirms how subjective the label is: a moral panic is what a writer claims one to be.

5.3 The diachronics of *moral panics*: were they the same or did they change over time?

The single most recurrent topic to be associated with the term *moral panic* in the SiBol 93 concordance is juvenile crime, both committed by young people but also upon young people. It is, in particular, dominated by items spawned by a seasonal occurrence: the murder of two-year-old James Bulger by two older children, an event which shocked the nation and to which a great deal of newspaper space was dedicated. *James Bulger* appears 794 times in SiBol 93 and *Bulger* occurs thirteen times in the SiBol 93 concordance of *moral panic(s)*, though many more entries are discussions of the consequences of the murder. Given that murders of children are quite rare, and murders *by* children are extremely rare, in the UK, journalists debated whether such attention was disproportionate and, therefore, indicated that a moral panic was in process. Goode and Ben-Yehuda (2006) include *disproportionality* in their list of indicators of moral panics, and Crichter calls it 'the key' to recognising them. However, (dis)proportionality is both extremely hard to measure and very largely subjective. James Bulger was but one murdered child, yet the murder of children and murder by children surely raises very many complex moral considerations about the nature of (in)humanity, of conscience, and, for those of a religious disposition, of evil. Moreover, if such an event crystallises a series of moral and social concerns in a large number of people, then to dismiss the response as disproportionate moral panic is also to miss its inherent news value:

(13) The political crisis has been compounded by a sense of foreboding about society. A specific event frequently serves to crystallise such

a feeling. Such an event was the killing of little James Bulger in Liverpool. The subsequent reaction had many of the qualities of previous **moral panics**. But it was more than that. The death gave expression to a feeling of social meltdown, that something was seriously amiss with society.

(SiBol 93, *Times*)

A second issue relating to the Bulger case to be talked of in terms of moral panic was that of whether violent behaviour correlates with, or can be caused by, watching violence, since a violent 'video nasty' was discovered in the house of one of the accused boys. The issue is portrayed as a moral panic:

(14) There's been a recurrent **moral panic** about violent images which looks to a mythical golden age of tranquil behaviour.

(SiBol 93, *Guardian*)

. . . but also, in the same newspaper, as a genuine concern, shared by 'anyone who actually works with kids':

(15) [. . .] the **moral panic** about screen violence is not, as some critics complain, a self-regarding media affair. Talk to anyone who actually works with kids and they will express a concern about what they see as the effects of the bombardment of violent imagery that today's youngsters are subject to.

(SiBol 93, *Guardian*)

A third issue frequently referred to as a moral panic in 1993, was that of 'lone parents', 'single mothers' and 'one-parent families', but only in the *Guardian*. The 'Tories' are seen as particularly prone to panic attacks on this issue, but on one occasion, '[t]his latest bout of moral panic has seen Labour MPs joining in'.

One writer in *The Times*, by contrast, takes up the cudgels on behalf of the 'traditional family', and rather dramatically dismisses the moral panic appellation as, as it were, too dismissive:

(16) Does the left now scoff that Britain is having a "**moral panic**" over lone parents? Wait until it becomes apparent that the British constitution is inextricably linked to the functioning of the traditional family: that Britain's free institutions literally cannot continue to exist when the traditional family no longer is the norm. The **moral panic** then will take Britain in directions that now can only be imagined, but all of which are likely to be ugly.

(SiBol 93, *Times*)

Another group mentioned twice as the object of moral panic, both by the *Guardian*, are 'travellers'.

The only other issue to be described on several occasions as a moral panic is the idea of a general physical or moral decline of society, variously referred to as 'urban decay' (*Times*), 'state of society' (*Times*), and alluded to in the following sarcastic piece from the *Guardian*:

(17) After [feminism] the Daddies couldn't find jobs [...] The Mummies said they would be better off on their own and the sobbing children were left with nothing to do but sniff glue and shoplift.

This, after all, is the kind of fairy tale that has been regurgitated at various intervals over the past few weeks. Such a **moral panic** could sustain itself only by attaching to some suitable target the free-floating anxiety we all felt at the James Bulger murder.

(SiBol 93, *Guardian*)

Issues which are mentioned just once as provoking moral panics include 'overmighty trade unions', abortion, prostitution, child abuse, the 'underclass' and 'dependency culture', and increasing drinking among young women.

Although in 2005 there is no major seasonal event like the Bulger murder, crime, and especially juvenile crime, was once again the issue most frequently labelled a moral panic – at least by the *Guardian*. In the *Guardian*, thirteen of the forty-four mentions relate to crime – including an ample discussion of 'unreasonable' fears aroused by 'hoodies'; this compares with two from eighteen and zero from twelve in the *Times* and *Telegraph*, respectively. In fact, concordancing *youth/juvenile + crime* reveals how much more seriously the phenomenon is taken by the *Telegraph* than the *Guardian*. The latter makes considerable play of Home Office statistics which reported a decrease in the number of juveniles cautioned or convicted in 2002 (105,700) compared to 1992 (143,600). For the former, in contrast, youth crime is a *serious menace* to be *tackled* and Home Office statistics are quoted which report how it is on the rise again, the paper stressing how only one percent of offences result in a court appearance.

Other issues which the *Guardian* in 2005 claims are objects of panic include Islam (2 mentions), the dangers to children posed by the Internet (2), binge-drinking (2), drugs (2), immigration (2), video nasties, the obesity epidemic and 'selfish working women' who wish to become 'late mothers'. Chavs[7] (young people again) also get a mention:

---

[7] The following definition is provided by the *Longman Dictionary of Contemporary English* (2009, fifth edition):

chav [countable] *British English*

an offensive word used especially by newspapers to talk about a young WORKING-CLASS person who is rude and AGGRESSIVE, has a low level of education, and who wears a certain style of fashionable clothing such as TRAINERs, SPORTSWEAR, and BASEBALL CAPS.

(18) The latest **moral panic** over hoodies echoes the last one over chavs. The genealogy of the chav is debated by sociologists. Manufactured **moral panic**, or last stand of the lost tribe of the white working class?

(SiBol 05, *Guardian*)

The *Times* also sees moral panics around drugs (2 mentions), alcohol consumption (2), children and sexuality (2), parenthood, immigrants, terrorism and sexual predators.

The *Telegraph* speaks of moral panics aroused by teenage pregnancies, 'affairs between pupils and teachers' and drug-taking among teenage girls.

All the papers have excursions into history. The *Guardian* cites Cohen's original example of the moral panic over Mods and Rockers, the *Times* claims that 'moral panics about booze are nothing new', whilst the *Telegraph* reviews a book which touches upon 'the Victorians' moral panic over masturbation by schoolboys', the only cure for which, apparently, was healthy sport and lots of it.

5.4 Conclusions on *moral panic* labelling

I began this section by noting that calling concerns over an issue a 'moral panic' was a way of downplaying their importance. But the question turns out to be much more complex. For journalists, labelling something as a 'moral panic' has a variety of attractions, chief among which is to distance themselves from a phenomenon which may well be of widespread topical interest, whilst continuing to consume much ink in writing about it. This marries with another ploy practised by the so-called quality papers – their predilection for reporting 'what the tabloids are saying', which allows them to talk of the same popular topics, celebrities, sport and sex, whilst maintaining a minimum of decorum. The *Guardian* and *Observer* are particularly tempted: in SiBol 05 they use the item *tabloids* 625 times, the *Times* (including the *Sunday* version) mention them 292 times and the *Telegraph* (including the *Sunday* version) a 'mere' 177 times. The tone is sometimes amused, sometimes scandalised, sometimes envious, but rarely approving.

The disaffiliative function of calling an issue a moral panic, then, expresses a sense of aloofness, of superiority over those engaging in the supposed panic, and also of collusion with a sophisticated readership: you and I know better.

Finally, it permits the writer to attack political or commercial opponents (the Tories, the 'right-wing press' and so on) either for wasting time and energy fussing over vacuities and/or arousing unwarranted hostility among some part of the public towards some specific group – be it hoodies, immigrants or lone parents. However, as we noted above, given how rarely either an instigator of a moral panic, or the group suffering from the panic, is specified, this function is a minor one compared to its uses to express disaffiliation and solidarity with readers.

6. Conclusions on MD-CADS

Returning to the main theme: to summarise and by way of definition, MD-CADS is the study of changes in linguistic habits or in social, political and cultural perspectives over a brief period of contemporary time, as illustrated in a particular discourse type or set of discourse types.

In this issue, Duguid (2010a) studies changes in the kind of evaluative lexis employed by papers between 1993 and 2005, and she discovers a noticeable increase in terms normally seen to indicate vagueness of expression. It must be stressed that, in contrast with its use in everyday speech, *vagueness* in a linguistic sense is by no means a negative thing. Speakers usually adopt the level of precision that they deem appropriate to the circumstances, and a low level of precision is typically employed in friendly conversation as a means of stressing common ground among participants. This may well be the stance towards the reader that modern UK papers are increasingly seeking to adopt.

Clark (2010) studies changes in news *evidentiality*, which may be defined as the study of the linguistic devices that a speaker or writer uses to attest to how he or she, or some other actor, came into possession of knowledge of some fact or event.

Marchi (2010) looks at changes in the use of the item *moral* and its related forms to see what the UK quality newspapers construed as moral issues in 1993 and then in 2005, and how they are evaluated. Although the main focus is diachronic she also looks at differences across individual papers.

Duguid (2010b), too, considers changes over time in evaluation and moral stance in examining the use in context of the prefix *anti* and poses the questions: what negative prejudices do the newspapers discuss? And do the targets of the prejudice and opposition expressed by *anti* change over the time period? She also notes in passing the importance of *anti* items in science reporting.

Finally, Taylor (2010) conducts an empirical investigation into how the rhetorical function of science itself in the news has changed, focussing, in particular, on how it is increasingly invoked to augment the moral significance of an argument.

All the papers in this issue shift back and forward between quantitative and qualitative data analyses, as outlined under Section 3.1, above, and they all employ both the inductive and the hypothesis-driven types of methodology described in the Abstract to this paper, (though in different measure and with different emphases). Duguid (2010a) and Clark (2010) start from overall keyword analyses before moving into closer qualitative reading, whilst Marchi (2010), Duguid (2010b) and Taylor (2010) all begin with more restricted research questions and then combine quantitative and qualitative analyses to shed light on them. All are not only eminently data-driven, but also, as Taylor (2010) puts it, *researcher*-driven.

A word of caution needs to be added. Both the methodology and the technology/software generally employed in MD-CADS tend to shed light on *changes* not only in prose style but also in socio-politico-cultural issues. In contrast, what stays unchanged may often remain invisible to the researcher. But as long as we are aware of this fact, it need not preoccupy us unduly. Humans, like all biological entities, tend naturally to be more interested in change than stasis, since changes of state often prove to be especially significant – for good or bad, threatening or rewarding, and so on. Change is also generally intriguing since it tends to demand explanation in a way that stasis often does not.

Finally, in terms of using corpora in teaching, Baker (2009: 315) makes the interesting point that, '[i]t could be argued that students would find corpus research more interesting and motivating if up-to-date corpora were available'. In other words, they may well prefer to study the kinds of argot evaluative items listed in Duguid (2010a), many of which they might use themselves, rather than those prevalent in the 1970s or 1980s. They will almost certainly appreciate reading about people and events, as well as modern attitudes to, say, sexual morality (Marchi, 2010), which they themselves recognise – rather than those wrapped in the shrouds of history, before their time. Should they happen across the following prophetic – indeed Sibylline – words from SiBol 05, it might even raise a smile or two:

(19) Yet there are signs that Obama is positioning himself to inherit Clinton's mantle as the next great Democratic presidential hope [. . .]

When Katrina struck, Obama was out of the country on his first foreign trip as a senator [. . .] On his way home he passed through London and paid a brief visit to No10 and a meeting with Tony Blair.

"They let me sit in Winston Churchill's reading chair," he proudly told reporters later. One day visitors may be told it was also the chair used by President Obama.

(SiBol 05, *Sunday Times*)

References

Alvarez-Cáccamo, C. and G. Prego-Vásquez. 2003. 'Political cross-discourse: conversationalization, imaginary networks, and social fields in Galiza', Pragmatics 13 (1), pp. 145–62.

Baker, P. 2006. Using Corpora in Discourse Analysis. London: Continuum.

Baker, P. 2009. 'The BE06 Corpus of British English and recent language change', International Journal of Corpus Linguistics 14 (3), pp. 312–37.

Bayley P. and C. Bevitori. 2009. '"Just war", or just "war": arguments for doing the "right thing"' in J. Morley and P. Bayley (eds) Corpus-Assisted Discourse Studies on the Iraq Conflict: Wording the War, pp. 74–107. New York and London: Routledge.

Biber, D. 1988. Variations across Speech and Writing. Cambridge: Cambridge University Press.

Biber, D., S. Conrad and R. Reppen. 1998. Corpus Linguistics: Investigating Language Structure and Use. Cambridge: Cambridge University Press.

Brown, P. and S. Levinson. 1987. Politeness: Some Universals in Language Use. Cambridge: Cambridge University Press.

Carter, R. and M. McCarthy. 2006. The Cambridge Grammar of English. Cambridge: Cambridge University Press.

Clark, C. 2010. 'Evidence of evidentiality in the quality press 1993 and 2005', Corpora 5 (2), pp. 139–60.

Cohen, S. 2006 [1973]. 'Deviance and panics' in C. Critcher (ed.) Critical Readings: Moral Panics and the Media, pp. 29–40. Maidenhead: Open University Press.

Critcher, C. (ed.). 2006. Critical Readings: Moral Panics and the Media. Maidenhead: Open University Press.

Critcher, C. 2006. 'Introduction: more questions than answers' in C. Critcher (ed.) Critical Readings: Moral Panics and the Media, pp. 1–24. Maidenhead: Open University Press.

Duguid, A. 2010a. 'Newspaper discourse informalisation: a diachronic comparison from keywords', Corpora 5 (2), pp. 109–38.

Duguid, A. 2010b. 'Investigating anti and some reflections on Modern Diachronic Corpus-Assisted Discourse Studies (MD-CADS)', Corpora 5 (2), pp. 191–220.

Fairclough, N. 1995. Media Discourse. London: Arnold.

Gabrielatos, C. and P. Baker. 2008. 'Fleeing sneaking flooding. A corpus analysis of discursive constructions of refugees and asylum seekers in the UK Press 1996–2005', Journal of English Linguistics 36 (1), pp. 5–38.

Goode, E. and N. Ben-Yehuda. 2006 [1994]. ' Moral panics: an introduction' in C. Critcher (ed.) Critical Readings: Moral Panics and the Media, pp. 50–59. Maidenhead: Open University Press.

Hardt-Mautner, G. 1995. '"Only connect." Critical discourse analysis and corpus linguistics', UCREL Technical Paper 6. Lancaster: University of Lancaster.

Leech, G. and N. Smith. 2006. 'Recent grammatical change in written English 1961–1992: some preliminary findings of a comparison of American with British English' in A. Renouf and A. Kehoe (eds) The Changing Face of Corpus Linguistics, pp. 186–204. Amsterdam: Rodopi.

McEnery, A. and A. Wilson. 2000. Corpus Linguistics. Edinburgh: Edinburgh University Press.

McEnery, A., R. Xiao and Y. Tono. 2006. Corpus-based Language Studies. London: Routledge.

McNair, N. 2003. News Journalism in the UK. London: Routledge.

Mair, C. 1995. 'Changing patterns of complementation and concomitant grammaticalisation of the verb help in present-day English' in B. Aarts and C. Meyer (eds) The Verb in Contemporary English, pp. 258–72. Cambridge: Cambridge University Press.

Mair, C., M. Hundt, G. Leech and N. Smith. 2002. 'Short term diachronic shifts in part-of-speech frequencies: a comparison of the tagged LOB and F-LOB corpora', International Journal of Corpus Linguistics 7 (2), pp. 245–64.

Marchi, A. 2010. '"The moral *in* the story": a diachronic investigation of lexicalised morality in the UK press', Corpora 5 (2), pp. 161–89.

Morley, J. and P. Bayley (eds). 2009. Corpus-Assisted Discourse Studies on the Iraq War. London: Routledge.

Partington, A. 2003. The Linguistics of Political Argument: The Spin-doctor and the Wolf-pack at the White House. London: Routledge.

Partington, A. 2006. The Linguistics of Laughter: A Corpus-Assisted Study of Laughter-talk. London: Routledge.

Partington, A. 2008. 'The armchair and the machine: Corpus-Assisted Discourse Studies' in C. Taylor Torsello, K. Ackerley and E. Castello (eds) Corpora for University Language Teachers, pp. 189–213. Bern: Peter Lang.

Partington, A., J. Morley and L. Haarman (eds). 2004. Corpora and Discourse. Bern: Peter Lang.

Scott, M. 2008. WordSmith Tools version 5. Liverpool: Lexical Analysis Software.

Someya, Y. 1998. E-Lemma. Available online at: http://www.lexically.net/downloads/e_lemma.zip

Stubbs, M. 1996. Text and Corpus Analysis. Oxford: Blackwell.

Stubbs, M. 2001. Words and Phrases: Corpus Studies of Lexical Semantics. Oxford: Blackwell.

Taylor, C. 2010. 'Science in the news: a diachronic perspective', Corpora 5 (2), pp. 221–50.

Westin, I. 2002. Language Change in English Newspaper Editorials. Amsterdam: Rodopi.

Wimsatt, W. and M. Beardsley. 1946. 'The Intentional Fallacy', Sewanee Review 54, pp. 469–70.

Newspaper discourse informalisation: a diachronic comparison from keywords

Alison Duguid[1]

Abstract

In this paper, I provide an overview of certain types of salient items found in the keyword lists of the SiBol 1993 and SiBol 2005 corpora with the objective of diachronic analysis of a particular text type, namely, that of British broadsheet newspapers. I analysed the keyword lists (see Partington, 2010: Section 2) in search of items that could be assigned to semantic sets, which could be glossed as hyperbole, vagueness and informal evaluation. The appearance of these sets in the keywords for 2005 seems to point to changes over time in newspaper prose style. The newspapers under consideration thus appear to have altered both in their function and in their relationship with their readership; and this is reflected in the salient lexis and its contexts of use. An increase in conversational and informal styles emerges, along with a notable increase in a particular kind of evaluative and promotional language as a result of a proportional increase in soft news, supplements and reviews.

1. Comparing the 1993 and 2005 corpora: corpus wordlists and keywords

A word list at first sight is a confusing animal, with its high-frequency items rising up like tusks and its hapax legomena lying as flat as fur; its patterns are weird and wonderful. Beneath the surface though its DNA reveals numerous regularities which can be useful to language researchers searching for patterns of importance in their own text corpora.

(Scott and Tribble, 2006: 31)

[1] Facoltà di Lettere, San Niccolò, via Roma 56, 53100, Siena, Italy.
Correspondence to: Alison Duguid,   *e-mail*: duguid@unisi.it

Corpora 2010 Vol. 5 (2): 109–138
DOI: 10.3366/E1749503210000419
© Edinburgh University Press
www.eupjournals.com/cor

In his consideration of the effects of corpus-based methods on language study, Mike Scott mentions two causes of what he calls an 'upheaval' (Scott and Tribble, 2006: 5): the first are the technological innovations that permit us to plough through vast quantities of text in a short time and to reduce it or 'boil it down' to lists and concordance lines; the second, meanwhile, is the way the pattern-perceiving predisposition of the brain comes into play when it examines such lists. To be useful for investigation, corpora the size of SiBol (see below) need a considerable degree of 'boiling down', and, inevitably, different patterns stand out to different researchers. In this paper, I will be looking at some of the differences between two comparable corpora that are differentiated by date, describing both the software-generated 'facts', in terms of relative frequencies and keyness scores, and looking at the linguistic patterns I perceived and use in commenting on such data in an attempt to make significant generalisations about the corpora. The two corpora are named after the universities (Siena and Bologna) that are involved in working on the project, and are called SiBol 93 and SiBol 05. The first contains around 100 million words (about twenty-seven million from the *Guardian*, thirty-four million from the *Telegraph* and *Sunday Telegraph*, and thirty-nine million from the *Times* and *Sunday Times*). The second contains about 145 million (forty-one million from the *Guardian*, thirty-seven million from the *Telegraph* and *Sunday Telegraph* and sixty-seven million from the *Times* and *Sunday Times*). Wordlists were compiled using WordSmith Tools 5 and two keyword lists formed using the Keywords tool: one of the key items in the 2005 newspapers, and the other of the key items from the 1993 set of texts. We decided to confine ourselves, initially, to analysing the first 2,500 items in each list although we recognise that this approach may have left out keywords at the same level of statistical significance as those included.

2. Language in the press

2.1 Language in the press: informalisation

Partington's (2010) overview of the project uncovered evidence of changes in the kind of language used by the broadsheets which make up our corpus, including an increase in the number of linguistic devices usually associated with informal registers. Some of the changes towards informality have been described as characteristic of the discourse of tabloids. The British tabloids are frequently differentiated from the broadsheets in terms of their involving readers rather than being detached from them – being emotional and subjective, rather than neutral, and for the use of humour (Morley, 1998: 35–47). Similar conclusions have been made about print advertising and how it exploits the features of oral language (Cook, 1992; and Myers, 1994). Lombardo (2001) summarises such advertising language choices as exemplifying 'strategies associated with orality, the informal language associated with face-to-face interaction'. Fairclough (2001) warned against this trend, which he saw as the overt marking of power through formality giving way to 'informality, as part of a hidden agenda'. He called this 'synthetic personalisation' – an informal conversational style used as a strategy to exercise power in more indirect, subtle and less explicit ways, and involving the construction of greater complicity. The writers who contribute to the SiBol 05 newspapers have chosen – by and large, and, in a sense, collectively – to project, in some circumstances at least, a conversational tone, marked by features of informal spoken language previously identified as a feature of the tabloids and of print advertising. The corpus does not reveal the processes by which these collective practices were encouraged, whether it was top-down through editorial guidelines as part of an attempt to make the newspapers more appealing, or whether it was bottom-up as a reflection of a wider informalisation in English use. As Carter and McCarthy have noted on the continuum between spoken and written language:

> Journalists also achieve impact and get on a 'conversational' wavelength with their readers by using common spoken discourse markers and purposefully vague language in a projected conversational exchange
>
> (Carter and McCarthy, 2006: 238)

Second-person pronouns are high in the 2005 keyword list. These are signals of informality in written discourse (see Trengrove, 1986), being typical of interactive spoken discourse and indicative of a conversational tone. They are deictic pronouns, and, thus, have variable reference according to their context. Their presence among the 2005 keywords means the corpus has many of the features of oral interaction. Hundt and Mair (1999), too, in their tracking of changes in newspaper prose between 1960 and 1990, noted a greater use both of contractions, and first- and second-person pronouns, where these oral features were adopted in an attempt to appeal to a wider reading audience. In this way, the dialogue between writer and readers becomes explicit, and is constantly being referred to by the writers, with the presupposed interlocutors projected to form a community of shared belief or value (Martin and White, 2005: 93). The writers expect those they address to respond to the value positions they propose. The projected relationship reflected in the corpus is also signposted by a set of items uniting informality and vagueness or lack of precision (see Channell, 1994). Vagueness is a strong indication of assumed shared knowledge, the referents of vague expressions being assumed to be known by the reader (Carter and McCarthy, 2006: 202) and can be used to soften expressions to avoid appearing too direct or unduly authoritative and assertive. A relationship is set up which will underlie all the evaluations and the language used to make them.

In this paper, I will look for other features of this relationship, beyond deictics and the contracted forms, which might be considered pertinent to language changes over time, focussing on sets of lexical keywords which have in common the semantic feature of evaluation.

2.2 Language in the press: evaluation

Evaluation, stance and appraisal are all terms which describe the ways the subjective views of speaker or writer, as well as the value systems of individuals and communities, are conveyed in language (Hunston and Thompson, 2000; Martin and White, 2005; Biber *et al.*, 1999: Chapter 12; and Mauranen and Bondi, 2003).

In highlighting the fact that evaluation is comparative, subjective and of course value-laden, Hunston and Thompson (2000) identify four parameters of evaluation (good/bad; certainty/uncertainty; expectedness; importance), but admit that, essentially, the good/bad parameter is the most basic and the one to which the others relate. Morley and Partington (2009) propose a means of indicating the precise reason for the positive or negative evaluation, which exploits a Linnaean-style binomial notation; for example, bad: dangerous (bad because dangerous), good: pleasurable (good because pleasurable), and so on. Bednarek's (2006) investigation of evaluation in media discourse, based on a small corpus of news items, employs a set of parameters that includes importance, expectedness, comprehensibility, necessity and reliability. Some of our keywords fit into these categories but many would be consigned to the category she has named emotivity, essentially meaning good or bad (all of which basically corresponds to Morley and Partington's Linnaean system, but without the helpful colon).

Hunston and Thompson (2000) identify three functions for evaluation. The first function, an ideational one of representing the world around us through language, also involves the expression of communal value systems, and every act of evaluation builds on that system; the second function is the interpersonal one of maintaining relations among participants; while the third function, which is textual or organisational, also serves to inform readers or hearers of the *point* of the discourse. To give an example which is highly relevant here, the increasing use of promotional material and the consequent intrusion of positive evaluations into newspaper language will affect the selection of content (ideational function), will alter the relationship between paper and readers (interpersonal function), and will indicate to readers what their attitude should be (part of the textual function).

The keyword analyses revealed how a large number of hyperbolic words have become more frequent in broadsheet language. Carter and McCarthy (2004) provide a useful discussion of what they call 'purposeful exaggeration' in everyday conversational British English. Using evidence from corpora, they demonstrate how speakers:

> exaggerate narrative, descriptive and argumentative features and make assertions that are overstated, literally impossible, inconceivable or counterfactual in many different types of discourse context. Such hyperbolic expressions usually pass without challenge by listeners, who accept them as creative intensifications for evaluative or affective purposes such as humour and irony.
>
> (McCarthy and Carter, 2004: 184)

At the same time, they remind us that hyperbole in written contexts was a feature of classical rhetoric, associated with persuasive speech and the exercise of power. Such rhetorical exaggeration has been examined in previous studies of broadsheet opinion pieces, including Duguid (2009), who looks at the kind of humorous opinion pieces where humour, especially humorous hyperbole, is a purpose in itself. McCarthy and Carter (2004) illustrate some of the most frequently recurring lexico-grammatical types of hyperbole in everyday contexts, finding that hyperbole (like metaphors) can be both conventional and creative. For them, what is of great interest is the evaluative context of hyperbole/overstatement and how speakers use it to express affective meanings, and how the interpersonal function is paramount in its use. In newspaper use of the rhetoric of the vernacular, the fact that such features of the spoken language appear to predominate among the 2005 keywords provides more corroboration for the hypothesis that broadsheet newspaper language is becoming conversationalised.

Among the items whose chief function is to evaluate are adjectives and adverbs (Hunston and Thompson, 2000: 16–19), and these categories account for the majority of the evaluative items among the 2005 keywords. The literature lists other grammatical features associated with evaluation, including intensifiers and quantifiers, comparators (such as comparatives and superlatives), ways of being vague, adverbs indicating affect, certainty and doubt, and hedges and emphatics. All of these are present in our 2005 keywords list. Grouping them as patterns into sets and subsets enables more powerful statements about changes in these newspapers' language habits to be made.

When we start to look at what is being evaluated, we see that the keywords of SiBol 93 contain many more items linked to the semantic fields of politics, economics and finance, as well as more references to foreign news. News reporting of such fields is what used to characterise the broadsheets. But this requires investigative reporters out in the field. It has been suggested (Lewis *et al.*, 2008; and Davies, 2008) that there has been a reduction in the number of journalists working for the British newspapers, while at the same time there has been an increase in the physical volume of the newspaper. Staff cuts have led to fewer correspondents and the increase in size has meant that those journalists remaining in their offices need to produce three times as much copy as previously. Although the actual figures and the way of calculating this have been disputed,[2] if fewer journalists are indeed responsible for more copy, then the temptation to use readily available PR material, or pre-packaged appraisals becomes progressively stronger. Press release material is being used more often as a basis for articles, and phrases are frequently taken *verbatim* by the journalists from a limited number of press releases. A report entitled *Quality and Independence of British Journalism*: *Tracking the Changes over 20 Years*[3] found that

---

[2] See: http://www.guardian.co.uk/books/2008/feb/09/pressandpublishing.society
[3] This report was prepared by Prof. Justin Lewis, Dr Andrew Williams, Prof. Bob Franklin, Dr James Thomas and Nick Mosdell at the Cardiff School of Journalism, Media and Cultural Studies.

60 percent of press articles come wholly or mainly from 'pre-packaged' sources. The findings suggest that public relations often does much more than merely set the agenda: it was found that 19 percent of newspaper stories were verifiably derived *mainly or wholly* from public relations material, while fewer than half the stories appeared to be entirely independent of traceable PR. The most PR-influenced topic was health, followed closely by consumer/business news and entertainment/sport.

This would account for the conventionalisation of certain positively evaluative terms which form part of the communicative function of promotion. If PR material is taken up and inserted on a regular basis, its style of language will be reflected in the over-use of certain items. Some descriptive items become perceived as promotional rather than descriptive, and newspapers, in turn, dedicate a certain amount of comment on their use. Ironic exploitation, with a reversal of evaluation from positive to critical, is perhaps also a result of irritation with PR's reiterated and strategic enthusiasm.[4]

3. The methodology of set identification: evaluative lexical keywords

Scott argues (2006: 25) that the medium frequency words in a wordlist tend to be lexical rather than grammatical items. He also calculates that 40 percent of the items in a frequency list will be *hapax legomena*, that is, items which occur only once. A wordlist will, therefore, always contain a small number of highly used items, the most frequently used of these being grammatical items, and a long list of items which occur very infrequently. In terms of lexical choice, the high frequency lexical items used over a wide variety of texts, such as in a corpus of one entire year of newspaper output, represent well-worn paths as opposed to new ones. In examining the keywords lists we can see how, over time, some little-frequented paths have become well-trodden, while, as it were, the grass has grown over others.

In analysing the 2005 keyword list, I identified three sets of lexical words which appeared to me to be distinct and which share the lexico-semantic properties of evaluation. All three sets also bear traces of informal register; and many items are described in the common reference works as being more frequent in spoken language. For this, I consulted Biber *et al.* (1999) and Carter and McCarthy (2006). These facts already tell us something about the changes that took place in the three broadsheets between 1993 and 2005. Grouping items in this way requires shunting back and forth between wordlists (in this case keyword lists) and concordance lines. It is a

---

[4] Similarly talk of 'giving 110%' (forty-three occurrences in SiBol 05) is assigned scare quotes and labelled as a cliché: 'The clichés of the post-match interview when people talk of "holding their hands up" and "giving 110%"'.

subjective process, in which generalisations about overall patterns in the data are reached by identifying shared attributes — characterising words as similar or related, much as a lexicographer might.

Following this methodology, under Section 4, I examine in some detail the sets and their subsets. I have included for the items concerned the keyness score provided by WordSmith Tools as well as the ranking in the keyword list to give an idea of the relative salience of the items; some of these will be illustrated also by concordance lines. In order to provide some external corroboration for the groupings, I checked the definitions given for each one in a corpus-based dictionary (*Macmillans English Dictionary for Advanced Learners*, henceforth MEDAL). I used terms which were repeated in the definitions to characterise the common features of the set. Definitions include the star rating MEDAL assigns to words indicating frequency in their corpus, where three stars are assigned to very frequently occurring words.

4. Patterns in the keywords list

I first divided the keyword items into two sets, Set A and Set B. Set A (see Table 1) contains items involving implicit superlatives (Carter and McCarthy, 2006: 443), which have a high intensity element in their meaning; for example, adjectives like *overjoyed* and *exhausted*, as opposed to *happy* and *tired*. They express some kind of extreme degree or exaggeration, and are frequently used for effect rather than description alone; and they are, also, often metaphoric (for example, *fantastic*, *fabulous* and *stunning*). With the exception of *desperate*, they all express positive (or, indeed, highly positive) evaluation. As Hunston and Francis (2000) have noted, we need to find a convenient descriptive umbrella term for what the items in a group have in common, and this may involve a degree of subjectivity. Here I chose 'hyperbole' as a convenient term.

The list consists of evaluative adjectives with intensity in their meaning (several are superlatives) and adverbs with what Martin and White (2005: 140–53) have called *force* — functions such as intensification, up-scaling and maximisation. I used the dictionary definitions to confirm whether intensification was carried in the meaning (the terms used in the dictionary definitions were *extremely*, *very*, *completely*, and so on), which I further subdivided into subsets, grouping similar items together for purposes of discussion.

A second set, Set B, was chosen because the items were identified as all being related to vagueness or lack of precision – including dictionary definition terms such as *imprecise* and *undefined* (see Table 2).

Having compiled these two sets, I found there was another set with some of the same properties, that is, they were for the most part adjectives with subjective evaluative meaning, being terms of praise or blame expressed

Ranking	Word	Frequency 05	Percent SiBol 05	Frequency 93	Percent SiBol 93	Keyness
55	*really*	58,326	0.0399	24,645	0.0249	4,083.19
94	*fantastic*	7,129	0.0049	1,120	0.0011	2,852.33
115	*so*	274,959	0.1882	159,337	0.1610	2,491.56
172	*best*	93,720	0.0642	49,963	0.0505	1,911.42
285	*iconic*	1,600	0.0011	52	0.0000	1,287.34
292	*top*	63,979	0.0438	34,277	0.0346	1,254.54
317	*biggest*	27,195	0.0186	12,825	0.0129	1,187.688
424	*huge*	24,681	0.0168	11,890	0.0120	965.6301
436	*world's*	17,963	0.0123	8,135	0.0082	949.17
535	*perfect*	14,163	0.0097	6,245	0.0063	839.01
606	*everything*	26,369	0.0181	13,407	0.0136	752.22
614	*everyone*	24,371	0.0167	12,248	0.0124	748.05
665	*amazing*	5,039	0.0034	1,686	0.0017	696.3
708	*hugely*	3,821	0.0026	1,154	0.0012	656.13
709	*definitely*	5,744	0.0039	2,076	0.0021	655.76
790	*gorgeous*	2,280	0.0018	522	0.0007	610.72
817	*fabulous*	2,657	0.0018	687	0.0007	597.84
834	*beautiful*	12,173	0.0083	5,620	0.0057	589.14
842	*very*	117,787	0.0806	71,177	0.0719	583.37
972	*every*	68,878	0.0472	40,443	0.0409	526.29
981	*real*	45,116	0.0309	25,594	0.0259	521.24
983	*super*	8,404	0.0058	3,669	0.0037	518.41
1,030	*actually*	20,631	0.0141	10,749	0.0109	498.96
1,153	*inspired*	8,950	0.0061	4,098	0.0041	450.06
1,226	*incredibly*	3,069	0.0021	1,026	0.0010	424.9
1,318	*giant*	9,803	0.0067	4,679	0.0047	402.66
1,467	*key*	25,108	0.0172	13,923	0.0141	364.88
1,470	*stunning*	3,247	0.0022	1,181	0.0012	364.46
1,569	*favourite*	15,889	0.0109	8,411	0.0085	341.99
1,592	*great*	72,804	0.0498	44,162	0.0446	337.54
1,604	*skinny*	1,200	0.0008	266	0.0003	335.18
1,656	*bestselling*	915	0.0001	163	0.0000	326.24
1,894	*groundbreaking*	420	0.0006	25	0.0002	287.2641
1,771	*compelling*	3,118	0.0021	1,191	0.0012	304.81
2,010	*incredible*	2,951	0.0020	1,149	0.0012	272.26
2,296	*desperate*	7,690	0.0053	3,859	0.0039	238.18
2,312	*never*	81,237	0.0556	50,446	0.0510	236.53
2,335	*pivotal*	1,180	0.0008	329	0.0003	234.65
2,342	*absolutely*	8,200	0.0056	4,169	0.0042	233.96
2,445	*terrific*	2,297	0.0016	877	0.0009	224.85

Table 1: Set A: hyperbole in the keywords

Keyword ranking	Word	Frequency in 05	Percent in 05	Frequency in 93	Percent in 93	Keyness
70	*bit*	36,862	0.0252	14,342	0.0144	3,409.296
181	*pretty*	17,386	0.0119	6,444	0.0065	1,853.438
206	*maybe*	14,704	0.0101	5,353	0.0054	1,646.515
228	*thing*	43,903	0.0301	21,578	0.0218	1,538.136
214	*something*	60,049	0.0411	30,833	0.0311	1,606.202
238	*things*	51,199	0.0351	25,998	0.0262	1,472.891
318	*couple*	25,816	0.0177	12,050	0.0121	1,185.978
616	*stuff*	11,307	0.0077	4,851	0.0049	747.0812
	subtotal	**26,1226**		**121,449**		
		0.1788%		0.1227%		

Table 2: Set B – vagueness in the keywords

in various ways. It is more difficult to find a convenient denomination for this set, Set C, but I settled on 'vague and informal evaluation'. The words have in common with the first two sets their informality (informality was in the definitions of most of these items in MEDAL). All but the last eight were found in the first 2,500 words of the keywords list (see Table 3).

Some of these items have come into the language recently (for example, *chav*, a pejorative term applied to working class young people,[5] and *bling*, another derogatory term used to describe ostentatious jewellery or accessories) and are the result of normal processes of neologisation. Others involve new exploitations or extensions of meaning in words that already exist (for example, *edgy* for an older generation means 'tense', 'nervous' but is now also used to mean 'cutting-edge', 'trend-setting' or 'challenging the norms', see discussion under Section 5.3). In such cases, close readings will disambiguate the meaning.

We also need to bear in mind that some of the items in our sets apparently derive from quotations of direct speech, that is to say, they are a written representation of spoken language and are not always directly attributable to a journalist. This represents the journalist's desire to provide another voice in the discourse, for the journalist judges that the actual words of the speaker are worthy of inclusion. However, as much as any real desire to reproduce someone else's direct speech accurately, it also heralds, often, a wish to be dramatic.

In the following section, we will look at some of the items from our sets in more detail to see in which phraseologies they occur and what they have in common. Evaluation can take many forms (Hunston and Thompson,

---

[5] See also Renouf (2007).

Key ranking	Word	Frequency in 05	Percent in 05	Frequency in 93	Percent in 93	Keyness
425	*scary*	2,106	0.0014	278	0.0003	965.6154
705	*bling*	669	0.0005	3	0.0000	659.0058
732	*cool*	8,163	0.0056	3,338	0.0034	642.1536
1,056	*chav*	472	0.0003	0	0.0000	488.2421
1,227	*weird*	2,722	0.0019	862	0.0009	424.6107
1,235	*funky*	958	0.0007	133	0.0001	423.293
1,290	*sexy*	2,577	0.0018	809	0.0008	409.3775
1,396	*funny*	7,516	0.0051	3,431	0.0035	383.1955
1,432	*chic*	2,448	0.0017	784	0.0008	372.8543
1,441	*fake*	2,683	0.0018	897	0.0009	371.4133
1,499	*different*	40,903	0.0280	23,770	0.0240	357.363
1,621	*dark*	13,082	0.0090	6,767	0.0068	332.6923
1,668	*cute*	1,326	0.0009	325	0.0003	323.2393
1,759	*moody*	1,775	0.0012	534	0.0005	307.102
1,832	*cheesy*	509	0.0003	45	0.0000	295.9402
1,910	*tricky*	2,761	0.0019	1,035	0.0010	285.0634
2,070	*upbeat*	1,831	0.0013	600	0.0006	265.2511
2,089	*fit*	12,707	0.0087	6,758	0.0068	263.9059
2,186	*hot*	12,669	0.0087	6,774	0.0068	252.3004
2,304	*quirky*	1,424	0.0010	437	0.0004	236.9216
2,461	*vibrant*	1,709	0.0012	585	0.0006	223.8059
2,675	*dodgy*	1,438	0.0009	473	0.0004	206.5683
2,692	*clunky*	305	0.0002	19	0.0000	205.3106
2,998	*crap*	1,039	0.0007	308	0.0003	184.9174
3,056	*edgy*	828	0.0005	218	0.0002	181.0731
3,968	*spooky*	582	0.0004	145	0.0001	138.5235
4,176	*classy*	1,053	0.0007	367	0.0003	131.962
4,538	*shiny*	1,427	0.0009	571	0.0005	120.7195
4,899	*sparkly*	213	0.0001	23	0.0000	111.2567

Table 3: Set C – informal evaluation

2000: 12–22) but some lexical items have evaluation as their chief function (for example, *splendid*, *happily*, *failure* and *succeed*). One question which will need to be addressed is why there should be such a group appearing in the keywords, why is *overt* evaluation so much what 2005 papers are 'about', there being considerably fewer *intrinsically* evaluative adjectives in the SiBol 93 keywords.

5. Keyword sets

5.1 Set A: hyperbole and extremes in evaluation in the keywords

One subset of Set A (Table 1) shows a concern with relative size or ranking as a parameter of evaluation, though this is often metaphorical and has to do with fame, importance or distinction; in short, this is a combination that I denominate as 'size and ranking' (see Section 5.1.1). It is possible to isolate another set of positive keywords used to construe objects and events in terms of rank or of exceptional, outstanding aesthetic quality, and I have called this subset 'amplified positive evaluation'. The third sub-set of Set A consists mostly of intensifying adverbs, and I have called it 'intensification'. A fourth subset consists of *all* and *every*, and other indefinite pronouns and quantifiers (*everyone* and *everything*) which present extreme case formulations. The MEDAL definitions for these items contain glosses which reflect their inclusive nature and often add the idea of emphasis, agreement or disagreement. All these suggest dialogistic features of engagement such as proclaiming, denying, pronouncing, *etc.*, (see Martin and White, 2005: 92–136). Such exaggeration also involves elements of intentional imprecision; the indefinite quantifiers allow language users to make generalisations.

5.1.1 Size and ranking

The following items are related to 'size and ranking'. Sinclair (1996: 87) introduced the term 'semantic preference' to identify the semantic field within which an item operates — the relation, not between individual words, but between a lemma or word-form and a set of semantically related words. Meanwhile, Hoey (2005: 22–4) uses the term 'semantic association' to describe the way in which words or word sequences tend to occur with particular semantic sets and, thus, become associated in the mind of a language user with that semantic set or class. Where I have found a semantic preference in the collocates I have indicated it.

biggest: Most occurrences are found in *The Times* and the collocates appear to belong to the financial domain (*company, group, bank, operator, retailer, market* and *shareholder*). There are some problem—solution related items (*biggest challenge, problem* and *mistake*). Most are defined geographically (*the world's, UK's, England's* and *Europe's*).

huge: (a MEDAL three star word) The collocates in R1 position suggest a semantic preference for words dealing with impact and effects, either emotional or in terms of fame or significance (*huge significance, scope, row, surprise, shock, sense, relief, pressure, demand, success, star hit, hits, setback, blow, loss* and *losses*).

super: (a two star word) MEDAL gives four uses: as an adjective 'informal and old-fashioned (still used by some older people)', and, indeed, we do not find many examples of this function in our 2005 data; *super* is also a noun, an adverb and a prefix, the last two being the most frequent in our data. It is also found in promotional/advertising contexts as a laudatory prefix. The general idea is that of 'big, with a positive connotation'.

giant: (a two star word) Used as a noun (among the most frequent L1 collocates are: *oil giant, supermarket giant, media giant, energy giant, software giant, insurance giant, phone giant, drinks giant* and *pharmaceutical giant*). The resulting noun phrases can act as premodifiers with company names such as *oil giant Yukos* and *supermarket giant Tesco*).

bestselling: In SiBol 05, this indicates the concern with success in commercial terms. It is both hyperbolic and vague. The main right collocates indicate a relatively restricted domain (*author, book, novel, writer, novelist, memoir, series, newspaper, album, single DVD*) and three words which reveal a seasonal distortion: *da, vinci* and *code*.

5.1.2 Positive and amplified evaluation

The following items all contain amplification in their meanings (that is, the definitions all contain a gloss which expresses intensity in one way or another such as *very, extremely, completely, extreme* and *great*) or are accompanied by intensifying adverbials.

world's: This item collocates with a number of comparative or superlative items such as *world's most, biggest, largest, top, best, first, leading, greatest, poorest* and *richest*, and has the meaning 'of the highest measure'. The writer using such units constructs an identity for himself or herself which suggests considerable knowledge of the world.

top: (three stars) The concordance lines reflect a penchant for lists (*top ten, two, four* and *three*) — the search for the best and the importance of striving. The principle domains are those of sport, the performing arts, cooking and restaurants, and travel; all of these areas are covered by supplements or dedicated pages.[6]

---

[6] We need to note that keyness is also affected by occurrences of a different use, the fashion item noun (*wrap-over top*).

iconic: (one star) This is a media word which has been the subject of much comment. Collocates are nearly all linked with fame, fashion and visibility, and most contexts are connected to the arts (*iconic status*, *image(s)*, *figure*, *brand*, *design*, *fashion*, *moment(s)*, *event*, *photograph(s)*, *film*, *movie*, *performance*, *piece* and *work(s)*).

key: As an adjective (three stars), it is inherently comparative in meaning, indicating a judgement concerning importance. It co-occurs with many general nouns: *key thing*, *man*, *question*, *point*, *element*, *moment*, *area*, *witness*, *worker*, *member*, *ingredient*, *component* and *difference*.

pivotal: R1 collocates appear to be related to strategic issues concerning people, places or times, often in a sports context (*pivotal role*, *moment*, *figure*, *point*, *part*, *position*, *player*, *year*, *figure*, *character*, *factor*, *decision*, *scene*, *stage*, *event*, *game*, *day* and *match*). Both *pivotal* and *key* seem to be serving the same function, that of claiming high ground and visibility by declaring importance.

best: By definition this item involves comparative evaluation (*best player*, *scorer* and *actor*), but it also serves to signal promotion and choice (*best bet* and *best bet of the day*). It is mostly concerned with connotations of competition and comparison.[7]

fantastic: This is categorised by MEDAL as informal. Here its use is prevalent with right collocates relating to sport (*fantastic player*, *team*, *club*, *season*, *players*, *game*, *football*, *season* and *club*), but also with life, travel and work experiences (*fantastic job*, *opportunity*, *experience*, *views*, *day*, *achievement*, *work*, *year*, *place* and *people*).

perfect: (three stars) This item displays a semantic preference for 'things to be sought after' (*the perfect risotto* and *the perfect roast chicken*), but it is also a sports metaphor (*a perfect 10*). One reason for the increase in the occurrence of this term seems to reflect the growth of the influence of PR in newspapers. In the SiBol 05 corpus, an article by Ben Goldacre reports on the topic of equation or formulaic stories.[8]

---

[7] Some occurrences, however, are simply seasonal and event-related in features about *George Best*, who died in 2005.

[8] '...documenting every single equation story to appear in the *Telegraph*, a serious paper that covers science properly. Their finds include such important breakthroughs in the field of mathematical modelling as: The Perfect Sitcom (quality $= (rd+v)f \div a+s$) to promote UKTV Gold; The Perfect Joke ($x = (fl + no)/p$) to promote some comedian; The Perfect Day (quality $= O + NS + Cpm \div T + He$) to promote ice cream; The Perfect Rugby Kick (KP $= CSP - s + w + r + yn + cr + sc + mt + xn + ctw$), which somehow has something to do with a research company called Qinetiq; The Perfect Marriage (some guy); The Perfect Chip (Tesco); The Perfect Football Penalty (odds of scoring $= (X + Y + S)*(T + I + 2B) \div 8 +$

amazing: (three stars) We find a wide range of collocates which are similar to those found with *fantastic*, but with less concentration on sport (*amazing things, experience, story, feeling, views, place, achievement, day, adventures, comeback, opportunity, feat* and *ability*).

fabulous: (one star) The salience of this item in terms of what gave it its place amongst the keywords is perhaps skewed by a number of titles repeated in the listings, event-related rather than evaluative items: a film, *The Fabulous Baker Boys*, and performances of the *Fabulous Beast Dance Theatre Company*, mentions of the sitcom *Absolutely Fabulous*, and the titles of various features in the papers.[9] Nevertheless, it is still important to note that the word in this case has been deliberately chosen for a title, often with ironic intentions. In most cases, however, the collocates relate to places, artefacts and appearance or sense data, with a bias towards travel promotion (*fabulous views, fabulous hotels, fabulous place, fabulous time, fabulous food, fabulous stay, fabulous view* and *fabulous beaches*).

inspired: When occurring as an adjective rather than a suffix, the R1 collocates include *inspired choice, idea, decision, move, piece, collection, casting, leadership* and *performance*.

beautiful: (three stars) MEDAL warns users that it is very general and suggests to their advanced learners other ways of expressing the idea because it is so undefined. It features in the names of cultural artefacts and is thus repeated as they are mentioned in reviews and listings: films, *A Beautiful Mind*, songs, programmes, and in the name of a feature in the *Telegraph* (the *Body Beautiful*). Its frequency perhaps suggests the importance of physical appearance and aesthetic reactions in the value system (its R1 collocates include *beautiful game, people, woman, place, things, day, city, house, daughter, places, beaches, country* and *girls*).

$V \div 2 - 1$) for, oh, Ladbrokes; How To Open Champagne ($P = T \div 4.5 + 1$) (Marks and Spencer); The Perfect Place To Shop ($D = f(m,b,c)$), Yellow pages; The Perfect Newspaper (it's the *Telegraph*, heh); How To Pour Gravy: (amount of gravy $= (W - D \div S) \div D * 100$), mmm Bisto; The Perfect Biscuit (where the formula was deemed too complicated for *Telegraph* readers), and many more. Then they've done exactly the same thing for the *Mail*. These stories tell us nothing about science. They are what PR companies call "advertising equivalent exposure", a way to get your brand into the paper without paying, and on to editorial pages. They are copied and pasted on to the page by hurried journalists with other deadlines to deal with...' (Bad Science, *Guardian*, 13 December 2008).

[9] It is always problematic when working from keywords to decide when the salience has been skewed so as to render any insight void. In more in-depth studies this should be dealt with manually and keyness recalculated after such items have been removed. In this case, if titles are removed, the keyness score would be higher (717.29) since many of the same items appear in both corpora. The status of titles as intertextual references merits further investigation.

gorgeous: (one star) In our material this item relates mostly to aesthetic or sense experiences (MEDAL gives it as an alternative to *beautiful*, especially with reference to clothes and hair). We also find the idiom *drop dead gorgeous*.

stunning: (one star) The R1 collocates include *views, victory, scenery, performance, view, display, success* and *location*.

great: (three stars) A polysemous adjective expressing importance or power as well as enthusiasm. In MEDAL, four out of the six meanings are labelled informal (right collocates belong to the arts, sports or travel, and include *great scenery, performance, success, display, effect, debut, win, catch, kick, shot, strike, view, landscapes, location, house, beaches, city, countryside* and *setting*).

terrific: (one star) This is nearly always connected with arts and aesthetics (*looks, sounds, performance*(s), *form, value, appearance, record, animation, film, cast, ensemble, story* and *achievement*).

favourite: (two stars) The R1 collocates include *favourite book, film, place, food, music, song, band, restaurant, piece* and *airline*.

compelling: The R1 collocates indicate a variety of contexts connected with argumentation, *compelling evidence, case* and *reason*(s), but they mostly concern the arts or literary artefacts, hence *compelling story, account, drama, narrative, viewing, performance, series, portrait, book, documentary, read, film* and *study*).

skinny: MEDAL gives the meaning of this item as 'very thin in a way that is not attractive'. In autobiographical accounts it seems to have such negative evaluation, whereas in fashion contexts it seems to be a desirable attribute. Its R1 collocates include the fashionable coffee choice *skinny latte*, but are otherwise mainly fashion items: *skinny jeans, trousers, scarf, scarves, models* and *drainpipes*.

incredible: (one star) There are frequent references to *The Incredible Hulk*, and *incredible shrinking* as an ironic epithet, but other collocates mostly relate to competition and performance. Its R1 collocates include *journey, amount, story, thing, run, success, speed, pressure, range, skill, strength, energy* and *achievement*.

Such open hyperbole can be contrasted with the limited number of evaluative adjectives from SiBol 93: *considerable, substantial, modest, cautious, satisfactory, inadequate, limited, large* and *small*. The only evaluations in the keywords of SiBol 93 which could be regarded as remotely hyperbolic are *distinguished* and *necessary*.

5.1.3 Intensification and emphasis

This subset involves a variety of intensifying features, usually adverbial:

really: (three stars) MEDAL classifies this as normally spoken and used for emphasis.

so: (three stars) This item is also used to emphasise a quality, feeling or amount, but there is considerable polysemy, and not all uses are emphatic. A keyness comparison of n-grams would provide further insights into the changing phraseology of broadsheets since we find the unit *so not*, employed to express a new emphatic negation with a variety of colligations, to be found mostly in first-person accounts or direct speech:

> (1) So we cut a deal. A fantastic deal, actually – **I am so not a victim**. In return for me going quietly -no threats of industrial tribunals and sex-discrimination claims – they're giving me a big payoff – a whole year's salary – and they're putting out the "spending more time with her family" stuff.
>
> (SiBol 05, *Sunday Times*)

> (2) I leave them plotting a "King Lear jolly" at the local bowling alley at which they will tease their Lear, David Warner, by calling him Dave ("**He's so not a Dave**").
>
> (SiBol 05, *Telegraph*)

> (3) The dining room was pretty much the communal place where the TV was and where we did our homework. The front room is the sacred zone. **You are so not allowed in the front room** – it was only used when there were visitors.
>
> (SiBol 05, *Sunday Times*)

hugely: This adverb shows similar semantic preferences to *huge* but with a stronger association with emotional impact (*hugely impressive, enjoyable, entertaining, disappointing, respected, satisfying, inhibiting, relieved, exciting* and *embarrassing*), or the extent of the impact (*hugely popular, successful, important, influential, significant, ambitious, controversial, powerful, inflated* and *competitive*).

definitely: (two stars) This item amplifies assertions, predictions and comparisons (collocates include *declared, remarked, told, called, played, asked, refused, dubbed* and *observed*) and is usually followed by evaluation, as shown under Figure 1.

N Concordance

1.018   under Angela Merkel. "I will not belong to the next government, definitely not," said an emotional Mr Schroder, addressing a trade
1.019   5, will return after sustaining neck and shoulder damage. "Graham's definitely out of this weekend's game but we won't know the full extent
1.020   than the Mile, with Makin saying: "He goes better on dirt than grass." Definitely bound for the Breeders' Cup is the British heroine of last
1.021   to spicy marinade pastes and to the relatively fierce heat of the grill. Definitely not a fish for the fish knife, then. METHOD: Combine the
1.022   like all of us, with strengths and weaknesses. "John Paul the Great"? Definitely not. Let us be truthful and not forget both aspects of his
1.023   not altered their relationship. "Tommy and I are enemies," he grins. "Definitely enemies." 27 February 2005, Sunday Times, p.55 You real
1.024   jumped better than he has done all season yesterday and fast ground definitely helps him. Whatever is decided, I have one more great
1.025   bidding for the radio stations owned by the Guardian Media Group? Definitely maybe is the answer. Chrysalis seems to want some, but

Figure 1: Concordance for *definitely*

N Concordance

9   he is fresh from his triumph as Wotan at Covent Garden. An incredibly versatile singer, Terfel excels at opera's jokers and servants
10   services and when he came back, he confessed everything. He was incredibly calm and just told his story. He seemed to be in control of
11   one of the most vivid moments of a series that has since swung incredibly. He thrust out a pad and watched with a mixture of horror
12   man ever to train as a noodle-puller. That's right. It's an incredibly rare skill for a Westerner, never mind someone originally
13   that autism is simply a disability. In fact, I believe that it may be an incredibly important asset for humanity. My life story doesn't conform
14   within a week. I didn't have any nausea or dizziness. But I was incredibly tired after the operation. You have to be very gentle with
15   colour, character and life leached out of them, you will recall just how incredibly, unutterably boring it was, even though at the time we
16   published on Monday, Lord Stevens says that the episode was "incredibly traumatic" for the whole force. He writes: "The
17   self-awareness. Course alumna's comment: "This course was incredibly helpful. I now have a much better understanding of what is
18   transformational surprise.Seen in silhouette against lambent light, an incredibly undulant woman slips effortlessly in and out of cactus- like
19   "I simply felt compelled to do it. It seemed right -it's incredibly funny, incredibly bleak, the emotional range is so huge. No pragmatic

Figure 2: Concordance for *incredibly*

incredibly: (one star) The concordance lines shown under Figure 2 indicate that it is often used to emphasise evaluations.

The R1 collocates include: *difficult, hard, well, close, important, lucky, high, good, exciting, beautiful, popular, fast, proud* and *moving*.

In contrast, only two intensifiers appear among the keywords of SiBol 93, namely *greatly* and *wholly*, which have a more written and formal tone; and there are also a number of downscaling adverbials (*scarcely, merely, nearly* and *virtually*), which exemplify a choice of focus rather than force.

Among the 2005 keywords we find another intensifier, namely *fucking* (keyness 327.83). MEDAL glosses this as 'extremely offensive' and 'used for emphasising'. This often involves a deliberate transgressive flout of politeness conventions. We should note that it occurs mostly in direct speech quotations or simulated speech. It seems to function as a generic intensifier and is not always used for negative evaluations; for example:

(6) It would be interesting to see how the world would be different if Dick Cheney really listened to Radiohead's OK Computer. I think the world would probably improve. **That album is fucking brilliant**. It changed my life, so why wouldn't it change his?

(SiBol 05, *Guardian*)

(7) Ferguson could not endure questioning of Juan Sebastian Veron. **"He's a great fucking** player," the Manchester United manager said.

(SiBol 05, *Guardian*)

There are a large number of censored versions of offensive language in the corpus which show up with asterisks. The *Guardian*, however, has an explicit policy of using the whole uncensored word so that the *Guardian* and the *Observer* account for nearly all occurrences.[10]

> *absolutely*: (three stars) This item appears to show a semantic preference for denial (*absolutely no*, *nothing* and *not*) and for justifying (*absolutely right, clear, necessary, sure, certain, essential, fine, vital, crucial, convinces, determined, confident, true, central, critical* and *correct*). It also adds emphasis by maximising words which already express strong emotion (*absolutely staggering, hilarious, ludicrous, horrendous, furious, disgusting, outrageous, fascinating, stunning* and *appalling*), especially strong emotion where intensification is already part of the basic meaning (*absolutely delighted, devastated, gutted, terrified, thrilled, knackered, shattered, stunned* and *gobsmacked*) and it is these last two preferences which account for most of the increase in use.

5.1.4 All and every

This subset of Set A comprises inclusive quantifiers used as indefinite pronouns: *everyone, everybody* and *everything*. According to Biber *et al.* (1999: 351) indefinite pronouns refer to entities which the speaker or writer cannot or does not want to specify more exactly and are most common in conversation and fiction (possibly due to the presentation of direct speech dialogue) and least common in academic registers. This suggests that news and academic prose writers more frequently opt for a precise expression consisting of determiner plus noun (Biber *et al.*, 1999: 353). It is possible, perhaps, that Biber *et al.* (1999) were examining corpora which deal more with hard news than with soft, and that this would account for their observations. Our data suggest that use of these items has increased over

---

[10] From the *Guardian* style guide:

'The editor's guidelines [on swearwords] are as follows:
First, remember the reader, and respect demands that we should not casually use words that are likely to offend. Second, use such words only when absolutely necessary to the facts of a piece, or to portray a character in an article; there is almost never a case in which we need to use a swearword outside direct quotes. Third, the stronger the swearword, the harder we ought to think about using it. Finally, never use asterisks, which are just a cop-out.'

See also http://www.guardian.co.uk/media/pda/2009/apr/03/research-digital-media where the use of expletives in the *Guardian* over a ten-year period is analysed.

time, which is a further indication of a shift to a more conversational register. We also find the hyperbolic *never* and *all* among the 2005 keywords.

5.2 Vagueness

Hyperbole is, by its very nature, vague to some extent. By including all, or most, or worst-case scenarios, it avoids precision. We can see in the next set, Set B keywords, how lack of precision can also be combined with understated vagueness.

bit: (three stars) This item appears in a number of evaluative patterns: *a bit* + evaluative adjective, *a bit* + of + evaluative noun, and also as a downtoner or hedge – *a bit worried, nervous, disappointed, tired, sad, surprised* and *mad*, which all indicate a need to avoid certainty in classifying emotions.

stuff: (three stars) This item often functions as a cohesive substitute for a general noun, but it also indicates informality. The most frequent cluster, *the stuff of*, involves a kind of counterfactual hyperbole, *the stuff of legend, dreams, nightmares, science-fiction, fairytales, fantasy, myth* and *Hollywood*, and, when preceded by demonstrative reference forms (*the, this* and *that*) it is used to express presumed shared knowledge of the world. In constructions with the definite article, for example, it collocates with dichotomies such as black/white, hot/cold and good/bad. *The white stuff* has variable reference deducible from context (snow, sugar, drugs), while *the black stuff* usually refers to oil. It collocates with items that indicate unusualness (*new, interesting* and *exciting*), as well as usualness (*usual, same, old, boring, basic, obvious, everyday, dull, familiar* and *routine*). A number of frequent clusters reflect a concern with emotional impact, both positive (*important, fascinating, gripping, stirring, weird, heady, interesting, impressive, thrilling, terrific, entertaining* and *wonderful*) and negative (*hard, bad, rough, tough, scary, heavy* and *dangerous*). This kind of evaluation comes in autobiographical narratives, in interviews (the clusters are frequently a part of direct speech reports) and in opinion-piece reviews.

thing: (three stars) All definitions contain glosses of imprecision. Like *stuff*, it is a general noun and is useful in creating lexical cohesion, enabling people to refer vaguely to categories, assuming shared categorisations. However, it is also a way of actually performing categorisation (*a boy thing, a Zen thing, a C4 thing, a Catholic thing, a status thing* and *a playboy thing*). In this data, it seems also to be used to contract dialogic space in assertions which either limit options (*the only thing* and *the right thing*) or to introduce hyperbolic evaluations (*the best thing, the most important thing, the biggest thing, the weirdest thing* and *the worst thing*), and also to generalise (*sort of thing* and *kind of thing*).

something: (three stars) As Hunston and Sinclair (2000) and Bednarek (2006) have pointed out, this item is often part of an evaluative pattern (*there's something* + adjective group), which, indeed, appears frequently in the dataset considered here. R1 and R2 collocates of *there's/there is something* include a number of clearly evaluative items, like *special, different, similar, wrong, good* and *sinister*. Many clusters also involve intensifiers where the vagueness of *something* is given focus and/or force by its collocates, and the informal imprecision can be juxtaposed with precise and formal choice of evaluative lexis. Examples of this include *something disappointingly prosaic, something commendably old-fashioned, something queasily imitative, something unsatisfactorily static, something laudably ambitious* and *something utterly beguiling*.

maybe: (three stars) This adverb is glossed in MEDAL as 'more informal than *perhaps*'.

5.3 Vague and informal evaluative lexis

The items in Set C of SiBol 05 keywords all share the features of informality and an underlexicalised vagueness in their definition, where the attitude of the writer is clear, but the grounds for that attitude are less clear. Many are the short words from the Old English part of the lexicon which are associated with informal language and are one- or (at most) two-syllable words, which have been defined as 'often of colloquial tone' (Quirk *et al.*, 1985: 1553, give the examples *meaty, comfy, gushy* and *runny* (as in nose)). In SiBol 2005, some, such as *bling* (Oxford Dictionary's word of the year 2009)[11] or *chav* (Oxford Dictionary's word of the year 2004), are neologisms, often discussed as such in the press, and are, therefore, salient because they did not exist in the previous corpus and also because they occur as objects of reflection – as citation forms in discussions of their use, rather than because they are particularly frequent.

big: We saw with Set A how size is an important parameter for evaluating, but the use of the word *big* itself seems mostly to be metaphorical. Rather than referring to size, it refers to importance, distinction and fame (clusters include *big enough to, the big screen,*

---

[11] www.askoxford.com:80/world of words/wordayear

*big business, the big time, the next big thing, a big name, the big issue,
no big deal, the big money, the big city, the big day, the big game* and
the big question).

Another subgroup of Set C is notable for shared morphology of its members,
that is, two syllables ending with *y*:[12] *sexy, easy funny, funky, tricky, dodgy,
quirky, cheesy, moody, creepy, clunky, edgy, grumpy, classy, spooky, yummy,
handy, shiny, sparkly, feisty* and *geeky*, which all give an adolescent, even
infantile, flavour to the evaluations.[13] An edited concordance of *sparkly* can
be seen under Figure 3.

N Concordance

1 Not bad. A bit dull." I turned to the woman on my other side. "He's not a sparkly person, is he?" she said, kindly. Yesterday he was not even a

2 know if they behave decently to the menial workers who keep their lives sparkly and drudge-free, those who Stephen Frears featured in his

3 its central premise the fact that all is not quite what it seems under the sparkly surface of the seemingly perfect family. The latest in a series of

4 sporadic bursts of monologue, Gareth Tudor Price's production is as sparkly and gaudily appealing as tinsel. As the day's celebrations

5 their fears. Wendy was invited to confront her phobia in the manner of a sparkly-handed Lady Macbeth; Sophie was persuaded to stick her hand

6 he may feel suffocated by a miasma of fashion, cosmetics and sparkly jewellery. Some people fear that there will be a psychological

7 full-on Highland regalia. The girls, meanwhile, are all looking suitably sparkly, but the famous Glaswegian preference for all things scanty is

8 death. What pathetic motives prompted these crimes: a love of "bling" - sparkly jewellery - in one instance, and in the other a wicked desire to

9 passive aggression - "Did I give you a wholly informative and sparkly interview? You know I did. I'm sorry, I'm not very sparkly . . ."

10 members rise from barmy stack- heeled monstrosities to the top of sparkly gussets. Bono kicks out the proverbial jams, Besneakered Neil

11 is in no doubt that she can make it in the grunt and groan world of sparkly spandex. "If she's as motivated at wrestling as she has been in

12 my narrative. Because I was planning new year home improvements: a sparkly-clean kitchen, properly-trained dogs, and, most of all, an empty

13 look is also one that works better in the plasticky world of LA, where sparkly things and sugary- pink velour don't look out of place. Us Brits

Figure 3: Concordance for *sparkly*

According to the *Oxford Corpus*, whilst the word *eccentric* is
associated with being elderly, rich or reclusive, *quirky* is associated with
being humorous or youthful, and with art and creativity, song lyrics, films
and novels.[14] In a number of these Set C items, it is not clear whether
their fundamental evaluation is positive or negative (for example, *edgy* and
moody), but, when used as part of a review or promotion, the evaluation
tends to be positive. The word *edgy* can have a positive sense of avant-garde
and unconventional, as opposed to a negative sense of agitated and nervous,
which is the meaning it nearly always has in sports reporting. *Edgy* came
into the Oxford corpus with this positive meaning in 2004, we are told, and
is identified therein as being informal. It is used in our corpus as a positive
term of appraisal (urban dictionary.com gives the meaning as 'involving a
tendency to challenge societal norms and reveal the dark side'), as in this
example:

---

[12] For a discussion of the *–y* suffix, see also Adams (2009).

[13] This might signal a distancing from or an ironic stance towards promotional language.
Sparkly seems to be used un-ironically in fashion and interior decorating texts but we see the
beginnings of an ironic distancing as it perhaps becomes less 'cutting-edge'.

[14] In spring 2006, the *Oxford Corpus* contained over two billion words. It claims to represent
all types of English from all parts of the world and to be the largest language research
programme in the world (see: www.askoxford.com).

(8) Nighty, Night is all infantile self-indulgence. Perhaps enthusiasts slap themselves on the back for enjoying such "**edgy**" fare. And, yet, far from being **edgy**, the result is curiously anachronistic, a mammary and member-obsessed world about which Benny Hill might have found himself tumescent.

(SiBol 05, *Times*)

(9) This is not an exciting series. It isn't **edgy** or groundbreaking and you won't find Davina McCall suddenly popping up in a woolly hat. It's the sort of programme, in fact, that the Prince of Wales would probably enjoy.

(SiBol 05, *Times*)

We can see with *edgy* a particular kind of meaning change in action. The word first denotes an emotion and, subsequently, comes to be used as a term of positive evaluation – praise for the ability to arouse or depict emotion. A similar progression is seen with *moody*:

(10) Starved of affection, and rarely in her clothes for ten consecutive minutes, the hapless waif is saved and damned by the kindness of strangers. A gruff local farmer in his twenties, Joe (Sam Worthington), duly comes to her emotional rescue. But he is spooked by her needy dependency, and wary of her trailer-trash roots. Their shy romance is charted in **moody** blue filters or saturated reds. Shortland paints a collage of regret: evocative snapshots of what might be; gritty footage of what is.

(SiBol 05, *Times*)

(11) Yet Paul's work is as personal as her subject matter. In **moody** chiaroscuro, she paints portraits of her son, four sisters and mother. And what other artist around today would title a picture, without any irony, My Mother And God?

(SiBol 05, *Guardian*)

(12) IN THE shadow of the San Siro stadium, in Milan, I collected my BMW. If I had hoped for something in **moody** black, I was disappointed. The bike was yellow as a bumblebee.

(SiBol 05, *Times*)

There appears to be a kind of evaluation reversal in play in these cases. Partington (2007) identifies evaluation reversal as the root mechanism in irony; here, unusually, the reversal is from bad to good (most irony uses surface positive evaluation to imply an underlying negative one). But the flip does not appear to be fully conventionalised, since the old evaluation sometimes co-exists alongside the new and perhaps even mocks the new usage. Many occurrences are used in distancing quotation marks or are direct quotations where the writer makes sure we know the choice of words is someone else's, as in the following concordance lines for *vibrant* and *edgy*:

(13) And when M&S does try to get its act together, it's excruciating. Every few months you would swear that some bright spark, who probably saw David Brent as a role model, has sent a memo to the shop floor telling the checkout staff to be "friendly" and, Lord help us, "**vibrant**".

(SiBol 05, *Times*)

(14) From all this delirium Barham brings home a reassuringly positive message. He liberally sprinkles his text with hurrah-words such as "**vibrant**" and "passion", and figures that whatever the kids want to do is OK.

(SiBol 05, *Guardian*)

(15) Perhaps enthusiasts slap themselves on the back for enjoying such "**edgy**" fare.

(SiBol 05, *Times*)

6. Interpretation of results

All items in Set A carry positive evaluation (with the single exception of *desperate*) – apparently in contradiction of the renowned claim that news values tend to favour the negative over the positive (Galtung and Ruge, 1973: 72). However, this may well be an indication of an increase in the proportion of soft news and magazine material relative to hard news, and that promotional material – which is, of course, largely positive in tone – might be the source of many of the stories. Amongst all of this positive promotion, there are items of negative evaluation outside the sets I have identified in the SiBol 05 keywords, such as *underperforming*, *obsessed*, *wannabe* and *struggling*. They do not really form a set of their own in any formal terms, although the last three involve representation of states of mind. The collocates are much concerned with business (*company*, *business* and *economy*) and with celebrity (*star* and *rapper*), and they express a sense of aspiration or competition gone awry – the unsuccessful side of striving. This, too, is an area which merits further research.

These hyperbolic keywords indicate a pronounced increase in the different ways of emphasising, amplifying, intensifying, maximising and generally up-scaling propositions. We might further examine the effects and functions of Set A items and their distribution in the corpora. The relative frequency of these items is 24.8 percent higher in SiBol 05 than that in SiBol 93 (see Table 4).

	Frequency per thousand words
SiBol 93 (with Sundays)	637450 ($=6.4426$ ptw)
SiBol 05 (without the *Observer*)	1174643 ($=8.0412$ ptw)
	Percentage increase $=+0.159864$

Table 4: Results for hyperbolic and emphatic items

Name of publication	Hyperbolic lexis (as percent)
Times	0.617
Guardian	0.663
Telegraph	0.673
Sunday Telegraph	0.709
Sunday Times	0.714
Observer	0.753
Average:	0.688

Table 5: Hyperbolic lexis in the 05 newspapers

Since it is possible to separate the data of the three broadsheets, I decided to investigate which of the papers indulged in the most hyperbole in 2005. For this purpose, I employed the 2005 version which includes the *Observer* (see Introduction, Section 2).

If we examine SiBol 05 using Xaira, which I have chosen because it can provide a useful graphic display of relative percentages, we find a total percentage of hyperbolic items of 4.1 percent of the corpus. On looking at the relative percentages for each specific newspaper, we find that *The Times* appears to be the most restrained (10.3 percent lower than average) and the *Observer* the most hyperbolic (9.4 percent above average). Although none of the differences are statistically significant (see Table 5), the Sunday papers are, clearly, where most hyperbole is to be found; this is probably due to the nature of the Sunday supplements, where we find the sports, fashion, culture, food, motoring, travel and arts features.

A closer search for other hyperbolic items, for example, *mega* and *uber*, reveals words that are on their way to becoming popular, though they are not yet frequent enough to appear among the keywords.[15] This suggests that journalists are less concerned with finding original phraseologies.

---

[15] In SiBol 93 we find 580 occurrences of *mega*, but most of these are part of the technology discourse (*sega mega drive* and *mega CDs*). In SiBol 05, there are 792 occurrences, still prefixed rather than given as one word, expressing size representation (force rather than focus); these appear to be a synonymous replacement for the rather old-fashioned *super*, as in *mega- yacht*, etc. As regards *uber*, in *SiBol 93* we find forty occurrences, nearly all of which are within quotations from German, about the Thomas and Uber Cup, or mentions of the German National Anthem, *Deutchland uber Alles*. In SiBol 05, we find 311 occurrences with

The hyperbole set of explicitly evaluative lexical items is used to perform exaggeration, but of a rather unfocussed type. Halliday and Matthiesson (2004: 319) classify interpersonal epithets as being those expressing the speaker's attitude, which, thus, represent an interpersonal element in the meaning of a nominal group. They point out that these tend to be reinforced by, for instance, intensifiers or swear words. It appears that *The Times* and *Guardian* delegate the hyperbole (or 'hype') to their Sunday sister papers, since they themselves are relatively restrained. The supplementisation of the broadsheets begins to appear as the main factor in the language changes from SiBol 93 to SiBol 05. Further diachronic work with similar corpora is needed if we are to account for the full range of possible changes.

The set of vague items are all MEDAL three-star words which appear in a number of phraseological patterns, and their frequency is a result of this ability to collocate in clusters which are informal and imprecise. The relative frequency of lexical items expressing vagueness in SiBol 05 is 45.7 percent higher than that of SiBol 93. This suggests that the tenor of the texts has changed since 1993. As Carter and McCarthy (2006: 202) remind us, 'being vague is an important feature of interpersonal meaning'.

The third set with its rather ad hoc definition ('vague informal evaluation') contains items which convey composite meanings rather than a well-defined quality, and these have variable context-dependent definitions. For example, the meanings of *cheesy* (applied to a television show, a lothario, portrait artists and an hotel) and *dodgy* (used as an evaluation for people, places and parts of the body) are really only clear to those who have both experience of the phenomena described and, more importantly, of the way the relevant discourse community (readers with experience of the particular newspaper) talks about them.

Many of the other items in the list evaluate in terms of fame, success, sexual attraction, unusualness, newness, excitement, style, quality and emotional impact. These might be said to represent some of the key values expressed in modern UK broadsheet discourse. They convey an attempt to differentiate some product or performance from the rest of what is on offer. If we extend our analysis of the keywords list from 2,500 to 5,000, we find yet more examples of promotional and informal discourse. We come across a group of words related to consumerism, materialism and competition: *elite, exclusive, classy, luxury, aspirational, wealthy, significant, upmarket* and *glamorous*. There is also a group of advertising-copy type words: *comfortable, natural, sleek, floral, proud, modern, festive, stylish* and *fairytale*. Another group of words is related to entertainment reviews: *brilliant, hilarious, talented, clever, wonderful* and *legend*.

When we look at the SiBol 05 keywords, it becomes apparent that the informal items are not just the modern equivalents of some older

---

items such as *trendy, cool, geek, hip* and *nerd* in R1 position, but also *rich*. It also seems to be a replacement for *super*, but is heavily ironic.

evaluative terms, given that there are very few explicitly evaluative items in the keywords of SiBol 93. So, have the new contexts (new supplements and features sections which account for the increase in size) and the new relationships created to attract readers (the emphasis on beauty, fame, size, importance, success, and the informality with which they are expressed) generated the values? Have the instances of evaluation increased as well as the targets of evaluation and new ways of expressing it? These parameters of evaluation do seem to belong to their time and, more pertinently, to their genre; there are no formal or high register alternatives in the 1993 data for the values expressed by the 2005 corpus, so there is not, simply, a different choice of register, but also a change of context. Whether this also indicates a new creativity is a moot point: the fact that many of the items are three-starred words for the MEDAL dictionary also suggests that this hype, far from indicating creativity in language use, denotes, rather, a well-worn and clichéd use of language.

The question remains, then, of why such emphasis, informality and familiarity has increased. Some mention needs to be made of the specific sub-genres of the data. The concordance lines come predominantly from articles dealing with leisure topics such as sport, fashion, entertainment, arts, health, lifestyle, food and travel. Another field seems to be that of financial advice or reviews.[16] The newspapers under investigation here have taken on a new role by 2005 – a comment and review rather than news reporting function, in an attempt to provide something the rolling news programmes cannot provide. This is reflected in the increase in size and variety of supplements.

The hyperbolic nature of advertising-speak and corporate jargon was detected by the *Oxford English Dictionary* monitoring programme, and was discussed in a book on language by Dent (2005) which was reviewed in the *Telegraph*:

(16) As part of the 'bigging-up' or 'supersizing' trend, she identifies the use of 'ova', 'uber' or 'mega' prefixes to beef up words. Miss Dent said: 'Linguistic supersizing is on the increase, and it may show the influence of advertising-speak and corporate jargon on language, in which everything needs to be hyped to get noticed. It means that some of our greatest words are losing their power. Add to this the "hyper-inflation" of our language, as just detected by the Oxford English Dictionary. Prefixes such as "ova" and "uber" and "mega" are diluting

---

[16] Some might account for the salience of these sets of informal, vague or hyperbolic items simply in terms of the growth in the *size* of the newspapers – given the addition over the period of magazine-style sections, whose registers might tend towards a conversational style. To check this, we made a list of comparative keywords from the one newspaper which had not increased in volume, namely, the *Telegraph*, and these sets of items were still found to be very prominent: of Set A, thirty-six of forty items were present; of set B, all eight were present; and of the informal evaluation items in Set C, fifteen of twenty-nine appear in the *Telegraph* 2005 keywords. Other indications of informal language, like personal pronouns and contracted forms, are to be found near the top of the keyword list.

the power of our words. One of its experts said this week that to be called a hero used to be the highest honour. Now you have to be a superhero to make an impact.'

(SiBol 05, *Telegraph*)

All three broadsheets include a review and comment on this book and reproduce many of the same examples and the same quotation, suggesting that, perhaps, the reviews themselves were taken from a press release.

7. Conclusions

The phenomena described above give us a preliminary view of the developments in newspaper language style highlighted by the 2005 UK broadsheet keywords. What the items considered here have in common is that they are all used to evaluate, many of them hyperbolically, and that they mimic spoken and informal language use. The appearance in the keywords lists of these high intensity items is a strong indication that a particular discourse function has grown considerably over the period. It is clear that if these words have become salient, then the nature of 'quality' broadsheet language has changed considerably, that it has adopted the use of less measured language, and has become more imitative of the orality and informal language that used to be a characteristic of the tabloids. A further useful study could be made using a parallel corpus of tabloids from the same period to check whether tabloid and broadsheet styles are converging or whether tabloid style, too, has undergone a shift, in their case, towards even greater informality than that with which they were already associated.

In review pieces, there is a fine distinction between how much they evaluate, (that is, give an opinion which the reader might want to follow), and how much they promote or advertise, (that is, project a product, performance or person into the public eye). At this stage of the research, the corpus has not yet been completely tagged according to the section from which items have come (hard news, foreign news, supplements, *etc.*) – though it is often obvious on reading the concordance lines. As already stated, there has been a large increase in the size of the newspapers, a corresponding increase in the proportion of non-hard-news content, and a boom in topics related to leisure. It would be reasonable to consider, therefore, that the increase in the use of evaluative language items reflects this expansion in the proportion of such opinion and review genres in the papers. But it also signals another kind of change, in the way writers construct themselves in a familiar relationship with their readers – as commentators and reviewers, rather than reporters. As evidence of this, one aspect which is very frequent in the data is that of ironic usage (following the definition of irony as reversal of evaluation, most generally from something good in the *dictum* to something bad and critical in the *implicatum* (Partington, 2007)), tongue-in-cheek evaluations or distancing-quote usage as we saw with *vibrant*. It is very difficult, however, to quantify this kind of knowing reversal of evaluation. Further research also needs to be done to discover how much of the evaluations are part of direct speech citation. Keyword lists serve as a springboard for the research process.

When the keywords are investigated in terms of their contexts and co-texts, they bear out the preliminary findings of a mixing of exaggeration and vagueness in the more recent data. We find small, incremental increases for each item over the twelve years between the two SiBols, but, thanks to the size and extent of the corpus, we can obtain, through a keyword analysis, an overall picture of a large build-up in the categories of hyperbole, vagueness and informality. This corroborates our hypothesis that the style is more conversational, that there is an imitation of the spoken language, and a more extensive use of individuals' opinions through direct quotation. The recurring semantic sets expressing size, beauty, fame, impact, importance, success, surprise, emphasis, emotions and aesthetics, also reflect an increase in 'advertisement-equivalent exposure' of one kind or another. And, finally, the frequent use of very common terms of evaluation (the three-star words from our reference dictionary) may suggest that the journalists are writing to ever more strict deadlines, and often resort, as a result, to dead metaphors and set phrases.

References

Adams, M. 2009. Slang: The People's Poetry. Oxford: Oxford University Press.

Bednarek, M. 2006. Evaluation in Media Discourse. London: Continuuum.

Bell, A. 1991. The Language of News Media. Oxford: Oxford University Press.

Biber, D., S. Johansson, G. Leech, S. Conrad and E. Finegan. 1999. The Longman Grammar of Spoken and Written English. London: Longman.

Carter, R. and M. McCarthy. 2006. The Cambridge Grammar. Cambridge: Cambridge University Press.

Channell, J. 1994. Vague Language. Oxford: Oxford University Press.

Cook, G. 1992. The Discourse of Advertising. London: Routledge.

Davies, N. 2008. Flat Earth News. London: Chatto and Windus.

Dent, S. 2005. Fanboys and Overdogs: The Language Report. Oxford: Oxford University Press.

Duguid, A. 2009. 'Loud signatures: comparing evaluative discourse styles – patterns in rants and riffs' in U. Römer and R. Schulze (eds)

Exploring the Lexis–Grammar Interface, pp. 289–315. Amsterdam: John Benjamins.

Fairclough, N. 2001. *Language and Power.* (Second edition.) London: Longman.

Galtung, J. and M. Ruge. 1973. 'Structuring and selecting news' in S. Cohen and J. Young (eds) *The Manufacture of News: Social Problems, Deviance and the Mass Media,* pp. 62–72. London: Constable.

Halliday, M. and C. Matthiesson. 2004. *An Introduction to Functional Grammar.* (Third edition.) London: Edward Arnold.

Hoey, M. 2005. *Lexical Priming: A New Theory of Words and Language.* London and New York: Routledge.

Hundt, M. and C. Mair. 1999. '"Agile" and "upright" genres: the corpus-based approach to language change in progress', *International Journal of Corpus Linguistics* 4 (2), pp. 221–42.

Hunston, S. and G. Francis. 2000. *Pattern Grammar: A Corpus-driven Approach to the Lexical Grammar of English.* Amsterdam: John Benjamins.

Hunston, S. and J. Sinclair. 2000. 'A local grammar of evaluation' in S. Hunston and G. Thompson (eds) *Evaluation in Text: Authorial Stance and the Construction of Discourse,* pp. 74–101. Oxford: Oxford University Press.

Hunston, S. and G. Thompson. 2000. *Evaluation in Texts: Authorial Stance and the Construction of Discourse.* Oxford: Oxford University Press.

Lewis, J., A. Williams, B. Franklin, J. Thomas and N. Mosdell. 2008. *The Quality and Independence of British Journalism: Tracking the Changes over 20 years.* Cardiff: Cardiff University Press.

Lombardo, L. 2001. *Selling It and Telling It: A Functional Approach to the Discourse of Print Ads and TV News.* Rome: Istituto di Lingue Moderne, Luiss.

McCarthy, M. and R. Carter. 2004. '"There's millions of them": hyperbole in everyday conversation', *Journal of Pragmatics* 36 (2), pp. 149–84.

Martin, J. and P. White. 2005. *The Language of Evaluation.* Basingstoke: Palgrave Macmillan.

Mauranen, A. and M. Bondi (eds). 2003. *Evaluative Language Use in Academic Discourse.* Special issue of *Journal of English for Academic Purposes* 2 (4). Amsterdam: Elsevier.

Morley, J. 1998. *Truth to Tell: Form and Function in Newspaper Headlines.* Bologna: CLUEB.

Morley, J. and A. Partington. 2009. 'A few frequently asked questions about semantic – or evaluative – prosody', International Journal of Corpus Linguistics 14 (2), pp. 139–58.

Myers, G. 1994. Words in Ads. London: Edward Arnold.

Partington, A. 2007. 'Irony and reversal of evaluation', Journal of Pragmatics 39 (9), pp. 1547–69.

Partington, A. 2010. 'Modern Diachronic Corpus-Assisted Discourse Studies (MD-CADS) on UK newspapers: an overview of the project', Corpora 5 (2), pp. 83–108.

Quirk, R., S. Greenbaum, G. Leech and J. Svartvik. 1985. A Comprehensive Grammar of the English Language. London: Longman.

Renouf, A. 2007. 'The chavs and the chav-nots' in J. Munat (ed.) Lexical Creativity: Texts and Contexts, pp. 61–92. Amsterdam: John Benjamins.

Scott, M. and C. Tribble. 2006. Textual Patterns: Key Words and Corpus Analysis in Language Education. Amsterdam: John Benjamins.

Sinclair, J. 1996. 'The search for units of meaning', Textus 9 (1), pp. 75–106.

Trengrove, G. 1986. 'What is Robert Graves playing at?' in C.J. Brumfit and R.A. Carter (eds) Literature and Language Teaching. Oxford: Oxford University Press.

Evidence of *evidentiality* in the quality press 1993 and 2005

Caroline Clark[1]

Abstract

In this paper, I adopt a diachronic approach to the analysis of the two large SiBol newspaper corpora, in order to examine and compare the expression of *evidentiality* (Bednarek, 2006; Dendale and Tasmowski, 2001; and Chafe, 1986) – that is, how the writer's knowledge is marked as having been 'seen' or 'heard', *etc.*, how the knowledge is attributed, and how it is passed on to the reader. Findings show an increased use of evidential markers over the thirteen-year period studied, and, at the same time, a shift in reporter usage of *evidentiality* towards hearsay evidence and the reporting of knowledge acquired by speculation. This is in keeping with other observations regarding an increased 'vagueness' in contemporary journalism (see Duguid, 2010), which is counterbalanced at times with an elevation of the newsworker's presence.

1. Introduction

The news story is popularly considered to be a means of transferring 'knowledge' about current situations and events to the reader – knowledge which may be intact, as recounted or witnessed, or may be manipulated by the writer. Despite claims to the contrary, particularly from within the industry itself, inherent in news reporting is the potential to influence the readers' beliefs and knowledge of the world, the way it is and the way it ought to be (see, among others, White, 2006; Hartley, 1982; Fowler, 1991; Iedema *et al.*, 1994; and Fairclough, 1995). A news story can position the reader to take favourable or unfavourable views by means of a more or less explicit evaluative stance, as argued by Iedema *et al.* (1994). Readers can be positioned to consider propositions within a story as true and credible

[1] Dipartimento di Studi Internazionali, Università di Padova, via del Santo 77, 35123 Padova, Italy.
Correspondence to: Caroline Clark,   *e-mail*: caroline.clark@unipd.it

Corpora 2010 Vol. 5 (2): 139–160
DOI: 10.3366/E1749503210000420
© Edinburgh University Press
www.eupjournals.com/cor

according to how the knowledge is presented, that is, its *evidential* status, intended as a general term for if, and how, evidence (or lack of evidence) for a particular statement or utterance is indicated, and the nature of this evidence (White, 2006: 21).

All languages mark evidentiality, or the source of information, in some way. In languages such as Macedonian, Quechua, Turkic and American Indian languages (for example, Pomo and Apache), evidentiality is expressed grammatically by the use of affixes, clitics or particles. The main verb, or the sentence as a whole, is marked for evidentiality, with an optional set of affixes for indirect evidentiality (see Aikhenvald, 2004, for an extensive summary).

The expression of evidentiality in English, on the other hand, is not generally considered to be a grammatical matter since it is optional and can be expressed in numerous ways, as Chafe notes:

> English has a rich repertoire of evidential devices. It expresses evidentiality with modal auxiliaries, adverbs and miscellaneous idiomatic phrases, although not, for example, with a coherent set of verb suffixes like those in some California Indian languages
>
> (Chafe, 1986: 261)

Markers of evidentiality 'are not the main predication of the clause, but are rather a specification added to a factual claim about something else' (Anderson, 1986: 274). They act as an indication of how a factual claim or proposition can be justified, that is, by citing the grounds on which the claim is based: whether the person/entity making the claim has direct evidence based on observation, which may be auditory or visual, for example; whether the evidence is indirect, and thus requires some inference; or whether it is a reasoned expectation based on logic, general knowledge or other facts (Anderson, 1986: 274–77).

In the context of the SiBol newspaper corpora, evidentiality has been interpreted loosely as the indication of how the writer has knowledge of what he or she is writing. This comprises both how the source of knowledge is marked and how the knowledge was acquired; for example, whether it was on the basis of perception (*we saw*), hearsay (*he said*), inference (*it sounds like*, *it appears*), general knowledge (*as we know*), cognition and speculation (*it is believed*) or discovery (*it turns out*).

I have adopted, here, the so-called 'narrow' view of evidentiality (Willet, 1988: 54–5; Chafe, 1986; and Mithun, 1986; 89), which acknowledges a conceptual difference between indicating the source of information and indicating the writer's assessment of the reliability of that information (Dendale and Tasmowski, 2001: 342). According to this view, evidentiality can be seen to 'assert evidence' while epistemic modality 'evaluates evidence', and indicates the writer's degree of confidence or belief in the knowledge upon which the proposition is based (Aikhenvald, 2004; de Haan, 1999: 4; and see also Mushin, 2000: 928). For example, *Tony Blair **must** be relatively happy* (SiBol 05, *Sunday Times*), indicates the writer's degree of confidence in the proposition (see also Section 7.5, below), while the invented example *Tony Blair **said** he is relatively happy*, identifies the source of the information and how it was acquired. In this paper, evidentiality (which may also allude to reliability of the knowledge or the writer's evaluative stance) is, therefore, treated as distinct from (or perhaps a sub-type of) epistemic modality.

Evidentiality is particularly relevant to news stories where it has important pragmatic and evaluative functions. 'Evidentials express the kinds of evidence a person has for making factual claims' (Anderson, 1986: 273) by encoding information about how the knowledge was acquired and the relationship between the writer and the knowledge (Mushin, 2001: xi), which affects, therefore, the relationship between the reader and the knowledge, as mediated by the writer. In this passage from source to writer to reader, knowledge is, necessarily, 'revised', and the selection, attribution and rewriting of story content, it has been argued, is aimed at positioning the reader to view the content and claims as highly warrantable, and to take a positive or negative evaluative position towards the participants, events and states of affairs (White, 2006: 21).

2. Research aims

The aim of this study was to take an overview of the use of evidentiality in newspaper language, and to investigate changes that may be found in the expression of evidentiality in quality newspapers. The investigation involved the two SiBol corpora – one containing data from 1993 and the other containing data from 2005. This thirteen-year period saw a number of major upheavals in the newspaper industry, including the relocation of the main UK newspapers from their Fleet Street base, changing ownership strategies, the breaking of the print unions, computerisation of production, and cost-cutting to finance price wars – all leading to massive staff cuts and general economic restraint (Davies, 2008). Some of the changes found in evidential markers, that is, writers' acknowledgements of how information is sourced and attributed, and how knowledge is acquired, may be a result of the widespread and profound changes in newsgathering.

Over the same period (and up to the present), newspapers have been criticised for a perceived 'dumbing down' and superficiality, linked to changes in production methods and staffing in particular. According to one study (Lewis *et al.*, 2008), fewer journalists now produce three times as many pages as they did twenty years ago, with about 80 percent of stories being partly composed from recycled wire or PR (public relations) copy, 'a trend that inevitably increases their dependence on 'ready made' news and limits opportunities for independent journalism' (Lewis *et al.*, 2008: 3). This criticism has, however, been contested by Peter Preston, editor of the *Guardian* from 1975 to 1995 (Preston, 2008).

3. Methodology

The methodology, which is similar to that employed in other studies in this issue, follows the combined quantitative and qualitative approach of MD-CADS, as outlined in Partington (2010). The principal research instrument used is WordSmith Tools 5.0 (Scott, 2008), allied with some use of Xaira 1.24.[2] Lemmatised wordlists were generated for the two SiBol corpora which then became the basis of keyword analyses. This was undertaken to compare the two corpora in order to reveal those items with a relative frequency that is significantly higher in one corpus or the other.[3] The lemmatised keyword lists became an essential starting point for the investigation, while the resulting data were analysed further, using the WordSmith Concord tools, to examine patterns of collocation and word clustering that resulted from the sorted concordances.

4. Corpora

The number of words printed by all the quality papers increased over the thirteen-year period, 1993–2005. In terms of wordcount, *The Times* was the largest of the papers in both years (with around thirty-nine million words in 1993 and around sixty-seven million words in 2005), as well as the paper with the greatest increase in number of words (over 70 percent). The number of words in the *Guardian*, which was the smallest paper in 1993, also increased significantly, by 53 percent: it grew from twenty-seven million words in 1993 to forty-one million words in 2005. In contrast, there was little change in the number of words in the *Daily Telegraph*: it contained thirty-four million words in 1993 and thirty-six million words in 2005.

To investigate how the increase in newspaper bulk was distributed, the *Guardian* was broken down into 'sections'. While the number of words in this paper increased by over 50 percent, the number of articles of *News* remained more or less unchanged, and the number of *Finance* articles decreased slightly. There was also a 135 percent increase in *Feature* articles and a 64 percent increase in *Sport* items. In terms of the composition of the paper, this means that while in 1993 *News* and *Features* each made up about a third of the paper bulk (with *Sport* and *Finance* together making up the remaining third), the situation in 2005 saw *Features* making up about half the paper, with *News* just a quarter.

This analysis could not be performed on the other papers (as they are not marked up in such a way as to make it possible); however, it could be presumed that a substantial increase in *Features* and *Sport* items may

---

[2] Xaira (XML Aware Indexing and Retrieval Architecture), created by L. Burnard and T. Dodd at Oxford University and now at version 1.25. See: http://www.oucs.ox.ac.uk/rts/xaira/
[3] The lemma list was compiled by Someya (1998). It contains 40,569 words (tokens) in 14,762 lemma groups, and was used as the basis for the lemma list.

be found across all papers, except perhaps the *Daily Telegraph*, (given that the number of words in this paper remained more or less unchanged). Since this study is based on the entire contents of all papers, it follows that these increases may affect results to some extent – that is, if usage of evidentiality is different across the various sections of the paper, then the changing bulk will in some way affect results.

5. Sources of information

Most research into evidentiality highlights the role of the 'source' of the information or knowledge as it is presented to the reader – whether the knowledge is attributed to a third party or whether the writer claims responsibility for the proposition. The evidence is, therefore, 'direct' when the writer reports his or her own experience of a situation, a bare assertion or, occasionally, an explicit opinion. On the other hand, 'indirect' evidence is based on a third-party account mediated by the writer, or by inference based on results and reasoning (Willett, 1988: 57).

The SiBol 05 keyword list contains the first-person pronouns *I* (keyness: 43.092) and *we* (keyness: 15.086) among the top keywords, indicating a significant increase in relative frequency over the thirteen-year period (the pronoun *you*, with a keyness of more than 47.000, was the second keyword after *www*).

This increased usage of *I* and *we* by newspaper writers in 2005 suggests that there could be a similar increase in quoted utterances, since it is mainly in this type of discourse that the first-person pronoun should be found in news writing, as in this example:

> (1) Mr Yorke said: "**I**'ve been a member for 20 years but when **I** watched Michael Howard trying to exploit the war for political advantage this week, **I** decided that **I**'d had enough [...]"
>
> (SiBol 05, *Times*)

In fact, as expected, *I* and *we* are found predominantly within quoted utterances. An investigation of random examples of *I* outside quotes, that is, where *I* represents the writer's voice, shows that it tends to be found in the context of soft news or feature articles, (i.e., news items not based on events, but rather aiming to satisfy reader curiosity or interest, or to provide information, opinion or advice).

A further analysis of both SiBol 93 and SiBol 05 lemmatised wordlists shows that *I* left-collocates with verbs such as THINK, KNOW (which are both SiBol 05 keywords) and BELIEVE. Therefore, if the source of knowledge is the first person, this knowledge was likely to be acquired on the basis of belief, speculation or inference (see Rooryck, 2001: 126).

The corpora were prepared for interrogation by having quotes which represent the start of a passage of direct speech marked up as such with a tag.[4] The 'open quotes' tag was then included in the word list and keyword analyses. The 'open quote' tag was among the ten most frequent 'words' in both corpora, with similar frequencies in all papers. Note, of course, that the frequency data refers to the number of quotes, not to their length, so it is not possible to ascertain with any precision the proportion of quoted language in relation to the entire corpora. Little difference was found in the numbers of quotes appearing in the Sunday and weekday editions, which suggests that the supposedly 'softer' Sunday papers did not use more quoted language. The relative frequency of quotes across all papers increased (SiBol 05, keyness: 4.047), but not to an extent which could explain the much greater increase in relative frequency of first-person pronouns. Therefore, writers either increased the length of quotes, with repeated instances of *I/we* within them (as in Example 1), or made a greater use of supposedly first-person accounts.

When using quotes, the writer attributes credibility to the story by re-porting the actual words of a newsmaker – that is, a protagonist or participant in the news – so that the source and content of the proposition are rendered much harder to challenge (Tuchman, 1978: 96). Quoting the accusations, criticisms, claims and denials of experts, witnesses and authorities, lends an air of neutrality to the proposition, since it is presented in what is purported to be the speakers' own words. Nevertheless, the writer retains responsibility for the content of the utterance (which may have been modified). Quoting is also a valuable device for disendorsing the same words. Since they are attributed to someone else, the writer is not responsible for the proposition and is effectively 'distanced' both linguistically and, at least as important, legally (Bednarek, 2006: 60; Fowler, 1991: 209; and Fairclough, 1995).

The sources quoted in news stories tend to be politicians, government authorities, police and judicial sources, sports people and celebrities, while it is less common for members of the general public – so-called *vox pops* – to be quoted (Glasgow University Media Group, 1980: 163). This contrasts with other media, in particular television news and the tabloid papers, which make a greater use of *vox pop* attributions (see Lewis *et al.*, 2004). The status of the source itself attributes varying degrees of credibility to the utterance while the writer's responsibility lies in the selection of which utterances to include and exclude (White, 2006: 21) and in the cleaning up and touching up of quotes, by abbreviating or adding glosses to aid comprehension; for example:

(2) He added: "They [the Bosnian government] want some more territory. I think they're entitled to [it] but I don't know if they can get it."

(SiBol 93, *Guardian*)

---

[4] The openings of quoted utterances were marked up to make it possible to calculate the frequency of the use of quotation using WordSmith Tools. Given the complexities of the different notations used by the various papers, it was not possible to distinguish between stretches of direct speech, scare quotes, quotes denoting specialised terminology, or quotes embedded within quotes.

However, investigating quotes for the source of evidence in large corpora is fraught with complexities, not least because of the various layers of 'embedded' discourse (Bell, 1991: 52) within a story. This can make it difficult to track accurately the first- and third-person sources, each with their own basis for knowledge, as can be seen here:

(3) The company's vice president, David Young, told investigators that a US naval officer at MIF told him that he "had no objections" to the shipments. "He said that he was sorry he could not say anything more. I told him I completely understood and did not expect him to say anything more," Mr Young said.

(SiBol 05, *Guardian*)

For this reason, a distinction is not made here between first- and third-person sources, except where the source of the evidence is an elusive, unrecognisable or unknown entity. Similarly, quotatives are collapsed into a more generic category of *hearsay* (comprising direct and indirect speech) to refer to knowledge based on the words of a third party.

6. Knowledge acquisition

How knowledge, information or evidence is acquired, or the *basis* (Bednarek, 2006: 637) or *mode* (Chafe, 1986: 263) of knowing is an essential ingredient of evidentiality – was the knowledge heard, seen or inferred, or was it presumed to be common knowledge to all readers? Given the changes in news production outlined above, it could be hypothesised that a combination of the source of the knowledge (direct or indirect) and how the knowledge was acquired may reflect some of the perceived changes over the thirteen-year period under investigation.

Scholars in the field have devised various categories for describing how knowledge is acquired, with quite substantial variations that are dependent on the material being studied (Willet, 1988; Chafe, 1986; Bednarek, 2006; and Rooryck, 2001). Given the nature of the SiBol corpora, this analysis is based mainly on the categories outlined by Bednarek (2006) in her work on news stories, and Chafe (1986), which are useful for organising the data. The writer of the news story can acknowledge that the information or knowledge was acquired by means of hearsay, or by perception, inference, speculation or discovery, or that it may be treated as general knowledge.

6.1 Hearsay

Information or knowledge of which the writer has no direct experience, but which is based on what another party has said (or written) regarding an event, state of affairs or condition, is referred to as 'hearsay' evidence. It can be based on written or spoken language and includes quoted utterances and indirect speech where the marker precedes or follows the proposition. This type of evidential is 'indirect' (Willett, 1988) since the source – or sayer – must be a third party; for example, *he said that*. The most frequently used markers of hearsay evidence found in both SiBol 93 and SiBol 05 are SAY, ADD, REPLY and TELL.

Overall, hearsay evidence predominates as a marker of evidentiality, both generally and in the two corpora. This is partly due to the sheer volume of usage and partly due to the effect of attribution. Where the content of the utterance is attributed to a third party, the writer retains some responsibility for the proposition simply by having selected it (presumably because it backs up the writer's, or the paper's, stance on an issue), and signalling either consensus or distance.

The reporting verb most frequently used by writers in both corpora is the neutral SAY, found predominantly before and after quotes, and in reported speech. Writers in 2005 used SAY significantly more (as reflected by a keyness[5] of 1.258 in SiBol 05). The relative frequency of SAY (4,207 per million words (henceforth, pmw) in 1993, and 4,619 pmw in 2005) increased to a similar extent as quotes, suggesting that there may well be some correlation between the two. When evaluated separately, we find a significant increase in relative frequency of *says* (keyness: 1.862), which is found to be high in the SiBol 05 keyword list. On the other hand, the relative frequency of the past *said* remained more or less unchanged. This reflects a general trend found across the papers, where writers in 2005 used present tenses to express evidentials, instead of past tenses (as found in 1993).

This is also the case for direct and indirect speech construction. In 1993, writers expressed more reported speech in past tenses (see Example 4), compared with 2005, when writers exhibited a greater tendency to report speech in the present tense (see Example 5).

(4) Mr Clinton **said** that a blockade **was** a term in international law
(SiBol 93, *Times*)

(5) Mr Kaloyev **says** that he **remembers** nothing of the killing
(SiBol 05, *Times*)

While the third-party sources of hearsay propositions reported in both direct and indirect speech tend to be political figures, celebrities and government authorities (Lewis *et al.*, 2008), the present tense form name + *says* + quote (proposition) is more frequently used when referring to sport, finance and local news. This form was used more by writers in 2005 (as per

---

[5] Keyness was calculated using WordSmith default settings: log-likelihood test, $p < 0.000001$.

Example 6), than those in 1993, who usually preceded quotes with *said* (see Example 7).

(6) Graham Secker, of Morgan Stanley, **says**: "There is clearly an economic cycle

(SiBol 05, Telegraph)

(7) Chris Dillow, economist with Nomura, **said**: "The effects of sterling's fall have yet to be seen fully

(SiBol 93, Guardian)

On the other hand, for political figures, the past form *said* (for example, *Mr Blair said*) is used to a similar extent in both corpora, where writers are less likely to quote their actual utterances, and prefer, instead, to employ indirect speech. This allows some flexibility in wording the proposition and, thus, reduces liability for misquoting.

The increased relative frequency of quotes (together with the increase in usage of SAY) suggests that writers in 2005 in fact interviewed (or at least appear to claim to have interviewed) more in 2005, and cited these interviews in quotes. Regarding indirect speech, which reports the words of third parties, other neutral reporting verbs, such as ADD, DESCRIBE, REPORT, as well as *according to*, have changed little in frequency over the thirteen-year period. However, writers in 1993 made a significantly greater use of illocutionary reporting verbs, such as THREATEN, WARN and ANNOUNCE, which are all found in the SiBol 93 keyword list (with a keyness of 756, 120 and 522, respectively).

The lower relative frequency of these illocutionary reporting verbs in the SiBol 05 corpora, may suggest the increasing use over the time period under investigation of a more vague form of writing by the 'quality' papers. This point is argued by Duguid (2010). It may, on the other hand, be an indication of a shift towards a more neutral and impartial writing style, where writers in 2005 preferred to report (quoted or indirect) speech (albeit copied from wire or PR copy), rather than to interpret the words uttered. This indicates a simplification of reporting. The writer's presence as interpreter or mediator of the utterances may be backgrounded in the 2005 papers.

In accordance with this hypothesis, among the SiBol 05 keywords, we find *reportedly* (keyness: 119), the relative frequency of which, while limited, increased over the period (from ten pmw in 1993 to fifteen pmw in 2005). *Reportedly* collocates highly in both corpora with TELL, SAY and, surprisingly, OFFER, and with the economy and finance, as in this example:

(8) Institutional investors said the higher price **reportedly** being discussed,

(SiBol 05, Times)

The word *reportedly* implies rumour or unverified claims, and although acquired by hearsay, it suggests the existence of an alternative truth or the need to consult other sources. It is a device by which writers avoid explicitly nominating the source – similar to using the agentless passive, such as *it was reported*. Further, by their use of *reportedly*, writers can avoid the constraints of temporal deixis (typically, *yesterday*, *last night*, and so on) which concordance results show are found to the left and right of *it was reported*, as in '*yesterday* it was reported that'.

Writers in 2005 were also more likely to use *reportedly* preceding or following quotes, creating a somewhat conflicting message. The source's (it is to be presumed exact) words are reported, but, by using *reportedly*, the writer is disendorsing himself or herself from the notion that anything was said at all, or that what was said may not match the quote exactly. Further, the removal of *reportedly* would transform the phrase into an assertion, as can be seen in the following:

> (9) he also **reportedly** added: "I'm on Osama Bin Laden's team."
> (SiBol 05, *Sunday Times*)

> (10) the Defence Minister, **reportedly** told the Cabinet: "The day after we leave [...]"
> (SiBol 05, *Times*)

A further marker of hearsay evidence which was used more by newspaper writers in 2005 was REVEAL, with a keyness of 646 in the SiBol 05 lemmatised keyword list. The writer rarely indicates whether the proposition was written or spoken (although contextual detail may do so). Use of the item REVEAL as a marker of hearsay evidence, suggests the mirative (a category of evidentiality in which *unexpectedness* is indicated), and the potentially scandalous, nature of the proposition:

> (11) A Ministry of Defence document obtained by this newspaper has **revealed** that the infantry is facing one of its worst recruiting crises
> (SiBol 05, *Sunday Telegraph*)

The revealing source is generally the offices of political figures, government authorities and institutions, and the surveys, analyses, reports and statistics they issue, whereby the exact identity of the 'revealer' remains unknown, and the proposition cannot, therefore, be verified. It can also be the papers themselves which 'reveal', as can be seen in Example 9, where it is suggested that the newspaper has an active role in uncovering secret documents, scoops and inside stories. Although this usage is very limited, it doubled in frequency over the thirteen-year period.

Evidence in the form of hearsay is that most commonly found in both corpora; knowledge based on the words of third parties, either quoted or reported, or on written language (in the form of press releases, parliamentary or company reports), makes the news story (and the writer) appear more credible. Writers in the quality newspapers in 2005 used expressions of knowledge acquired by hearsay evidence more – as is reflected in the increase in relative frequency of quotes, and, to a similar extent, the use of neutral reporting verbs – than writers in 1993, who made a greater use of more specific illocutionary reporting verbs. Further, the increase in frequencies of *reportedly* and REVEAL suggest a change in writer style towards obscuring the source on the one hand, and mirativity (the marking of a proposition as new or unexpected, see DeLancey, 2001), on the other.

6.2 Perception

It has been noted in languages with grammaticalised evidentiality that evidentials appear to derive, predominantly, from verbs of saying – as seen above – or verbs of perception (Botne, 1995; and Rooryck, 2001: 126). Evidentiality in the form of perception comprises visual and non-visual markers (Chafe, 1986; and Bednarek, 2006), where the writer indicates that the knowledge or proposition was *seen*, *heard* or *felt* either by the writer, or by a third party as reported by the writer. The source, the 'experiencer' (Bednarek, 2006: 644) or 'perceiver', is usually unspecified, and so the proposition can be construed as being the perception of the writer. When the evidential is embedded in a quote, we find a first-person perceiver who is then quoted by the writer, as opposed to the writer perceiving, although it is not common for the writer to use *I/we* + perception referring to self, such as *I hear that*.

'Hearing', as a form of non-visual perception, is closely related to hearsay, whereby *I/we heard* corresponds to something 'having been said' as a formal announcement, or informally as something 'overheard'. However, in contrast to the increased use of hearsay evidentiality over the time period which I have reported above, the relative frequency of HEAR (261 pmw in 1993 and 281 pmw in 2005) and *audibly*, which can be glossed as, 'in such a way that I could hear', remained more or less unchanged.

On the other hand, evidentiality in the form of visual perception, that is, knowledge gained from events seen or witnessed, is more commonly found in news stories. Writers in 1993 used the item *visibly* (glossed as, 'was seen to be'), as a marker of sensory evidence more than their counterparts in 2005, and in both corpora it collocates with unpleasant feelings in the form of *shocked*, *shaken* and *upset*. By using *visibly*, the writer indicates that, while some witnessing agent was assumed to be present, this witness or source is unknown or is unspecified, and could be construed as the writer.

The verb of visual perception most frequently used by writers in the quality papers in both SiBol corpora is the neutral SEE (1,023 pmw in 1993 and 1,183 pmw in 2005). It was used more often by writers in the 2005 papers (keyness: 1.286), with the greatest increase in relative frequency being found for the forms *see* (482 pmw in 1993 and 625 pmw in 2005) and *seen* (277 pmw in 1993 and 282 pmw in 2005). Similarly, writers in 2005 used WATCH more frequently (keyness: 1.057), which increased in frequency from 198 pmw in 1993 to 262 pmw in 2005, and LOOK (keyness: 3.062). The latter was among the first 100 keywords in SiBol 05, and increased in frequency from 790 pmw in 1993 to 1,014 pmw in 2003. On the other hand, writers in 1993 made greater use of APPEAR (317 pmw in 1993 and 301 pmw in 2005). The increased relative frequency of LOOK may be accounted for by a tendency towards the use of phrasal verbs, such as *look for* and *look after*. On the other hand, in SiBol 05 WATCH collocates highly with the fields of television and sport, which appears to contribute to the increased frequency.

Evidentiality in the form of perception is less common and is restricted to verbs of visual perception. In the 2005 data, writers made greater use of this type of verb than in the 1993 data. This point is discussed further under Section 7.3.

6.3 Inference

Knowledge acquired by perception may be further elaborated, or processed mentally, which we might refer to as 'inference'. This type of knowledge implies actively having 'worked through' an observation, and having inferred a state of affairs from visible or tangible evidence. While not a static mental assessment (such as *know* or *think*), inference involves some form of cognitive processing of the observation, as can be seen in the prevalence of denotational forms of the markers of visual perception such as LOOK, APPEAR, *etc*. When the writer indicates that the knowledge was acquired by perception, or by the senses (visual and non-visual), there is a barely hedged suggestion that the proposition is highly reliable, or very likely to be fact. For example, 'he looks shabby' (SiBol 93, *Times*), differs little from the assertion 'he is shabby' (Chafe, 1986: 267), although it is clearly charged with author subjectivity. However, this reliability, or the likelihood of it being the case, is removed once *like* is added to LOOK, SOUND and SEEM, as in the following examples:

(12) It **sounds like** a straightforward, Newtonian case of "what goes up, must come down"

(SiBol 05, *Guardian*)

(13) from another it **seems like** a rebellion against academic orthodoxy.

(SiBol 05, *Guardian*)

(14) it **looks like** they might be up to the same old tricks again

(SiBol 05, *Times*)

Although the knowledge appears to be acquired by perception (*sounds* and *looks*), the addition of *like* indicates inference, or a conclusion drawn from sensory perception (see Chafe, 1986); Example 12 is such a case.

The relative frequencies of LOOK (which collocates closely with *like*, *as* and *though*), and SEEM/SOUND *like*, are significantly higher in SiBol 05, as seen above, as both a simile and a hedged inference. The relative frequency of LOOK *like* increased from sixty-four pmw to eighty-six pmw over the period covered, while SEEM *like* and SOUND *like* increased from twelve pmw to eighteen pmw, and twenty pmw to thirty-two pmw, respectively.

Similarly, there is an overlap, or blurring of the boundaries, between evidentials of perception and inference. The item SEE is synonymous with 'consider' or 'understood' in Examples 15 and 16, and LOOK (Example 17) is closer to mental inference than to visual appearance. The item APPEAR (Example 18), which is more frequent in SiBol 93, is more commonly used to infer evidence than to report sensory perception:

(15) It was **seen** as an indication that in future the credit would rise

(SiBol 05, *Telegraph*)

(16) The Warrington bombing has been widely **seen** throughout Ireland as a propaganda disaster

(SiBol 93, *Times*)

(17) "It **looks** increasingly **like** this 20th century chancellor is running out of answers

(SiBol 05, *Guardian*)

(18) it **appears** that the committee may have themselves found no evidence

(SiBol 93, *Telegraph*)

In these examples, the source of the knowledge is generally unknown or not indicated, and can usually be attributed to the writer. The writer's commitment to the proposition is not particularly strong: there is an indication of limited reliability, and the writer's 'impressions' rather than verified facts. It is apparent from the data that writers in 2005 made greater use of evidentiality in the form of visual perception. It was, however, not in the form of providing eye-witness accounts, but in the vague recognition of the contribution of visual evidence to inference.

On the other hand, the frequencies of usage of APPEAR, *apparently* and SEEM changed little over the thirteen-year period (except for, as noted above, the forms *looks like*, *seems like*, and so on). By using these words, the writer suggests that some logical reasoning has been used to reach a conclusion, based on observation or reliable information. The writer implies that there is limited certainty about the conclusion, and the evidence, like the source, is unknown or not made explicit. Further forms of inference can be indicated by adverbs, such as *plainly*, *evidently*, *obviously* and *clearly* (see Examples 19 to 21), which underline the 'obviousness' (Bednarek, 2006: 641) of the evidence. The relative frequency of *obviously* changed little (fifty-five pmw in 1993 and fifty-six pmw in 2005), but writers in 1993 used *clearly* (116 pmw in 1993 and 109 pmw in 2005), *evidently* (keyness: 42; eleven pmw in 1993 and nine pmw in 2005) and *plainly* (keyness: 56; nine pmw in 1993 and six pmw in 2005) more frequently, although the relative frequencies were themselves low.

> (19) the present policy of no military intervention has so **plainly** failed to deliver
>
> (SiBol 93, *Guardian*)

> (20) They are **evidently** not aware that snow is an entirely normal phenomenon in November
>
> (SiBol 05, *Telegraph*)

> (21) "...we have made that outwardly clear so we are **obviously** there for the long haul"
>
> (SiBol 05, *Times*)

In these examples, it is implied that the proposition is shared knowledge that requires no further qualification, or that the proposition should be known, or is known to an informed circle, including the writer, but probably excluding the reader. It is interesting to note that writers in the 2005 quality papers used evidentials of inference, in general, less than their counterparts in 1993.

6.4 General knowledge

When the writer appeals to shared, or common, knowledge we find an overlapping of speculation and inference. The propositional content is marked as pertaining to general knowledge, which the writer presumes to share with the reader, or indicates that it is important for the reader to know it (while it is presumed that it is currently unknown) – a rhetorical technique that is common in journalistic writing. This function of evidentials is found in the two corpora in the adverbs *notoriously* (nine pmw in both corpora), *famously* (seven pmw in 1993 and twenty-seven pmw in 2005) and *infamously* (seven pmw in 1993 and ten pmw in 2005), with limited frequency, as well as SAY (4,207 pmw in 1993 and 4,619 pmw in 2005). Evidentials of this type, or the rhetorical use of this type of general knowledge, are found more often in the SiBol 05 corpora. The item *notorious*(*ly*), which collocates with unfavourable personalities and states of affairs, showed a very slight increase in relative frequency (eight pmw to nine pmw). On the other hand, writers in 2005 made greater use of (*in*)*famously*.

The item *famously* (keyness: 572) collocates highly with speech acts, such as SAY, DESCRIBE, REFUSE and REMARK, as well as unfavourable situations.

The adverbs *notoriously* and *(in)famously* may be used to mark propositions which are not shared knowledge, or even presumed to be well-known, but, rather, knowledge which is available in certain informed circles. The source of the proposition cannot usually be identified, beyond the suggestion that it is generally known in these circles – for which the writer is a spokesperson. The reader is invited to accept the evidential basis of the proposition on the grounds of its status as a purported 'fact'.

Similarly, the writer can reiterate general or shared knowledge with SAY, including BE + *said to*, *they* SAY (where *they* is a generic set of people and an explicit *sayer* cannot be traced) and *it* BE *said*. While the relative frequency of SAY increased significantly, these instances were found to be less frequent in the later corpus.

Although journalists do not refer to information acquired by general knowledge very frequently, when they do, the adverbial form is more widely used, with the only significant difference between the two corpora being in the increased frequency of *(in)famously*.

6.5 Cognition and speculation

In news stories, we find that thoughts, beliefs and indications of the mental processing of evidence, as well as the expression of knowledge, accompany propositions. The reader gains, therefore, knowledge according to the belief or knowledge of others. To the left (and occasionally to the right) of the proposition will be markers of belief, mindsay, knowing or speculation, such as *I guess*, *I know* or *I believe*. These markers of evidentiality, grouped here as 'cognition and speculation', include a wide range of markers which have also been called 'belief' (Chafe, 1986), 'mindsay' (Bednarek, 2006), and 'speculation' (Rooryck, 2001).

The items KNOW, GUESS, THINK, SUPPOSE and BELIEVE have the higher relative frequencies in lemmatised word lists for both corpora, and it is in this area of 'knowing and speculating' that the greatest difference between the two corpora is found, as lemmatised keyword analyses show.

At one extreme of the cline of mental processing we find 'knowing', where the writer implies that there is little doubt as to the source's commitment to the proposition. Writers in the 2005 quality papers used the item KNOW significantly more frequently (keyness: 1.869), and the relative frequency of *know* (keyness: 2.277) increased from 395 pmw to 534 pmw. KNOW collocates with personal pronouns, and in particular the frequency of *I/we know*, which is found predominantly within quotes, increased from eighty-six pmw in 1993 to 130 pmw in 2005.

The writer signals a weaker commitment to the information by referring to 'belief', where the source's commitment to the proposition has the possibility of being countered. Writers in 2005 used THINK significantly more frequently (keyness: 3.729) than in 1993 (826 pmw in 1993 and 1,078 pmw in 2005). In the same thirteen year period, the frequencies of both *think* (414 pmw in 1993 and 586 pmw in 2005) and *thinking* (seventy-nine pmw in 1993 and 113 pmw in 2005) also increased (keyness: 3.378 and 678, respectively). The same writers in 2005 made more frequent use of GUESS (keyness: 288; twenty-seven pmw in 1993 and thirty-eight pmw in 2005). On the other hand, newspaper writers in 1993 used more frequently SUPPOSE (keyness: 52; eighty pmw in 1993 and seventy-three pmw in 2005) and BELIEVE (keyness: 174; 491 pmw in 1993 and 458 pmw in 2005).

As expected, THINK, used more frequently by writers in 2005, is mainly found to the right of *I* and *we* (46,001 instances to the right – of which 30,668 are 1R – and 5,768 to the left in a span 5L–5R), and within quotes, indicating that the source is therefore indirect or a third party, such as:

> (22) "I **think** he will carry on as long as he feels strong and has the support of the party," Mr Blunkett replies
>
> (SiBol 05, *Telegraph*)

The item BELIEVE, which is of greater relative frequency in 1993, collocates with third-person authorities, institutions and experts as sources, such as:

> (23) Psychologists also **believe** that practice and the passage of time improve scores
>
> (SiBol 05, *Telegraph*)

When suggesting 'speculation', the writer is more likely to refer to an unspecified source, where the evidential marker is a form of agentless passive, and, thus, unknown and unverifiable (see Examples 24 and 25) where it can also be noted that what is *thought*, *known* or *believed* is generally a negative state of affairs that is in keeping with news values.

> (24) **It is believed** that Mr Major phoned Jim Molyneaux, UUP leader
>
> (SiBol 93, *Guardian*)

> (25) **It is known** some Tory MSPs are in despair over the appointment
>
> (SiBol 05, *Times*)

When indicating that knowledge is acquired by speculation, writers are less concerned with the evidence supporting the proposition, which is often 'based on something other than evidence alone' (Chafe, 1986: 266). Generally, readers will accept beliefs if the views are uttered by a person or an entity which they respect, or even irrationally (or perhaps *proto-rationally*) – because the belief 'suits' them. The evidence may be secondary to the elaborating and processing of that evidence, as can be seen in the very high frequency of the agentless passive and unknown 'believer'.

6.6 Discovery

News writers may mark that the proposition or knowledge is the result or culmination of investigation or discovery (see Bednarek, 2006). These markers of evidentiality, which are less frequently used in both corpora, indicate that the proposition is based on some form of 'hard evidence' or proof. The writer may refer to the process of demonstrating proof, which leads to a supposedly verifiable statement, by using markers such as SHOW, DEMONSTRATE and FIND, which are the most frequently used forms in both corpora.

Writers in 2005 made greater use of FIND (the relative frequency of which increased from 829 pmw to 923 pmw in 2005) and SHOW (707 pmw in 1993 and 793 pmw in 2005), both of which have a keyness of 504, while the relative frequency of DEMONSTRATE changed little (fifty-eight pmw in 1993 and fifty-four pmw in 2005). In these cases, the source may be explicitly cited (such as 'researchers have found that') or, as is more common, the agentless passive may be used (for example, 'it was found that'), implying that an (unidentified) agent was responsible for the proposition. Again we find that the newspaper writer in 2005 is less likely to identify the source of the proposition, and tends to maintain what could be described as 'neutrality'—that is, a stance which is deliberately non-evaluative, impartial and perhaps even 'vague' (see Duguid, 2010).

The knowledge, on the other hand, may be based on a general suggestion of available proof or evidence, without further specification of the source of that proof, as expressed typically by *it turns out that* and *it has emerged that*. The items EMERGE (127 pmw in 1993 and 130 pmw in 2005) and TURN OUT do not necessarily suggest the availability of hard evidence, nor the termination of some investigation, but a situation which has evolved, or a discovery which has been made. The source, or producer, of the results may be obscured by the use of *it emerges*. A comparison of the two corpora shows that writers in 2005 used both EMERGE and TURN OUT more frequently, implying unexpectedness or mirativity (grouped together, the frequency of third-person *emerge*/turn* out* increased from 109 pmw in 1993 to 124 pmw in 2005).

This form of evidential implies a basis of proof, and is, therefore, hard-impacting but, at the same time, the absence of a source, or any process of investigation, weakens the proposition. The source of the knowledge is generally not stated, and the evidential is used to strengthen the apparent 'validity' of the proposition. Newswriters in 2005 made greater use of these forms, suggesting that they may have placed less importance on the nature of the evidence, or the precise sourcing of information, than writers in 1993. While there are relatively few examples of 'discovery' to be found in the two corpora, this area of evidentiality is important since the proposition is marked as being highly reliable and is strengthened by its basis on some commitment to 'proof'. It is implied that this result is verifiable, although in reality it may not be.

7. Discussion

As we have seen, the quality papers in 2005 relied more on hearsay evidence in the form of quotes and indirect speech than in 1993; this is the most frequent form of knowledge acquisition to be found in both corpora. Writers used quotes significantly more frequently in 2005 (keyness: 4.047), which was mirrored by an increase in the neutral reporting verb SAY. These findings suggest that journalists either had greater opportunity to interview, had first-hand access to sources, or that quotes were taken as soundbites from press releases and wire copy, as claimed by some Media Studies research (Lewis et al., 2008).

The item SAY is economical and allows the writer to maintain neutrality – thus being safeguarded from error of interpretation, assuming that the quote is indeed accurate. At the same time, writers in 2005 used illocutionary reporting verbs much less frequently than those in 1993, implying that they interpreted hearsay knowledge less, and appear to have taken a more impartial stance. This latter observation contrasts the generally held view that journalists 'interpret' the news more than they did in the past, since it is assumed that readers are already aware of the main events as they have been reported in other media, such as the Internet, radio and television news.

The greater use by newspaper writers of less specific evidentials seems to indicate a generalised and reduced specificity in news reporting, or levelling, whereby writers are less inclined to flag interpretation, and where the boundaries between reporting and interpreting become blurred.

Writers in the 2005 quality newspapers also made more frequent use of LOOK/SOUND/SEEM *like* where the source can usually be attributed to the writer – whose commitment to the proposition is not particularly strong, and the proposition is more one of 'impressions' than verified facts. Further lack of specificity is found in markers of speculation, which suggests that writers in 2005 may have been less concerned with the actual evidence supporting the proposition and more with suggesting widespread common knowledge of the proposition. For example, writers in 2005 made greater use of some agentless passive forms such as *it is thought* (which increased in frequency from 5.8 pmw to ten pmw in 2005). In these cases, the source is unspecified and a type of approval is instilled in the proposition – the 'knowing' cannot be easily verified, nor does there appear to be the desire to verify it.

The greatest differences in evidentiality between the SiBol 93 and SiBol 05 corpora lie in the reporting of knowledge acquired by speculation, (that is, according to the beliefs and opinions of others), where the source is often unknown. The SiBol 05 keywords GUESS and THINK signal an opinion, and, thus, the possibility of the proposition being countered. Both normally collocate with *I/we* and are found within quotes. But it follows that, although the opinion is attributed to a third party, the writer claims some responsibility for the proposition. Offering opinion is a legitimate form of newspaper writing, although it suggests a shift in reporting style towards hedging one's views, or the views of others, and the writer presuming to know the thoughts of newsmakers, especially when using third-party forms such as *she thinks*.

A further finding is a change in reporting style where writers seem to elevate the importance of their own position (presumably unintentionally) which compensates for a perceived vagueness. The main evidence for this can be found in the increased frequency of evidentials of general knowledge and mirativity. The increase in markers of general knowledge (such as *famously*) suggests that writers in 2005 were more inclined to signal their membership of an informed group. The reader is invited to accept the evidential basis of the proposition on the grounds of its status as a purported 'fact' – known to others but not necessarily known to the reader.

Similarly, the position of the writer is elevated by evidentials of discovery, which often have an element of mirativity, such as EMERGE and TURN OUT, both of which are among the SiBol 05 keywords. These forms, which suggest great evidential reliability, underline the writer's participation in the discovery of something, which, at some point may have been unexpected. The focus on the writer/reporter is also highlighted when the evidential indirectly evaluates the 'means of reporting', with verbs such as REVEAL, for example. The focus once again is on the writer's profession, and the ability to participate in events, rather than on the original source.

The explanations for these observations could lie in several areas. The changes outlined above may simply be a reflection of 'fashion' and a physiological evolution in reporting style, whereby periphrastic forms of evidentiality are more commonly used; this is in keeping with a generalised tendency towards 'conversationalisation', which has been noted in many fields from journalism to education. This recalls the view that the quality papers may be moving towards the perceived style of language found in the tabloid papers (McNair, 2003), which, in turn, will be evolving.

8. Conclusion

The aim of this investigation was to observe evidentiality in the field of news stories, in particular to investigate and examine any changes that may be found in the expression and usage of evidentials in the quality newspapers in 1993 and 2005. Although loosely defined in this study, evidentiality is the key to how knowledge is presented to the reader, including how the writer has knowledge of what he or she is writing, how the source of knowledge is marked, and how the knowledge was acquired.

It was found, overall, that writers in the quality newspapers in 2005 used more evidential forms than writers thirteen years earlier in 1993 – an increase which, on the surface, suggests a greater reporter presence as a mediator of news stories. Writers in both years rarely made explicit reference within the text to the provenance of the story, (that is, whether it was supplied by press release, an agency or wire service), and they seldom acknowledged that the information or knowledge was acquired by others, and not by himself or herself, colleagues or the newspaper.

The findings do not point to massive changes in reporting style. However, they do seem to point to a shift towards a style of writing which could be described as 'vague', as outlined by Duguid (2010), a tendency which many see as contributing to the 'dumbing-down' of newspaper copy. A lack of specificity in reporting style can be traced in evidential markers across all the so-called quality papers considered here, for example, in the increase in the relative frequency of the apparently neutral and non-committal item, SAY.

These changes could also be seen as a form of 'neutrality', whereby the sources of propositions are not explicitly identified, and the evidentials are not illocutionary. That is, writers may be seen to take a deliberately non-evaluative or impartial stance, in keeping with best journalistic practice. However, rather than neutrality, this comes coupled with a tendency towards not explicitly outlining sources, and a preference for the agentless passive and the anticipatory *it* constructions. This suggests, instead, that while moving away from the use of illocutionary reporting verbs (such as *threaten*), which imply interpretation, and constructions which require a third person (such as evidentials of perception), there is a trend towards indicating the writer's own presence. This can be seen in the increased use of evidentials which express mirativity (for example, *reveal* and *emerge*) that foreground the writer's role – something *emerged* that was unexpected to me, the writer – while backgrounding the source.

A further observation is that the changes in usage of evidential forms may well reflect changes in sourcing, with primary material coming from television rolling news, such as the services of the CNN, Sky and the BBC. There have been many widely documented and profound changes in news management and production over the past two decades, and it has been suggested that the role of reporters and journalists has borne the brunt of these changes in the news-working environment: reporting has become less a job of investigation, enquiry and writing, and more one of re-writing wire stories and press releases within rigid time constraints (Lewis *et al.*, 2008) with consequent changes in newspaper prose style.

References

Aikhenvald, A. 2003. 'Evidentiality in typological perspective' in A. Aikhenvald and R. Dixon (eds) Studies in Evidentiality, pp. 1–32. Amsterdam: John Benjamins.

Aikhenvald, A. 2004. Evidentiality. Oxford: Oxford University Press.

Anderson, L. 1986. 'Evidentials, paths of change, and mental maps: typologically regular asymmetries' in W. Chafe and J. Nichols (eds) Evidentiality: The Linguistic Coding of Epistemology, pp. 273–312. Norwood, NJ: Ablex.

Bednarek, M. 2006. 'Epistemological positioning and evidentiality in English news discourse', Text and Talk 26 (6), pp. 635–60.

Bell, A. 1991. The Language of News Media. Oxford: Blackwell.

Botne, R. 1995. 'The pronominal origin of an evidential', Diachronica 12 (2), pp. 201–21.

Chafe, W. 1986. 'Evidentiality in English Conversation and academic writing' in W. Chafe and J. Nichols (eds) Evidentiality: the Linguistic Coding of Epistemology, pp. 261–72. Norwood, New Jersey: Ablex.

Davies, N. 2008. Flat Earth News. London: Chatto and Windus.

DeLancey, S. 2001, 'The mirative and evidentiality', Journal of Pragmatics 33 (3), pp. 369–82.

Dendale, P. and L. Tasmowski. 2001, 'Introduction: evidentiality and related notions', Journal of Pragmatics 33 (3), pp. 339–48.

Duguid, A. 2010. 'Newspaper discourse informalisation – a diachronic comparison from keywords', Corpora 5 (2), pp. 109–38.

Fairclough, N. 1995. Media Discourse. London: Edward Arnold.

Fowler, R. 1991. Language in the News: Discourse and Ideology in the Press. London: Routledge.

Glasgow University Media Group. 1980. More Bad News. London: Routledge.

de Haan, F. 1999. 'Evidentiality and epistemic modality: setting boundaries', Southwest Journal of Linguistics 18, pp. 83–101.

Hartley, J. 1982. Understanding News. London: Methuen.

Iedema, R., S. Feez and P. White. 1994. Media Literacy. Sydney, Australia: Disadvantaged Schools Program, NSW Department of School Education.

Lewis, J., K. Wahl-Jorgensen and S. Inthorn. 2004. 'Images of citizenship on television news: constructing a passive public', Journalism Studies 5 (2), pp. 153–64.

Lewis, J., A. Williams, B. Franklin, J. Thomas and N. Mosdell. 2008. The Quality and Independence of British Journalism. MediaWise (Journalism and Public Trust Project). Accessed 1 May 2008, at: http://www.mediawise.org.uk/display_page.php?id=999

McNair, N. 1996. News Journalism in the UK. London: Routledge.

Mithun, M. 1986. 'Evidential diachrony in Northern Iroquoian' in W. Chafe and J. Nichols (eds) Evidentiality: The Linguistic Coding of Epistemology, pp. 89–112. Norwood, New Jersey: Ablex.

Mushin, I. 2000. 'Evidentiality and deixis in narrative retelling', Journal of Pragmatics 32 (7), pp. 927–57.

Partington, A. 2010. 'Modern Diachronic Corpus-Assisted Discourse Studies (MD-CADS) on UK newspapers: an overview of the project', Corpora 5 (2), pp. 83–108.

Preston, P. 2008. 'Review Flat Earth News'. The Guardian, 9 February. Accessed 17 June 2009, at: http://www.guardian.co.uk/books/2008/feb/09/pressandpublishing.society

Rooryck, J. 2001. 'Evidentiality, Part I.', GLOT International 5 (4), pp. 125–33.

Scott, M. 2008. WordSmith Tools version 5. Liverpool: Lexical Analysis Software.

Someya, Y. 1998. E-Lemma. Accessed June 2008, at: http://www.lexically.net/downloads/e_lemma.zip

Tuchman, G. 1978. Making News: A Study in the Construction of Reality. New York: The Free Press.

White, P. 2006. 'Evaluative semantics and ideological positioning journalistic discourse' in I. Lassen, J. Strunck and T. Vestergaard (eds) Mediating Ideology in Text and Image: Ten Critical Studies, pp. 37–67. Amsterdam: John Benjamins.

Willet, T. 1988. 'A cross-linguistic survey of the grammaticalization of evidentiality', Studies in Language 12 (1), pp. 51–97.

'The moral *in* the story': a diachronic investigation of lexicalised morality in the UK press

Anna Marchi[1]

Abstract

In this paper, I explore the discourses surrounding whatever is explicitly identified as a *moral issue* in the SiBol corpora. This analysis is mainly diachronic but will combine a variety of parameters in order to access patterns of change/stability across different newspapers, within a single newspaper in time, across different news types, across topics and in the broader context of recent history. I adopt the Corpus-Assisted Discourse Studies (CADS)[2] methodology – merging, and shunting between, quantitative and qualitative approaches. The analysis investigates morality-related lexical items, their collocations, the surrounding contexts, and the news items and topics they are framed within, in an attempt to offer a general picture of the topic, while also aiming to provide an in-depth understanding of what the press means or projects by *moral*.

1. Introduction

Morality is an inescapable feature of mortality. Adam becomes the protagonist of the Bible story the moment he becomes a moral being – and a mortal, fully human, being – by eating from the tree of knowledge of good and evil. In recent times, Steven Pinker, in advocating the notion of a universal moral grammar, similarly links human moral instinct to the very conception of the meaning of life:

> Moral goodness is what gives each of us the sense that we are worthy human beings. We seek it in our friends and mates, nurture it in our children, advance it in our politics and justify it with our religions.

[1] c/o ab via Pietralata 32, 40122 Bologna, Italy.
Correspondence to: Anna Marchi, *e-mail*: a.marchi@lancaster.ac.uk
[2] See: http://en.wikipedia.org/wiki/Corpus-assisted_discourse_studies

Corpora 2010 Vol. 5 (2): 161–189
DOI: 10.3366/E1749503210000432
© Edinburgh University Press
www.eupjournals.com/cor

A disrespect for morality is blamed for everyday sins and history's worst atrocities. To carry this weight, the concept of morality would have to be bigger than any of us and outside all of us.

(Pinker, 2008)

Framing a topic or an issue as moral (or immoral) implies that we are to address something fundamental, 'the very conception of the meaning of life'. The purpose of this paper is to analyse a number of items deriving from the core word *moral*[3] as used in the SiBol corpora – namely, *moral* itself, along with *morally*, *morality*, *immoral*, *immorally* and *immorality* – in order to trace a diachronic profile of what the British broadsheet press in the years 1993 and 2005 portray as the domain of morality.

After briefly discussing the concept of discourses of morality, I describe in this paper the analytical processes that were followed in order to carry out this piece of corpus-assisted research. The analysis begins with an examination of the difference between MORAL and ETHICAL.[4] I then move to focus on the MORAL set, and, through keywords, collocational analysis and close reading of concordance lines, focus the investigation on specific topics in order to offer a portrait of the two time periods.

2. Dissecting morality

[S]cratch the surface of most news stories and you find a moral agenda.

(Marr, 2005: 62)

It is, nowadays, widely accepted that there is no such thing as objective journalism: news gathering and news writing imply human judgment and, thus, may well involve moral evaluation. Morality and journalism are intertwined. In his pioneering and much quoted (even by the media themselves) study on what he calls 'moral panics' (see also Partington, 2010), Cohen (1972: 17) says that the mass media constitute 'a main source of information about the normative contours of a society [...] about the boundaries beyond which one should not venture and about the shapes the devil can assume'.

The debate on whether the media or, more specifically, media discourse, construes or represents society and morality is wide and open, and there is a long tradition of research aimed at uncovering ideology

---

[3] For simplification, in this paper the ensemble of items will be referred to as the MORAL set or just MORAL. The set comprises the most frequently occurring terms which contain the word *moral* and also refer to the concept of morality (*moral, morality, morally, immoral, immorality* and *immorally*), while it excludes other words such as the verb *moralise*, because the negative evaluation it seems to imply would not correspond to the research question that I am investigating. The word *amoral* was taken into consideration, but excluded from the analysis due to its relative infrequency.

[4] Mirroring the MORAL set, and including *ethics, ethical, ethically, unethical* and *unethically*.

(see Hall, 1982; Fowler, 1991; and van Dijk, 1998; amongst others) and the moral agendas underlying the news. News-media discourse both reflects and shapes a society and its mores, since it functions as a social barometer – that is, an indicator of existing conditions or existing orders of discourse that are socially shaped. But at the same time it is also socially shaping, because the cumulative power of the media discourse reinforces and reproduces the status quo (Fairclough, 2001).

News discourse in particular has an important role in the definition and hierarchisation of reality, because it 'incorporates assumptions about what matters, what makes sense, what time and place we live in, what range of considerations we should take seriously' (Schudson, 1995: 14). It seems relevant, therefore, to understand how powerful symbolic agents such as newspapers present the moral domain, since this allows us to understand better the 'common sense' of an era, which is defined by Gramsci (2000: 344) as 'the conception of the world which is uncritically absorbed by the various social and cultural environments in which the moral individuality of the average man is developed'.

Morality is an abstract category and is conceptualised in texts in a number of ways. It can be seen as a subcategory of *evaluation*, in the sense described by Hunston and Thompson (2000), very generally, as 'the indication that something is good or bad' (Hunston, 2004: 157). Evaluative judgments of goodness and badness are likely to be inscribed and reiterated in newspaper prose, sometimes more overtly (so phenomena may be described as *fair*, *improper*, *dreadful*, *right*, *wrong*, a *virtue*, a *sin*, etc.) but more often subtly, either unconsciously or consciously with a manipulative intent. 'Evaluation is often implicit and it relies for its effect on intertextuality, and, in many texts it is multilayered' (Hunston and Thompson, 2000: 117).

It is not the intention, here, to investigate how moral discourses are constructed/reproduced by the press, nor to scrutinise the hidden moral implications of newsmaking. Instead, *explicit* references to 'morality' are addressed in order to access what is projected as morality, and what is described as moral (or immoral). The research questions in this paper are, therefore:

(1) What does the British broadsheet press explicitly frame as being within the moral sphere? And,

(2) Has the discourse about morality changed over time (specifically, between 1993 and 2005)?

3. Method, corpus and process

As Partington (2010) states in his overview, CADS aims to investigate non-obvious meanings within specific discourse types. The analysis is, by its nature, comparative, and, in the case of Modern Diachronic Corpus-Assisted Discourse Studies, the comparison is primarily a diachronic one. CADS methodology combines the quantitative approach of Corpus Linguistics with the qualitative approach of Discourse Analysis. As with other examples of mixed methodology in applied linguistics (Hart-Mautner, 1995; Stubbs, 2001; and Baker *et al.*, 2008), the idea behind complementing discourse analysis with corpus techniques is to allow us to consider larger amounts of data, to put a greater distance between the observer and the data, and at the same time to allow for an in-depth analysis that does not lose contact with the rich wider extra-linguistic context.

In CADS there is a continuous shunting between quantitative and qualitative approaches which interact and inform each other in a recursive process: we start with a research question, we turn to the data, (i.e., to the 'boiled down extract' (Scott and Tribble, 2006: 7) of the data), and look for patterns. When something that is potentially interesting is found, we look more closely, expanding the analysis to the larger stretches of text and considering contextual elements. Close reading and extra-textual elements implement the original research question and open new paths, and the process starts again.

The tools used in this research are Xaira[5] and WordSmith 5.0,[6] which offer complementary approaches. These tools also favour the 'funnelling' process, which involves examining the data, finding specific patterns, restricting the analysis to that phenomenon/portion and then expanding the analysis again; this allows us to move from the general to the particular, retaining a general picture while working on fine-grained aspects. Specifically, WordSmith was used to produce wordlists and keywords while Xaira was employed for collocation and concordance analysis. Xaira also allowed the XML mark-up of the corpus to be exploited to best advantage.

SiBol (the Siena–Bologna Modern Diachronic Corpus of British newspapers) contains the complete output of major British national broadsheets – *The Guardian*, *The Daily Telegraph* and *Sunday Telegraph*, *The Times* and *The Sunday Times*, and the *Observer* – in two different, but recent, moments in time: 1993 and 2005. The *Observer* was only available for the year 2005, since the corpus compilers had no access to the 1993 texts. The SiBol 93 corpus contains approximately 100 million orthographic words; SiBol 05 is somewhat larger with about 155 million orthographic words (10 million of which are accounted for by the inclusion of the *Observer*). The corpus is XML-valid[7] and TEI-conformant;[8] all texts have been marked-up in order to retrieve specific news types or parts of the newspapers, and specific portions of individual news items. The newspapers have been

---

[5] Xaira (XML Aware Indexing and Retrieval Architecture) developed at Oxford University is the XML version of Sara, the software that was originally developed for interrogating the British National Corpus. For further information, see: http://www.oucs.ox.ac.uk/rts/xaira/
[6] See the manual for WordSmith 5.0, which is available at:
http://www.lexically.net/downloads/version5/HTML/index.html
[7] eXtensible Mark-up Language (see: http://www.w3.org/XML/).
[8] Text Encoding Initiative (see: http://www.tei-c.org/index.xml).

encoded according to a variety of parameters. This categorisation permits comparison across the defined partitions, (i.e., at a diachronic level, or on the basis of the papers' political orientation, or across individual newspapers). Since, as Lakoff (2002) notes, politics is about morality, political leaning is a very important variable, and it would be interesting to compare newspapers comprehensively on the basis of their orientation. This study's primary focus is diachronic, but I will try where possible to involve the specificity of each newspaper and of its readership. For the sake of clarity, as well as space, a decision was made not to crowd the analysis with too many variables – although it is important to emphasise that when undertaking discourse analysis we deal with a complexity that goes beyond the boundaries of discourse. It is sometimes useful, therefore, to 'step out of' the texts and to take into account contextual variables such as social, cultural and political aspects, elements of media production (e.g., news values) or reception (e.g., readerships).

4. *moral** versus *ethic**

The *Oxford English Dictionary* defines *moral as*:

> of or relating to human character or behaviour considered as good or bad; of or relating to the distinction between right and wrong, or good and evil, in relation to the actions, desires, or character of responsible human beings; *ethical*.

Its definition of *ethical* is, 'of pertaining to *morality* or the science of ethics'. *Morality* is, in turn, defined as, '*ethical* wisdom, knowledge of *moral* science'. These dictionary definitions are somewhat circular, taking the reader back and forth between morals and ethics. However, they suggest that any corpus-assisted analysis of morality would also, perhaps, benefit from an examination of ethics, since the two terms appear to be so strongly connected.

So before focussing on words relating just to morality, I wanted to understand whether the two groups of words are treated as synonyms in the corpus and, if not, how they differ. In which contexts do journalists refer to *morality* rather than *ethics*? And has the usage changed over time?

Figure 1 shows the absolute frequencies of *moral**[9] and *ethic**, respectively, in SiBol 93 and in SiBol 05. In both corpora, the incidence of *moral** is much greater (in the figure the size of the columns corresponds to the weighted frequencies within the corpora: 99.1 per million words (pmw) *moral** versus 28.1 pmw *ethic** in SiBol 93 and 67.8 pmw versus 41.1 pmw in SiBol 05), just as *moral** is much more frequent in language in general,

---

[9] The asterisk represents a wild card. The simplification was adopted in order to be able to make quick comparisons between SiBol and the BNC.

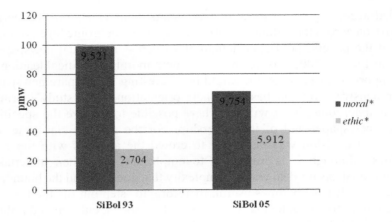

Figure 1: Frequency of *moral** and *ethic** in the two corpora

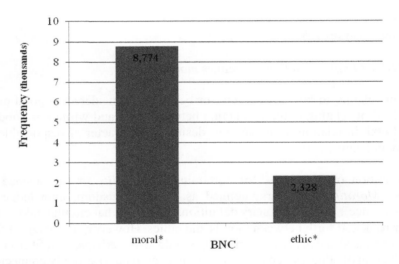

Figure 2: Frequency of *moral** and *ethic** in the BNC

compared to *ethic** (see Figure 2, which shows the absolute frequencies found in the BNC).

While the relative frequency of *moral** decreased in SiBol 05 compared to SiBol 93, *ethic** is nearly twice as frequent in the 2005 data than it was twelve years before.

Having noted the growing popularity of *ethic**, rather than comparing the two sets of terms diachronically I decided to focus on the differences between the two sets (*moral, morally, morality, immoral, immorally* and *immorality* versus *ethical, ethically, ethics, unethical* and *unethically*). All concordance lines containing the target words were retrieved, and then saved in two XML files (one for each set). Wordlists were created for each file and then compared using WordSmith Keywords, in order to access the different usage of the two sets of terms and their 'aboutness' (Scott, 1999). Taylor (2010), who adopts a similar procedure in her contribution to this issue, has called the output 'concordance keywords'.

Concordance lines containing the ETHICAL set elicit keywords which suggest that ethics is referred to when news is about:

- Business, economy and finance: *fund(s), investment(s), invest, companies, investors, company, bank(s), corporate, business, trading, financial, managers, market, supplier, management, industry, sector, services, brand(s), business, marketing, workers, portfolio, profits, employees, income, money, firms, pension, savings, stocks, multinational, prices, supplier and sales*
- Behaviour and life-style: *consumer(s), living, products, buy(s), fair, fairtrade, coffee, fashion, food, buying, using, clothing, shopper, tourism, jeans, cook, supermarkets, shopping, Tesco* and choosing
- Environment(alism): *green, environmental, organic, animal(s), PETA, sustainable, growth, eco, fur, renewable, environment, recycled, ecology, recycling, environmentally* and energy
- Science: *research, medical, cells, embryos, transplant(s), stem, testing, technology, science, scientists, medicine, doctors, cloning and genetic*

The MORAL set is preferred when news is about:

- Religion: *church, authority, Pope, spiritual, God, Catholic, truth, encyclical, faith* and *belief*
- Feelings and virtues: *values, courage, sense, fibre, duty* and *obligation*
- Communication: *story, play, tale, character, book, writer, novel, judgements, art, film(s), words, theatre, hero* and *history*
- People: *man, family, boys, children, men, father* and *women*
- Time or age: *young, modern, old* and *century*
- Political sphere: *war, conservative, political, terror, torture, Bosnia, Tory* and *state*
- Moral panics: *panic* and *crime*
- Sexuality: *sexual* and *sex*

Interestingly, the keywords for the MORAL set also include a variety of personal pronouns, as shown in Table 1.

The two sets of words are quite clearly different: they belong to different spheres and to different discourses. ETHICAL tends to relate to things that are created (commodities, inventions, discoveries, solutions, *etc.*) or chosen (behaviours and attitudes) by humans, while MORAL is applied more to intrinsic aspects of human life – identity, tradition, values, various fundamental institutions of society (religion and politics) and to fears.

Keyword Rank	Keyword	*MORAL* set	*Percent*	*ETHICAL* set	*RC* *Percent*	*Keyness*
2	*his*	4,250	0.57	627	0.29	285.12
4	*he*	4,707	0.63	849	0.4	172.86
10	*him*	910	0.12	114	0.05	85.97
30	*her*	1,364	0.18	251	0.12	46.23
54	*us*	1,128	0.15	214	0.1	33.74
77	*our*	1,489	0.2	310	0.15	28.27

Table 1: Keywords pronouns in the MORAL set text compared to the ETHICAL set text

Breaking down the frequencies of ETHICAL for the individual newspapers, we notice that it is relatively more popular in the left-leaning *Guardian* and in the centrist *Times*, compared to the right-leaning *Telegraph* (24.3 pmw in the *Guardian*, 20.8 pmw in the *Times* and 12.7 pmw in the *Telegraph*). But while we must note that the increased usage of one term over the other sets the political and ideological tone of an issue, we cannot conclude that the liberal press substitutes the use of MORAL with ETHICAL. It is true that the *Guardian* seems increasingly to prefer to express the idea of right and wrong by using a term that is less charged with traditional and religious values, (hence their choice of ETHICAL over MORAL), but the lexical choice is also related to the constraints of the topic. When dealing with the categories listed for the 'moral set' above, the *Guardian* sticks to the same rules or habits as the *Telegraph*.

The portrait presented here is just one possible interpretation – a generalisation based on the grouping of words – and, as with all classifications, it is subjective. But being based on and supported by data, the interpretation can be checked and reformulated by a return to the dataset.

This first step of the analysis allows us to obtain a rough idea of the discourse surrounding morality in the press, but it also opens up a series of possible paths. We must once again, though, acknowledge that to select and follow one thread is a subjective choice, with associated implications, benefits and limitations.

A corpus approach is not a neutral one, selection comes into play throughout the process and early stages of analysis (e.g., the choice of the lexical items to investigate) can heavily determine the progress of the research. The patterns we identify and the findings we generate implement and shape subsequent questions; each previous step informs the next, possibly excluding other threads.

(Marchi and Taylor, 2009: 4)

The categories identified above will inform subsequent analysis and some of the issues that have been related to the sphere of 'morality' (such as religion or sex) will be pursued in greater detail as a result of the accumulation of patterns throughout the investigation.

5. The moral sphere

Figure 1 showed a considerable decline in the use of *moral** in 2005, compared with 1993, (−31.3 pmw), whilst this is compensated for by the increase of *ethic** (+13 pmw). However, as we have seen, the two sets tend to refer to different kinds of news, contributing towards different types of discourses. From this point onwards, the analysis will be focussed only on three MORAL words, (*moral, morally* and *morality*), which will be examined individually.

An initial analysis of collocates for *moral* in the two time periods revealed more regularities than striking differences. An initial exploration consisted of looking at items preceding or following *moral and* (or *and moral*), using a procedure similar to that adopted by Baker (2005), in identifying groups associated with *gay(s)* and *homosexual(s)* by means of the co-ordinating conjunction *and*. The aim, here, was to obtain insights into what other qualifications are related to issues defined as being *moral*. As Table 2 shows, the picture in 1993 and 2005 is analogous, with just minor variations in terms of relevance. This initial exploration of the term, *moral*, was undertaken in order to gain insights into what other qualifications are related to issues qualified as being *moral*.

SiBol 93	Freq.	z-score	SiBol 05	Freq.	z-score
political	89	95.6	political	77	87.8
social	84	106	social	58	77.5
spiritual	81	323.7	ethical	53	253.9
ethical	57	257.2	spiritual	36	152.6
legal	43	63.5	religious	29	72.7
intellectual	33	113.7	intellectual	27	98.7
religious	22	51.8	physical	27	70.2
economic	20	27.7	legal	22	34.2
emotional	19	53.1	financial	19	24.8
physical	16	39	economic	18	26.5
psychological	15	57.7	emotional	16	47.4
cultural	13	33.2	psychological	13	53.1
material	13	30.6	material	11	27.4
financial	13	15.7	cultural	10	27

Table 2: Words following or preceding *moral + and*

Amongst the top collocates (within a span of L5 to R5) there is also considerable correspondence; but a closer examination points to some interesting differences, too. A general point is, again, the high presence of pronouns found in SiBol 05, although, as Partington (2010) notes, the increased presence of personal pronouns has to be seen as a general trend of the so-called quality press which is going through a process of informalisation that is sometimes referred to as 'tabloidisation'[10] (Curran and Sparks, 1991; Connell, 1998; and Esser, 1999).

The next step was to investigate the differences in usage of these items over the two periods. Collocates of the word *moral* were retrieved, and then ranked by frequency. A number of cut-off points were then applied in order to reduce the amount of data to a manageable size, as well as to remove weaker collocates. First, all collocates co-occurring only once (4,706 words for SiBol 93 and 4,939 for SiBol 05) were eliminated. Then, any collocates with a z-score lower than two were removed. Finally, grammatical collocates were excluded. As with all cut-off decisions, the process is based on subjective judgment, but these judgments are consistent and thus replicable. This procedure resulted in the lists shown under Table 3, which represents the collocates that are significantly more present in each of the two periods. The words in bold are unique collocates of the word *moral* in that particular reference period (taking into consideration the top 150 collocates for each period).

Some words in the lists suggest the presence of dominant semantic fields. Going through the list while checking against the broader context of concordance lines, two potentially interesting groups were indentified for each period. In SiBol 93 there are a number of words relating to religion (*values*, *spiritual*, *intellectual*, *church's*, *theology* and *theologians*) and to normativity (*values*, *principles*, *standards*, *guidance*, *norms* and *doctrine*). What seems to characterise SiBol 05, instead, is the reference to personal virtues (*courage*, *fibre* and *seriousness*), which, once again, possibly echoes the focus on the individual sphere that was noted with the increased presence of personal pronouns. What interested me most in SiBol 05 is a group that could be labelled relativism *versus* universalism (or absolutism) with a long list of items: *dilemma*, *dilemmas*, *equivalence*, *relativism*, *ambiguities* and *certainty*.

A similar result emerged by looking at R1 collocates of the word *morally*. Once again, collocates are largely shared between the two periods (for example, *wrong*, *bankrupt*, *reprehensible*, *dubious*, *right*, *repugnant*, *superior*, *repugnant* and *acceptable*). It remains to be seen 'what' is morally wrong, acceptable or unacceptable and whether that has changed over time. It is in fact 'important that we do not over-interpret collocational data' (Baker,

---

[10] Tabloidisation 'is precisely that kind of journalism in which the personal is not only the starting point but also the substance and the end point' (Sparks, 1998: 9).

SiBol 93	Freq.	z-score	SiBol 05	Freq.	z-score
values	227	130.6	high	319	52.5
spiritual	112	97.8	ground	282	83.3
intellectual	56	41.4	courage	81	63.8
principles	55	43.5	dilemma	74	77.7
crusade	52	89.7	dilemmas	59	127.2
judgments	50	73	fibre	55	77.9
framework	40	43.8	equivalence	48	268.9
decay	24	44.3	relativism	48	219.2
rectitude	23	95	seriousness	22	33.5
suasion	8	131.7	ambiguities	13	50.5
standards	95	38.8	**compass**	96	139.8
judgment	55	30.6	**purpose**	55	31.3
vacuum	51	68.5	**universe**	35	35.9
stance	40	37.9	**ambiguity**	32	74.2
guidance	39	34.1	**certainty**	27	31
church's	35	57.7	**hazard**	17	28
justification	28	35.4	**intrinsic**	13	33.8
theology	27	47.4	**crusader**	12	35.9
theologians	22	70.7	**laxity**	10	65
norms	20	59.2			
doctrine	19	28.7			
certainties	18	44.4			

Table 3: Selection of collocates for *moral* (span of L5 to R5)

2006: 118–9) and no conclusion should be reached before we have checked the context of the extended concordance lines.

Evidence for a growing reference to relativism is provided by a group of collocates of the adverb *morally* in SiBol 05 – *ambiguous, questionable, ambivalent, complex, equivalent, indistinguishable* and *confused* – all words that could be classified as tokens of the relativism *versus* absolutism debate. When progressive findings fit in well with previous ones, we should particularly guard against potential 'corroboration drive' – that is, the tendency to advance the research through steps that confirm previous findings, while disregarding other paths of analysis. The phenomenon is similar to confirmation bias, but it is not limited to confirmatory evidence: it also refers to the analytical process itself – 'a systematic search for elements that validate previous findings' (Marchi and Taylor, 2009: 4).

6. Moral relativism

The data discussed above only give a picture of frequencies and not of relevance, and the two are, of course, rather different beasts. To use an aphorism that has been attributed to Einstein, and to paraphrase a common criticism raised against Corpus Linguistics, 'not everything that can be counted counts, and not everything that counts can be counted'. It has emerged that in SiBol 93 explicit MORAL discourse is more present than in 2005; statistics also tell us that in SiBol 05 the association of morality with relativism is prominent.

It was decided, then, to analyse the unit *moral relativism* (occurring altogether twenty-eight times in SiBol 93 and forty-five times in SiBol 05), taking into consideration how the individual newspapers treat the issue, who the actors involved are, and whether the tone was positive or negative. In the *Guardian* data for 1993 there are only three occurrences of *moral relativism*, and they are all positive. This is shown as in Example 1, where *moral absolutism* is portrayed as definitely bad and, by contrast, *moral relativism* takes on a positive aura:

(1) If we are going to talk morality, then – to some of us – valuing a female life as less than an eight-week embryo is in itself immoral. Yet the battle between the pro-choice lobby and anti-abortionists is a thoroughly modern one between moral relativism and moral absolutism.
(SiBol 93, *Guardian*)

The *Telegraph* data for 1993 also contains three occurrences, but they are consistently negative – as in Example 2, where by association *moral relativism* is as bad as a lie:

(2) Compassion requires the suspension of censoriousness, but does not require either the propagation of lies ('Aids is not prejudiced') or complete moral relativism – according to which, one kind of behaviour is as good as another.
(SiBol 93, *Telegraph*)

The much smaller sub-corpus of the *Sunday Telegraph* for 1993 has twelve occurrences, and, much the same as its conservative sister paper, the evaluation assigned to the concept is unequivocally negative, as in Example 3:

(3) The application of moral relativism to sex and family life leads to the modern welfare slum.
(SiBol 93, *Sunday Telegraph*)

The *Times* contains seven occurrences of the item and also sees the concept as a bad thing:

(4) In teaching our children moral relativism we have placed them in the world without a moral compass, even hinting that there is no such thing.

(SiBol 93, Times)

In most cases the reference to *moral relativism* is made within a single topic, such as family, single parents or the religious authority's views on the concept; the following example is about the publication of the Papal Encyclical *Veritatis splendor*:

(5) The Pope stands for absolute values in a world penetrated by moral relativism, and is thus a hate-figure for the intellectual elite who offer us guidance through the pandemonium they have created.

(SiBol 93, Times)

The liberal *Guardian* seems to be the only voice to legitimise moral relativism. The fact that all occurrences of *moral relativism* are positive in this newspaper, does not imply, though, that *relativism* itself is seen as good by the progressive press. Looking at *relativism* on its own, among the twenty-two occurrences in the *Guardian* for 1993, we find a considerable number of examples with negative connotations, as here:

(6) The trouble with "pure" relativism, however, is that it leaves no room for any kind of moral vision.

(SiBol 93, Guardian)

What characterises the *Guardian* in 1993, then, is not a pro-relativist attitude, but the fact that a pro *versus* anti debate is still conceivable. This has changed by 2005, when the fifteen occurrences of *moral relativism* in the *Guardian* are all negative. It seems to have become an expression used by conservatives to label liberals, and, consequently, for liberals to be charged with *moral relativism* is undesirable:

(7) The first thing to say is that these putative British neocons sometimes have a point. The left can be reluctant to assert the superiority of liberal democracy, thereby laying itself open to the charge of moral relativism.

(SiBol 05, Guardian)

However, *Guardian* writers can still view moral relativism as acceptable provided that it is not named explicitly as such. In the following example, (derived from the concordance lines retrieved when analysing the collocates for *moral* in the category previously defined as 'relativism *versus* universalism'), *moral relativism* is not mentioned, but it is paraphrased as *non-absolutist ethics*:

(8) Morality is based on the natural sympathy we have for our fellow creatures, nothing more and nothing less. We all have reasons to be good and to seek accommodations with each other. His case cannot be made quickly because it is neither simple nor simplistic. But the mere fact that these, and countless other non-absolutist ethics exist is enough to show that there are plenty of principled alternatives to moral absolutism.

(SiBol 05, *Guardian*)

As a general methodological point, it is interesting to take into consideration omissions as well as occurrences, acknowledging, of course, that it is far more difficult to see what is not there.

Basing an interpretation on empirical data, no matter how generalisable, does not guarantee objectivity; one should be careful not to overestimate the findings, and it is always important to reinscribe findings in their broader extra-linguistic context. In this case, for instance, it should be noted that both 1993 and 2005 were potentially sensitive years for 'moral relativism'. In 1993, Pope John Paul II issued the famous encyclical about moral truths. In 2005, that Pope died, and the press gave him considerable coverage and tribute. To guard against the risk of over-interpretation (O'Halloran and Coffin, 2004) we should, therefore, wonder whether the discourse around moral relativism would be different in another 'season'?[11]

7. Morality and sex

Unusual or unique events which contribute to making a particular 'season' uncommon might be problematic in terms of representativeness, but it is also interesting, since the response to such events (and the selection of events to which to respond) is emblematic of an era. Speaking of newsworthiness, Hartley (1982: 75) notes that, 'Events don't get into the news simply by happening, no matter how frantically. They must fit in with what is already there [...]. Events need to be known and registered'. The year 1993 was a salient one for events falling under the umbrella of morality. Hunt (1994) registers 1993 as the origin of a conflation of morality and panic. But what are the 'claims of moral decline leading to moral panics' (McEnery, 2006: 20) in 1993 and 2005? In order to answer this question, I examined the collocational patterns of *morality* in the two time periods; in both cases the first lexical word to be found was *sexual* (see Table 4).[12]

Since collocation is directional (Scott and Tribble, 2006), I also decided to check the patterns for *sexual*. In this case, *morality* ranks twenty-

---

[11] Gabrielatos and Baker (2008) define 'seasonal collocates' as co-occurring words that are related to specific events.

[12] In addition *sex* ranks twentieth in position L2 in SiBol 93.

ninth (R1) amongst the collocates for *sexual* in SiBol 93 and forty-ninth in SiBol 05.

In order to obtain a comprehensive picture of sex and morality, the corpora were searched for all articles containing MORAL and SEX.[13] In terms of quantity, there are more articles presenting the co-occurrence of the target words in 1993 (but we need to take into account the higher frequency of MORAL *per se* in SiBol 93), and, taking the newspapers individually, there are more in the Sunday papers and in the *Guardian* (at a glance in Figure 3).

Having mapped the distribution, I repeated the operation I used for MORAL and ETHICAL to obtain Concordance Keywords. I retrieved, using Xaira,[14] all the news items presenting the co-occurrence of MORAL and SEX, and downloaded them all into two XML files (one for SiBol 93 and one for SiBol 05). I then derived wordlists and compared them using WordSmith's Keywords, in order to access what morality and sex were discussed in relation to in the papers in 1993 and 2005. Three main groups of keywords were identified for each period. In SiBol 93 articles containing the terms *sex* and *morals*, the news topics include:

- Education: *education, pupils, homework, discipline, school, alumni, curriculum* and *teaching*
- Family: *parent, child, family* and *families*
- Cultural industry: *films, television* and *Hollywood*

The discourse of education is related to John Patten's (then Education Secretary) guidelines on how schools should treat sex education; the main points of Patten's initiative were thus synthesised by the *Times*:

(9) CRUSADE to ensure that schoolchildren are taught about sex within a clear moral framework that promotes family values was launched yesterday by John Patten, the education secretary. Under guidelines proposed yesterday, pupils must be told that the law forbids sexual intercourse with girls under 16 and homosexual acts between males if either party is under 21.

(SiBol 93, *Times*)

---

[13] SEX defines a set of words including *sex, sexual, sexuality, sexually, heterosexual(s), homosexual(s), homosexuality, homosexually, gay(s), lesbian(s), lesbianism, transsexual(s), transexuality* and *transexualism*.

[14] Xaira XML query allows us to search for words, phrases and patterns within a marked-up portion of text – in this case individual articles, tagged as < div3 >.

SiBol 93	L5	L4	L3	L2	L1	Centre	R1	R2	R3	R4	R5
1	THE	THE	THE	OF	OF	**MORALITY**	OF	THE	THE	OF	THE
2	A	TO	OF	AND	THE		AND	A	OF	THE	OF
3	TO	OF	TO	TO	A		IS	IS	AND	IN	AND
4	TO	OF	TO	TO	A		IN	IN	A	TO	IN
5	IN	IN	AND	ABOUT	SEXUAL		THE	AND	IN	AND	TO
6	IS	IS	IN	A	ON		BUT	BE	TO	A	A
7	AND	AND	IS	ON	PUBLIC		TALE	TO	IS	IS	IS
8	AS	ON	ABOUT	IS	CHRISTIAN		THAT	THAT	AS	AS	THAT
9	IT	FOR	ON	SENSE	THAT		TO	IT	BY	BY	WITH
10	THEIR	NOT	NOT	IN	TO		AS	NOT	NOT	WITH	NOT

SiBol 05	L5	L4	L3	L2	L1	Centre	R1	R2	R3	R4	R5
1	THE	THE	OF	OF	OF	**MORALITY**	OF	THE	THE	THE	THE
2	TO	OF	THE	A	THE		AND	A	A	OF	OF
3	OF	A	A	THE	AND		TALE	AND	OF	A	AND
4	AND	TO	TO	ABOUT	A		IS	OF	IN	AND	TO
5	IS	AND	AND	AND	SEXUAL		IN	IS	TO	TO	A
6	A	IS	IN	TO	PERSONAL		PLAY	TO	AND	THAT	IS
7	IN	IN	ABOUT	ON	ON		BUT	IN	IS	IS	IN
8	THAT	ON	IT	IN	ABOUT		THAT	IT	AS	IN	THAT
9	BE	WITH	IS	MODERN	MODERN		OR	THAT	THAT	AS	AS
10	HIS	IT	AS	IS	THAT		TO	ABOUT	NOT	HIS	HE

Table 4: WordSmith Pattern output for *morality* in SiBol 93 and SiBol 05

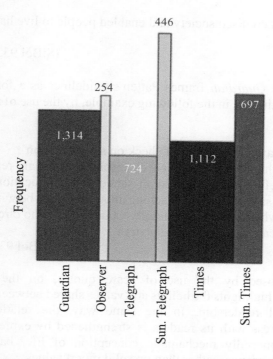

Figure 3: MORAL and SEX co-occurring in individual articles in 1993 and 2005 in the specific papers. The width of each column represents the size of each sub-corpus, whereas the height represents the frequency of the search term

(10) But sex education should encourage pupils to consider "the importance of self-restraint, dignity and respect for themselves and others", the guidelines say. Pupils should be helped to recognise the physical, emotional and moral risks of promiscuity. "Schools should foster a recognition that both sexes should behave responsibly in sexual matters. Pupils should be helped to appreciate the benefits of stable married and family life and the responsibilities of parenthood."

(SiBol 93, *Times*)

The *Telegraph* makes its views towards the topic quite explicit, describing the implementation of the guidelines in terms of parents recapturing their right to educate their children:

(11) The more successful schools were in complementing the role of parents, the less likelihood there was of parents exercising their right under the 1993 Education Act to withdraw their children from sex education. Mr Patten said schools should teach pupils to appreciate the importance of moral values. They provided ideals to live up to, were the

hallmark of a civilised society and enabled people to live harmoniously together.

(SiBol 93, *Telegraph*)

Conversely, the *Guardian* frames Patten's guidelines as a form of control, which is strengthened, in the following example, by the use of modals *should* and *must*:

(12) Patten says parents should check on sex education
PARENTS should be able to check teaching materials related to sex education before they are used in schools, the Education Secretary, John Patten, said yesterday. Teaching about sex must be within a moral framework which encouraged family values and "in no circumstances" should advocate homosexual behaviour

(SiBol 93, *Guardian*)

The stress, posed by the use of scare quotes, on the 'dangers' of homosexuality highlights the beliefs and values shared between the *Guardian* and its liberal readership. In the same way, the relationship of the conservative press with its readers is strengthened by expressing aversion towards a supposedly mechanistic conception of life, based solely on knowledge and science, rather than on solid moral values:

(13) Sex education, including lessons on HIV and Aids, will be removed from the science curriculum and become a separate subject. Mr Patten's aim is to ensure that pupils learn about sex within a moral framework. The move reflects concern that too much emphasis is currently placed on teaching the mechanics with too little stress on the responsibilities and consequences. Mr Major believes that traditional family values have been subverted by a combination of liberal thinking and political correctness. The drive also follows attacks by the Tory Right on single-parent families.

(SiBol 93, *Sunday Telegraph*)

The *Sunday Telegraph*'s aversion to liberal thought and policies (which it labels as Political Correctness – a pejorative term according to Cameron (1995) and Suhr and Johnson (2003)) and their ominous consequences is occasionally made explicit, as it is in its position towards homosexuality:

(14) The lie is not without consequences. The whole environment in which an American child is brought up today is radically different from that which prevailed just a decade ago. Schools now distribute condoms to children as young as 11 without the consent of parents, actively promoting a sort of animal copulation of the lowest kind, all in the name of Aids prevention. Are they taught to avoid the one thing that is truly dangerous, a homosexual affair with an older man? Teachers would lose

their job suggesting any such thing. Political Correctness demands that they furnish pupils with a positive view of homosexual life.

(SiBol 93, *Sunday Telegraph*)

Moving on to 2005, in the SiBol 05 list of concordance keywords, once again, and unsurprisingly, we find personal pronouns (*I*, *he*, *you*, *his*, *my* and *she*). We find, in addition, keywords that may be grouped into two categories:

- Politics: *Blair*, *Iraq*, *Africa*, *UN*, *African*, *Bush*, *muslim*, *Rwanda*, *Abu Ghraib* and *Guantanamo*
- The Vatican: *Wojtyla*, *pope*, *Paul*, *Krakow*, *evangelical*, *Rome*, *cardinals* and *Benedict*

It is clear at first glance that the 2005 list of concordance keywords is imbued with references to current events – it is of course predictable that *Bush* and *Blair* are key items in the press of 2005 compared to 1993 – but what is interesting is that *Major* and *Clinton* are not key in the query comparing 1993 with 2005. In SiBol 05, many of the concordance keywords are also 'seasonal', relating, for instance, to the sexual tortures perpetuated at Abu Ghraib. As already mentioned, 2005 was also the year of the death of Pope John Paul II, that is Karol *Wojtyla*, the Pope from *Krakow* and the election of the new Pope *Benedict* XVI. Both are newsworthy events, and so the Vatican is a dominant topic in general in that period, and it specifically dominates news dealing with sex and morality, because of both Popes' commitment towards the protection of Catholic values in the sphere of sexual and conjugal ethics.

There is, also, a series of interesting items in the concordance keywords lists, which characterise the two periods and, especially in SiBol 93, indicate the era's specific concerns in the association of morality and sex (see Tables 5 and 6).

In SiBol 93 the reference is to *single* mothers, birth *control* and *artificial* insemination. The 'moral panic' here is the destabilisation and disappearance of the traditional family. The frame is the political context of the time, with Major's 'Back to Basics' campaign. In 1993, the issue of single mothers received particular attention in the media, so much so that it has been dubbed 'the year of the lone mother' (Mann and Roseneil, 1999: 99).

The Back to Basics campaign, and Patten's guidelines, echoes (or is echoed by) the Papal Encyclical,[15] which aimed to 'reflect on the whole of the Church's moral teaching, with the precise goal of recalling certain fundamental truths of Catholic doctrine which, in the

---

[15] The English version of the encyclical is available at:
http://www.vatican.va/holy_father/john_paul_ii/encyclicals/documents/hf_jp-ii_enc_06081993_veritatis-splendor_en.html.

Keyword	Freq. SiBol 93	Percent	Freq. SiBol 05	Percent	Keyness
VIOLENCE	308	0.06	198	0.02	82.02
ADULTERY	77	0.01	25		50.5
CONTROL	167	0.03	105	0.01	46.44
WOMEN	844	0.015	920	0.12	35.19
AIDS	149	0.03	104	0.01	33.3
ACTS	101	0.02	59		32.13
INSEMINATION	21		1		30.51
PROZAC	25		3		28.84
SINGLE	185	0.03	152	0.02	26.91
PROCREATION	24		4		24.2

Table 5: Keywords for 'sex and morality' news items from SiBol 93

Keyword	Freq. SiBol 05	Percent	Freq. SiBol 93	Percent	Keyness
SURGERY	77		10	36.72	36.72
CANNABIS	53		4		33.87
PEDOPHILE	36		1		30.41
GAY	466	0.06	212	0.04	26.65

Table 6: Keywords for 'sex and morality' news items from SiBol 05

present circumstances, risk being distorted or denied'. Among these 'present circumstances' the encyclical enumerates, 'contraception, direct sterilization, autoeroticism, pre-marital sexual relations, homosexual relations and artificial insemination'. The press broadly reports the Pope's words, but with a stance that corresponds to their political leaning. For instance, according to the *Guardian* the Pope issues rulings, he condemns and uses inappropriate hyperboles (see Example 15), whilst, according to the *Telegraph*, he fights 'evil' (see Example 16):

(15) Rome accused of failing to understand role of sex
THE Pope's latest ruling on morality condemns artificial birth control and other acts forbidden by the Church as "intrinsically evil". It mentions sexual perversion and genocide in the same context.

(SiBol 93, *Guardian*)

(16) In rejecting moral relativism, the Pope is not thinking merely in terms of sexual behaviour. He is fighting against evil in all its forms.

(SiBol 93, *Telegraph*)

In 2005, one government policy that bears heavily on newspapers' moral agenda is that concerning homosexuality. There are two reasons for this. First, there is the Vatican's strenuous condemnation of homosexuality, which was defined by Pope Benedict XVI as an 'intrinsic moral evil'. The *Guardian*, the *Observer*, the *Times* and the *Sunday Times* mentioned this (Examples 17, 18 and 19), while the issue does not appear to have been reported in the *Telegraph* and the *Sunday Telegraph*:

(17) His homily in St Peter's basilica before the cardinals went into conclave made it clear that he intends to tackle the secularism, moral laxity and consumerism of contemporary Europe head-on. He has described homosexuality as tending towards an "intrinsic moral evil".

(SiBol 05, *Guardian*)

(18) It is hard to see how the hand of God could have guided the 115 cardinals to elect a former member – albeit involuntary – of the Hitler Youth who believes homosexuality to be an intrinsic moral evil, other religions to be defective and other churches – including the Church of England – not proper.

(SiBol 05, *Times*)

(19) This because the Pope believes, and has constantly stated, that homosexuality is a disordered inclination towards moral evil. Couple that with the evident view that, because this inclination lacks the biological imperative of procreative heterosexual relations, gay people are more carnal and promiscuous, and you can instantly understand the Vatican's extraordinary antipathy towards them.

(SiBol 05, *Sunday Times*)

The second seasonal cause of news interest in homosexuality was the discussion over civil partnerships, with the Civil Partnership Act 2004 coming into force in December 2005. The law enabled same-sex couples to register as civil partners. Again the *Guardian*'s take on the issue embodies the newspaper's ideal reader (see Example 20). While the other newspapers debate the morality of same-sex civil partnership, the *Guardian* considers moral changes within the gay community:

(20) One by-product of the Civil Partnership Act is this introduction of a new morality into gay and lesbian society, traditionally somewhat casual in its relationships – precisely because its relationships have hitherto been denied any social glue. Indeed, the act is dividing the gay community, and not only between those who resent its not being called "marriage" and those who do not wish to ape heterosexual ties so closely.

(SiBol 05, *Guardian*)

Of course, these examples provide only a partial picture: they were chosen as representative of the individual newspapers' views and moods. It should be noted, though, that these choices have tended to overstress differences; however, there are also commonalities. For instance, the papers seem to agree that there is more to morality than sex, but this idea is interpreted and represented differently:

(21) MORALITY is the cornerstone of all politics. [...] Instead of a history of morality, we get a history of moralising. [...] morality is not simply sexual morality [...]

(SiBol 05, *Observer*)

(22) Secularism has become more illiberal, more persecutory, more fundamentalist. In its response the church must no longer be defensive, but try to set its own agenda. It must argue that modern Christian societies compare more than favourably with secular ones. The task of doing God's will has been interpreted too narrowly, exclusively in terms of sexual morality.

(SiBol 05, *Times*)

8. Moral compass

To finish, I want to illustrate one of the ideas I derived from this exploration by means of a metaphor. We have seen that SiBol 05 was characterised by a discussion about *moral relativism* and we have also seen how the term was characterised by negative semantic prosody.

In SiBol 05, there is also a considerable increase in the number occurrences of the expression *moral compass*:[16] it appears just eight times in SiBol 93 but ninety-six times in SiBol 05. The metaphor 'moral compass' implies the idea of a unique, objective morality – the purpose of a compass is to point in one single direction: 'A compass has a true north that is objective and external, which reflects natural laws or principles, as opposed to values that are subjective and internal. Because the compass represents the eternal verities of life' (Covey, 1990: 94). Just as there is one 'true' north, the term *moral compass* could imply that 'good' morality is in a single direction and must be 'found'. Those who do not have a working moral compass will, therefore, get lost.

This interpretation fits with our earlier discussion of relativism and its perceived negativity. The threat of relativism corresponds to the need for a moral compass. An examination of the concordance lines reveal, indeed, that most occurrences are about the lack or the loss of it, where lacking and losing reinforce the idea that a moral compass pointing north is something good. It

---

[16] Case sensitive.

is also a concept which is often personalised – it is something one can carry around in one's pocket:

> (23) Mr Blair did not strive to become Prime Minister just so he could tell the Sun that he makes love to his wife five times a night. He does have a moral compass, even if he doesn't always take it to work with him. He genuinely means it when he says he wants to end world poverty or improve literacy, or when he says he feels the hand of history on him. He gets side-tracked by gimmicks and he does, as Brian Sedgemore, says, "Tell big porkies as easily as he tells small porkies", but he is trying to make a difference.
>
> (SiBol 05, *Telegraph*)

That *moral compass* is something to be owned is made clear by the abundance of possessive pronouns among its collocations: *his (13)*, *its (10)*, *her (4)*, *our (2)*, *my (2)* and *their (2)*; see Examples 24 and 25:

> (24) We are in dangerous waters here, and nobody knows how Clinton will navigate when his moral compass can no longer guide him.
>
> (SiBol 93, *Telegraph*)

> (25) [speaking of Gordon Brown] By the end, he also went back in time to take credit for ending slavery and child labour. The really bad news is that he has found his moral compass and he wants us to find ours too.
>
> (SiBol 05, *Times*)

We do things with a compass: we can lose it, break it, leave it on the counter, it is something we hold and in this sense it represents a metaphor of 'liquid modernity' (Bauman, 2000), an era of flexibility and movement and an era of consumerism. Bauman claims[17] that the metaphor that best suits the contemporary citizen is an 'anchor', (while before post-modernity and its end it was 'roots'), where the anchor – like the compass – stands for something we carry around, and we use according to our needs: we choose where to throw it, and when to lift it and leave. It is not something that we belong to, but something that belongs to us.

In the corpora, the moral compass too is constructed as an instrument and a commodity to possess. Sometimes we receive it from something or someone:

> (26) Just as Pope John Paul II's moral compass was forged in Cracow, with its proximity to Auschwitz and also after the war to the communist steel-town Nowa Huta, so Pope Benedict's compass was set by Traunstein and its Nazi past.
>
> (SiBol 05, *Times*)

---

[17] Lectio magistralis: 'Vite di corsa. Le sfide all'educazione della modernità liquida', Bologna, 13 November 2008.

Staying within the conceptual metaphor of morality as being a journey, but in stark contrast with the *moral compass* in terms of semantic implications, the corpus contains mentions of the term *moral maze*. The moral maze is also a place and, thus, external to the self and independent from it: it is not something we have, but something we *enter, are stuck in, navigate, are dragged, pitched* or *plunged into, become lost in* and *foxtrot round*.

> (27) The Prime Minister's call for the country to go 'back to basics' has plunged the Conservatives into a moral maze.
>
> (SiBol 93, *Telegraph*)

> (28) We don't know what we're doing. It's a moral maze out there. And it isn't even May 5 yet.
>
> (SiBol 05, *Guardian*)

'A maze normally refers to a network of pathways, which, by their complexity, open and closed routes, and invisibility of orienting landmarks, obstructs access to a predetermined goal or point of arrival' (Harvey, 1999: 7). If the moral maze is the problem, the moral compass is the solution. Interestingly, the metaphor *moral maze*[18] is slightly more frequent in SiBol 93 (thirty-three occurrences) than is SiBol 05 (twenty-three occurrences).

The evidence here is too limited (both in terms of absolute frequencies and of relative decrease) to allow for any real generalisation, and it seemed worth extending the question beyond the boundaries of the corpus. In order to test the validity of the finding, the phrases *moral maze*[19] and *moral compass* were searched on Lexis Nexis database, looking at all the British broadsheet newspapers available in a large time span (from 1989 to 2008).[20] Figure 4 shows a constant increase in the number of articles making reference to *moral compass*.

Newspapers have become progressively larger in size over time, so the increasing frequency of *moral compass* is not revealing *per se*. However, what is more interesting is how the term changes over time in comparison with the trend for *moral maze*. Far from suggesting a correlation between the rise of one item and the fall of the other, it seems interesting, nevertheless, to highlight the growing popularity of the *compass* metaphor, which has largely surpassed the use of the *maze* one. A simple Google search could have told us that *moral compass* is far more common than *moral maze*, but it would have failed to reveal that this popularity seems to be fairly recent.

---

[18] The search term used is case sensitive in order to exclude from the search all references to the BBC Radio 4 programme, *Moral Maze*.

[19] All occurrences of *moral maze* were checked manually, in order to separate the mentions of the BBC Radio 4 programme, from the metaphoric use of the expression.

[20] The broadsheets available on Lexis Nexis for the whole time period are: *Guardian, Observer, Times, Sunday Times, Independent* and *Independent on Sunday*. Unfortunately, the *Telegraph* and *Sunday Telegraph* are only available from year 2002, and so had to be excluded from the query.

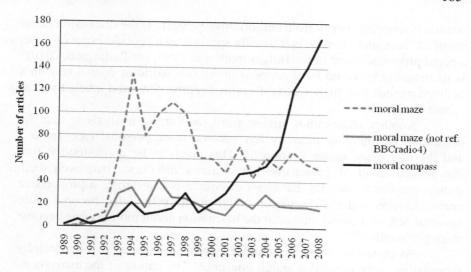

Figure 4: Broadsheets'[21] articles mentioning *moral maze* or *moral compass* from 1989 to 2008

Metaphorically we could see the 'compass' as what we need to navigate in the 'maze', and to get out of it. It goes beyond the aims of this paper to attempt a sociological explanation, but the findings hint at an interesting area for further investigation in our quest for an understanding of morality.

9. Conclusion

It was the intention of this article to both sketch the explicit representation of morality in the press at twelve years distance, and also to give an impression of the way CADS methodology can help us to explore something like 'discourse about morality', by opening a variety of windows on a particular socio-cultural (and political) question. Far from being comprehensive, this analysis does not aim to produce conclusions, but to outline processes of analysis and to raise further productive questions.

The findings are open to interpretation; for instance, the proportional decline of explicit reference to morality could at first sight be read in terms of change in media language (that is, as a fashionable tendency to favour ETHICAL terms over MORAL ones) but could also be related to broader social or political issues. Does the fact that in 1993 there was a new Conservative government while in 2005 there was an old Labour one influence journalists' use of such terms (particularly in view of the fact that much of what is

---

[21] All hits retrieved on Lexis Nexis for the broadsheets available on the database for the whole reference time period (*Guardian, Observer, Times, Sunday Times, Independent* and *Independent on Sunday*).

written is reported speech from authoritative voices)? Is the discussion about morality 'seasonal', that is, is it usually sparked by a specific event (such as a papal pronouncement or the Bulger murder in 1993, see Partington, 2010)? Is its meaning based on what happens in the real world or does it rely on a codified agenda that makes certain events become news and labels them as 'about morality'?

Another observation arising from the current analysis is that the discussion surrounding morality has become more personal (see Table 3 and the discussion under Section 5). This needs to be understood within the general trend of personalisation of news discourse; but, even then, should our conclusion be that news discourse is registering a progressive personalisation and the discussion about morality has *also* become more personalised, or, instead, that *even* the discussion about morality has become more personalised?

As concerns the methodology I employed, I started this research by formulating some general research questions. The nature of the analysis is, therefore, bottom up and inductive, since I did not have an initial hypothesis to either corroborate or falsify. I looked at the data, patterns emerged that caught my eye, and I followed them down the funnel, skimming and filtering with closer attention and, to use Scott and Tribble's terms, 'imagination':

> [W]hen one examines the boiled down extract, the list of words, the concordance. It is here that something not different from the sometimes scorned 'intuition' comes in. This is imagination. Insight. Human beings are unable to see shapes, bits, displays or sets without insight, without seeing in them 'patterns'. It seems to be a characteristic of the homo sapiens mind that is often unable to see things 'as they are' but imposes on them a tendency, a trend, a pattern.
>
> (Scott and Tribble, 2006: 7)

Finding patterns, choosing paths, putting together findings, making sense of them is necessarily partial and subjective. CADS allows us to exploit the strengths of both quantitative and qualitative approaches, while compensating some of the reciprocal weaknesses; but it also multiplies the potential paths we can take and often (as in this case) there is no unequivocal point of arrival. What we have is a series of choices, where one choice leads to another and opens new questions or modifies the initial question. It is, in other words, not simply about providing new answers, but, as with all valid scientific methodology, about generating new questions. This is research 'serendipity', defined as a 'not just a lucky find, but a lucky find that enables fresh questions to be asked in the field' (Partington, 2009: 292). This capacity to raise new puzzles (Kuhn, 1970) and discover further complexity 'helps guarantee that the linguistic scientist will never be out of a job' (Partington, 2009: 292). The problem from the researcher's perspective might be 'where does it end?', because there will always be new questions to be asked.

References

Baker, P. 2005. The Public Discourses of Gay Men. London: Routledge.

Baker, P. 2006. Using Corpora in Discourse Analysis. London: Continuum.

Baker, P., C. Gabrielatos, M. Khosravinik, M. Krzyzanowski, T. McEnery and R. Wodak. 2008. 'A useful methodological synergy? Combining critical discourse analysis and corpus linguistics to examine discourses of refugees and asylum seekers in the UK press', Discourse and Society 19 (3), pp. 273–305.

Bauman, Z. 2000. Liquid Modernity. Oxford: Blackwell.

Cameron, D. 1995. Verbal Hygiene. London: Routledge.

Cohen, S. 1972. Folk Devils and Moral Panics: The Creation of the Mods and Rockers. Oxford: Martin Robertson.

Connell, I. 1998. 'Mistaken identities: tabloid and broadsheet news discourse', The Public 5 (3), pp. 11–31.

Covey, S.R. 1990. Principle-Centered Leadership. New York: Simon and Schuster.

Curran, J. and C. Sparks. 1991. 'Press and popular culture', Media, Culture and Society 13 (2), pp. 215–37.

van Dijk, T.A. 1998. 'Opinions and ideologies in the press' in A. Bell and P. Garrett (eds) Approaches to Media Discourse, pp. 21–63. Oxford: Blackwell.

Esser, F. 1999. ' "Tabloidization" of news: a comparative analysis of Anglo-American and German press journalism', European Journal of Communication 14 (3), pp. 291–324.

Fairclough, N. 2001. Language and Power. London: Pearson/Longman.

Fowler, R. 1991. Language in the News: Discourse and Ideology in the Press. London: Routledge.

Gabrielatos, C. and P. Baker. 2008. 'Fleeing, sneaking, flooding. A corpus analysis of discursive constructions of refugees and asylum seekers in the UK Press 1996–2005', Journal of English Linguistics 36 (1), pp. 5–38.

Gramsci, A. 2000. The Gramsci reader: selected writings, 1916–1935. New York: New York University Press.

Hall, S. 1982. 'The rediscovery of "ideology": return of the repressed in media studies' in M. Gurevitch, T. Bennet, J. Curran and J. Woollacott (eds) Culture, Society and the Media, pp. 56–90. London: Routledge.

Hartley, J. 1982. Understanding News. London: Taylor and Francis.

Hart-Mautner, G. 1995. ' "Only connect": critical discourse analysis and corpus linguistics', UCREL Technical Paper 6. Lancaster: University of Lancaster.

Harvey, M. 1999. 'How the object of knowledge contains the knowledge of the object: an epistemological analysis of a social research investigation', Cambridge Journal of Economics 23 (4), pp. 485–501.

Hunston, S. 2004. 'Counting the uncountable: problems of identifying evaluation in a text and in a corpus' in A. Partington, J. Morley and L. Haarman (eds) Corpora and Discourse, pp. 157–88. Bern: Peter Lang.

Hunston, S. and G. Thompson. 2000. Evaluation in Text: Authorial Stance and the Construction of Discourse. Oxford: Oxford University Press.

Hunt, A. 1994. ' "Moral panic" and moral language in the media', British Journal of Sociology 48 (4), pp. 629–48.

Kuhn, T. 1970. The Structure of Scientific Revolutions. Chicago: University of Chicago Press.

Lakoff, G. 2002. Moral Politics. How Liberals and Conservatives Think. Chicago and London: Chicago University Press.

Mann, K. and S. Roseneil. 1999. 'Poor choices? Gender, agency and the underclass debate' in G. Jagger and C. Wright (eds) Changing Family Values: Difference Diversity and the Decline of Male Order, pp. 98–118. London: Routledge.

Marchi, A. and C. Taylor. 2009. 'If on a winter's night two researchers... a challenge to assumptions of soundness of interpretation', Critical Approaches to Discourse Analysis across Disciplines 3 (1), pp. 1–20.

Marr, A. 2005. My Trade. London: Macmillan.

McEnery, T. 2006. Swearing in English: Bad Language, Purity and Power from 1586 to Present. London: Routledge.

O'Halloran, K. and C. Coffin. 2004 'Checking overinterpretation and underinterpretation: help from corpora in critical linguistics' in C. Coffin, A. Hewings, K. O'Halloran (eds) Applying English Grammar: Functional and Corpus Approaches, pp. 275–97. London: Hodder Arnold.

Partington, A. 2009. 'Evaluating evaluation and some concluding thoughts on CADS' in J. Morley and P. Bayley (eds) Corpus-Assisted Discourse Studies on the Iraq Conflict: Wording the War, pp. 261–303. London: Routledge.

Partington, A. 2010. 'Modern Diachronic Corpus-Assisted Discourse Studies (MD-CADS) on UK newspapers: an overview of the project', Corpora 5 (2), pp. 83–108.

Pinker, S. 2008. 'The moral instinct' in The New York Times, 13 January 2008. Available online at: www.nytimes.com/2008/01/13/magazine/13Psychology-t.html

Schudson, M. 1995. The Power of News. Cambridge Massachusetts: Harvard University Press.

Scott, M. 1999. WordSmith Tools Help Manual version 3. Oxford: Oxford University Press.

Scott, M. and C. Tribble. 2006. Textual Patterns: Key Words and Corpus Analysis in Language Education. Amsterdam: John Benjamins.

Sparks, C. 1998. 'Introduction', The Public 5 (3), pp. 5–10.

Stubbs, M. 2001. Words and Phrases: Corpus Studies of Lexical Semantics. Oxford: Blackwell.

Suhr, S. and S. Johnson. 2003. 'Re-visiting "PC": introduction to the special issue on "political correctness" ', Discourse and Society 14 (5), pp. 5–16.

Taylor, C. 2010. 'Science in the news: a diachronic perspective', Corpora 5 (2), pp. 221–50.

Investigating *anti* and some reflections on Modern Diachronic Corpus-Assisted Discourse Studies (MD-CADS)

Alison Duguid[1]

Abstract

In this study, I use WordSmith Tools 5.0 (Scott, 2008) and Xaira to examine the prefix *anti*, its collocates, contexts and quantitative profile in the SiBol corpus.[2] First, I discuss the problem involved in investigating a prefix, and I follow this with an examination of the prefix itself. Although the overall proportion of *anti* prefixing has remained fairly similar over time, (unlike *pro* which has decreased), there are key changes in the stems or 'targets' of the prefix which reflect changes in social and political concerns. Among the findings are changes in the way that antibiotics are talked about, and an increase in the discourse about products designed to deal with age-related problems. The study also examines co-texts and contexts of *anti* terms expressing opposition to groups distinguished by their nationality, religion or ethnic origins, and differences in the ways such opposition is constructed. The analysis illustrates how modern diachronic corpus-assisted discourse studies (MD-CADS) can contribute to research into socio-cultural and political language and highlights the value of investigating prefixes.

1. Introduction

This paper is an expanded version of research that formed part of a two-year interdisciplinary project at the Faculty of Political Science University of Siena entitled *In the Eyes of the Beholder*: *Anti-Americanism in Western*

---

[1] Facoltà di Lettere, San Niccolò, via Roma 56, 53100, Siena, Italy.
Correspondence to: Alison Duguid, *e-mail*: duguid@unisi.it
[2] The two corpora are named after the universities (Siena and Bologna) working on the project and are called SiBol 93 and SiBol 05. See Partington (2010) for further details. The first corpus contains around 100 million words (about twenty-seven million from the *Guardian*, thirty-four million from the *Telegraph* and *Sunday Telegraph*, and thirty-nine million from the *Times* and *Sunday Times*). The second, contains about 145 million (forty-one million from the *Guardian*, thirty-seven million from the *Telegraph* and *Sunday Telegraph*, and sixty-seven million from the *Times* and *Sunday Times*).

Corpora 2010 Vol. 5 (2): 191–220
DOI: 10.3366/E1749503210000444
© Edinburgh University Press
www.eupjournals.com/cor

Europe and the United States during the Iraq Crisis which involved the compilation of a corpus based on the search term *anti-Americanism* over the period 1999 to 2007 in twelve different newspapers in Britain and the USA. In preparation for a project seminar, a longer time span was considered, in which the terms *anti-Americanism* and *anti-American* were examined in the SiBol corpora. This analysis was mainly quantitative, but an attempt was made to look at the evaluative force of the terms and their collocations. The study of the prefix suggested that it had the rhetorical function of summarising and labelling identity, action, stance and policies, and this raised questions about its exact meaning.

As the title of the initial project highlights, *anti* is often an outsider or 'over-the-fence' term (Partington, 1998: 74–5) applied to others and by beholders. The process of investigation provoked some consideration of methodology. Further stimulus came from Tribble (2006: 166) who, on comparing a newspaper (the *Guardian Weekly*) with the British National Corpus (BNC), found that *anti* was a strong keyword, probably, in part, because no prefixes are included in the BNC wordlists. Tribble (2006: 166) stated that, 'a view of the collocates of *anti* gives an immediate view of the issues that dominated news reporting between 1966 and 2001'. This provided encouragement for using the *anti* prefix as a path into the diachronic investigation of changes in the issues that dominated reporting in the SiBol corpus, (in parallel with other studies of the keywords to be found in this issue of *Corpora*). A corpus of this kind and size stimulates researcher-driven, inductive research of the kind outlined by Partington (2009) and discussed by Partington (2010) and Taylor (2010).

Both the anti-Americanism project and Tribble's finding indicated that there was also potential for investigating at a synchronic level, since, if the *anti* prefix is a characteristic feature of newspaper language, then it merits some kind of investigation into how it is used. The research questions thus suggested are: on a diachronic level, does the *anti* prefix give a view of the issues that dominate news reporting and what changes can be found in the stems or 'targets' of *anti*-labelling and their relative salience in the British broadsheets between 1993 and 2005, and what does this tell us about the way these social, cultural and political issues are represented in the broadsheets? And, on a synchronic level, what are the patterns of use of *anti* as a prefix, how are the polarised stances which are constructed with the *anti* prefix referenced, in particular, those regarding race or religion, what strategies of representation are used and how do these differ according to the target?

1.1 Investigating a prefix: methodological concerns

1.1.1 Form

One of the first questions involved in corpus investigation is often, 'what exactly is a word?' Clearly, prefixes are not words, but parts of words. Most work on affixation is done as part of studies in morphology and lexicography, though it is of interest in language acquisition studies and the discussion of levels of vocabulary (see Gardner, 2007, for a useful survey). Linguists have employed corpora to investigate individual affixes: the BNC has provided data on derivational morphemes and their distribution in different registers (Plag *et al.*, 1999) and derivational affix combinations (Hay and Plag, 2004). Such studies have mostly employed general reference corpora such as the BNC or Lancaster–Oslo/Bergen (LOB) corpus (Bauer and Nation, 1993). In Bauer and Nation's (1993) classification scheme of word family recognition, *anti* is placed on level five of seven as one of the 'regular but infrequent affixes'. The main questions that have been considered have concerned productivity (Nishimoto, 2004; Prcic, 1999; and Baayen and Liebor, 1991) and productivity constraints (Plag, 1999, 2003; and Lipka, 2002). Among specific corpus studies, Baayen and Renouf (1996) have carried out studies on a newspaper corpus looking at different aspects of lexical productivity over time, including on neologisms. Renouf (2007) is particularly interested in affixation and its role in phrasal creativity. Stvan (2006) studies a corpus of brand names, investigating the suffix *–ex* and looking at domain types, productivity and meanings.

Prefixation involves adding a prefix to a base or a stem; it does not, usually, change the class of the word. Derivational prefixes may usually be paraphrased, although 'being lexicalised units prefixed nouns may acquire meanings which cannot be fully understood by combining the meanings of the prefix and the base' (Quirk *et al.*, 1985: 790). In fact, the prefixation of *anti* and *pro* often generates items with a different function from the stem; consider *cellulite* and *anti-cellulite* (*cream*), *life* and *pro-life* (*activist*), *abortion* and *anti-abortion* (*campaign*).

Prefixes pose particular problems for the corpus researcher. The prefixed forms can be written as a single word or can be hyphenated. Since there are variable uses in prefixation, the presence or absence of a hyphen and the presence or absence of a space after a hyphen, and the fact that hyphens can be encoded differently by different software, can make the search process and compilation of quantitative data very time-consuming, and may lead to unstable results. Some researchers, when working on relatively small corpora, make the decision to alter their corpus (using a search and replace function) to ensure they have identified all possible variants, but, given the size of the corpora, here, and the fact that two different software packages were being used (involving both simple text and XML marked-up text), that option was not applied here. The SiBol research group had already made the decision to use WordSmith Tools and Xaira to interrogate the corpus, depending on the research requirements at any given moment. As Taylor (2010) points out, WordSmith permits one to move with ease from concordance to text, and Xaira permits sorting collocates quickly by *z*-score and by frequency. Both sets of software required more than one search procedure to identify all cases of the *anti* prefix while eliminating all non prefixed forms, such as *Antibes*, *antique* or *anticipate*. Word Query and Phrase Query in Xaira were used, and the search item *anti** with WordSmith (the asterisk representing a wildcard function ensuring any combination of characters in its place) to ensure that items with a hyphen, with a space or as whole-word forms were all retrieved.

A question arises with regard to whether the choice of hyphenated over non-hyphenated forms has any linguistic significance. As Quirk *et al.* (1985: 970) point out, some derivational prefixes are only loosely attached to their base, which is why one can find examples like *pro-* and *anti-establishment*. Quirk *et al.* (1985: 1537) also believe that, as a sequence of items becomes more established, it might become hyphenated as an intermediate stage before being written as a single word. One would expect, therefore, that any hyphenated forms would perhaps appear more frequently in the earlier corpus as the same words in the later corpus might be expected to have a more established form. However, this is not borne out by examination of this corpus. According to Quirk *et al.* (1985: 1613), the rules for this use of the hyphen are subject to considerable variation in the practice of publishing houses and of individual writers, as well as in dictionaries and style manuals. If hyphenation were, simply, a matter of house style, one paper would contain more hyphenated versions; but even this hypothesis is not borne out, given that the same word can appear in different forms in different parts of the newspaper. This suggests that the different sections of a paper follow the personal style of the section editor rather than any overall policy. In some cases, it depends on how important the issue is to the newspaper's identity; for example, the Euro-sceptic *Telegraph* always uses a hyphen for *Euro-* compounds where other broadsheets do not (Taylor, 2005). This reflects the more distant, and less accepting, stance of this particular newspaper to the European Union.

Since we are not starting with a complete word, or even a stem, we cannot begin with keywords – as is usual in corpus-assisted discourse studies (CADS) methodology. The only *anti* prefixed word to appear in the keywords lists for SiBol is *antisocial* (connected with the government's Anti-Social Behaviour Order policy (ASBO)) in the 2005 corpus. Instead of keywords with their relative salience, it is the prefix itself which is the point of entry into the data. The form *anti* appears as a word in the wordlists obtained by using WordSmith Tools, as Tribble found in relation to his corpus. It is ranked in the SiBol 93 wordlist in the top 1,000 words at position 909 with a frequency of 12.169, and in SiBol 05 wordlist at position 874 with a frequency of 19.626. In terms of relative percentage, there has been a very slight increase from 0.01231 percent in SiBol 93 to 0.01240 percent in SiBol 05. There has been little change, essentially, in terms of the frequency of the form; but, as with all such prefixes, it is not the form itself which sheds light on its use, but the various roots with which it will combine. What can the corpus reveal through the collocates and concordance lines with *anti* about the way newspapers construct the world?

1.1.2 Meaning

Quirk *et al.* (1985: 1543) classify *anti* as one of the prefixes of 'orientation and attitude', along with *contra, counter* and *pro*, so we would expect it to express aspects of subjectivity – to be an indicator of stance. However, although *anti* is used primarily to suggest opposition to some entity or practice, it became clear on analysing the corpus data, through examining both the words that contain *anti* and their concordance lines, that the nature of the opposition varies.

In the corpus data, the prefix is used principally to represent a metaphorical fight against elements of the physical world, often with the sense either of preventing or curing something. The main semantic field the prefix occurred with in both SiBol corpora was that of medicine. It appears with nouns or adjectives (*antibacterials* and *antibacterial*) and, in these cases, a corpus investigation can to a certain extent reveal changes in the deployment of resources or in the representation of awareness of the medical sphere. *Anti* can also mean, as Quirk *et al.* (1985: 1543) tell us, 'something designed to circumvent or to destroy' and we find in the data: *anti-lock, anti-tank* and *anti-aircraft*. This use can signal particular technological concerns, and it is found in different discourse types. The item *anti-lock* was found in the discourse concerning cars, mostly in review sections, whilst the other two are part of the vocabulary of war reporting.

Anti is also used to describe an attitude of opposition to something or someone – to individuals or groups. The corpus-based *Collins 2009 Advanced Dictionary* states that the 'anti (prefix) is used to form adjectives and nouns that describe someone or something that is opposed to a particular system, practice or group of things' and, as a second meaning, it forms 'adjectives and nouns that describe things that are intended to destroy something harmful or to prevent something from happening', which we have already seen appears in the data in the medical and technological fields, but it also appears in the dataset in the field of law and legislation (*anti-crime* and *anti-poaching*).

In the political and social world, instead, the dataset suggests that it is used where opposition is expressed by criticism of ideas, measures, behaviour, or social groups that are seen to have too much power (as with, for example, *anti-trust* and *anti-union*), but also nationalities and individuals (*anti-Syrian* and *anti-Bush*) or religious and ethnic groups (*anti-Catholic, anti-Muslim* and *anti-Semitic*). By its nature, the Press tends to simplify complex situations, and to present polarised and adversarial representations of events. This is one of the reasons why *anti* was chosen as a way of seeing what areas of research might prove useful for investigation. As well as delimiting such areas, it also provides data about how different kinds of opposition are characterised, which I can now make an attempt to outline. It might also be interesting to consider whether the fact that, in both corpora, the *Guardian*, which uses more *anti* forms (0.013 percent), and the *Sunday Times*, which uses the least (0.008 percent), is an indication that the former tends to present the world in a more polarised fashion. In any case, there is a wide range of different kinds of opposition in the data. From a preliminary attempt to classify the uses, it appeared in the data that the target of the opposition may have inbuilt evaluation, good or bad, (*anti-racism, anti-torture, anti-poverty* and *anti-slavery*). In other cases, the target might not be good or bad in itself, but it might be perceived that there is too much of it, or it is perceived as having particular privileges so that opposition is presented as having a protective and/or a limiting rationale (*anti-trust* and *anti-union*). The target might be an abstract concept, and the ways in which it has been put into practice might make opposition to it a reasonable thing. It might be an abstract concept which is generally viewed as morally wrong (*anti-apartheid*) or have unforeseen effects (*anti-globalisation*).

Systems that are supposedly binary often compete with each other, so that being *for* one entails being against the other. The target might be actions or behaviour that is considered to be negative in one way or another, and opposition to these can be presented as reasonable (examples from the data include *anti-bullying* and *anti-poaching*). The target might be a group (national, religious, ethnic, or based on sexual preferences), so that being *anti* such a group might well be regarded as discrimination against all members of that group (for example, *anti-gay, anti-Muslim, anti-Catholic* and *anti-English*). There are also objections to individuals for what they represent and what they have done (as in SiBol, *anti-Blair* and *anti-Bush*). The evaluation is context-sensitive and will depend on which or whose side is being taken. The nature of the opposition may be ethical, aesthetic or emotional (as in Martin and White's (2002, 2005) Appraisal framework), but which of these applies is not clear from the prefix itself. The polarising nature of the term can also be seen from the fact that we find items such as *anti-anti-American* and *anti-anti-globalisation*.[3]

The polysemic nature of the prefix is reflected in some of the political discussion of *anti* items. It is not possible to assume a single inherent meaning for *anti* beyond a generic 'against' meaning, and production and reception values cannot be assumed to be identical in different cases. Does the expression 'anti-Israel sentiments' imply that the author would like to see the country destroyed? Do *anti-capitalists* necessarily want to *smash* capitalism? Does criticism of Islam equal being *anti-Islam*? Is being *anti-anti-racism* the same as being racist? Does stance lead inexorably to action? The ways in which the terms are used often confuses the issue by suggesting that such questions have only one answer.[4] Polarised *anti*-sentiments can

---

[3] *Anti* words with headword status in *Collins 2009 Advanced Dictionary* include *anti-abortionists, anti-social, anti-trust* and *anti-virus* (software).

[4] The distinctions between sentiments words and actions, and the suasive use of words were considered when the racial and religious hatred bill was amended by the House of Lords on 25 October 2005 to include the change, 'Only threatening words or behaviour will be classified as criminal. Generally abusive or insulting words about religion that are not actually threatening will not be illegal.' See Section 3.3, below.

be found under other guises too, in various other prefixes and suffixes; for example, *misogynist*, *homophobic* and *racist*. Moreover, prosodic issues can come into play in reality. The anti-abortion lobby in America began to use the more positive label *pro-life*, whilst the pro-abortion lobby began to use the term *pro-choice* to represent their positions as part of a positive political framing, suggesting that opponents were *anti*-life and *anti*-choice, respectively; clearly, *pro* is seen as having a more positive evaluative prosody than *anti*.

Looking at *anti* terms in their contexts of use can give us a detailed picture of the forms that are in 'opposition to something'. In this investigation, we shall now go on to examine diachronic changes using the forms found in the wordlists: their relative frequencies (not all of which may be statistically significant in comparing the two corpora). We shall also consider the synchronic patternings which emerge by comparing the ranking of the different forms, and will consider in more detail the nuances of the range of meanings by examining concordance lines and, where appropriate, larger portions of text, too (for, as Partington (2010: 88) points out, '[...] corpus-assisted studies of discourse tend to deal in larger chunks of meaning than is typically required in standard lexical grammar analyses').

2. Different *anti* targets: changes over time and synchronic comparisons

There are different issues raised for each of the different types of target. I chose to look first at the science terms, which constitute the lion's share[5] of *anti* items in our corpora – partly out of curiosity related to the questions raised by Taylor (2010) concerning the representation of *science* and scientificity by the press. The relative frequency for the most frequently occurring items was examined for each year, as well as the range of coverage in months, to see whether any particular health issues were receiving more coverage than others. The diachronic thrust of this research means we are looking at what has changed over the period, whilst the synchronic aspect of the investigation demands that we are able to see how the various collocates are ranged in relation to one another in any one year (this is part of an ongoing project which will be, it is to be hoped, updated with new corpora); relative frequency data are given so that changes over time can be seen. However, there are often only incremental or infinitesimal differences, since the *anti* prefix is infrequent (Gardner, 2007: 246) and the relative frequencies of its R1 collocates only reveal something about the particular combination of *anti* and change over time. In order to look at differences in common targets of *anti* within each year so that an overall picture of *anti* usage appears, a different sampling strategy was employed (see Taylor, 2010) based on

---

[5] For *anti*- there were ninety-seven science terms out of the 903 word forms found in 2005, whilst there were fifty-eight science terms out of 643 *anti* word forms in 1993.

a ranking in the two corpora. This involved taking the top 100 *anti* items for each year (see Appendix A) and examining those where the change in ranking has been greatest – that is, those which have gone up or down at least twenty-five places in the *anti* 'charts' (see Table 1). In this way, synchronic patternings of *anti* use become clearer: the rankings in any one year can be compared to another ranking, and be seen as part of a pattern rather than in terms of individual items. This exercise is involved with the research question concerning what the targets of *anti* can tell us about the social and political concerns of broadsheets.

2.1 Changes in the reporting of the scientific or medical sphere

The items which relate to the physical world are the largest set of *anti* collocates and so to a certain extent represent what is being reported in the medical sphere in particular.[6] The first step was to see what changes there were between the two corpora (see Table 2). Since the relative frequency was not always a guide to the range of coverage; the number of months in which the term appears gives a better idea of how much interest there is in a given topic.[7]

We can, thus, see that the items *antibiotic* or *antibiotics* have increased in relative frequency (though less markedly so in the spread of months). In terms of the detailed profile which might account for the change, we find that collocates of these two items in 2005 suggest a difference in attitude and indicate the increasingly problematic nature of antibiotic use. Collocates and clusters of *antibiotics* (using the WordSmith Concord Tool) in the 1993 corpus include *treatment* and *courses of antibiotics*, whereas in 2005 the discourse focusses more on concerns about the *overuse* of antibiotics, (present in six out the twenty most frequent clusters), and the problems of hospital infections, since, among the collocates, we find *resistant, resistance to MRSA, hospital infections* and *overuse*.[8] *Antibacterial* is also much more frequent in the 2005 data and it, too, is related to the topic of hospital infections; but it is also part of a discourse of do-it-yourself and alternative treatments involving remedies such as propolis, tea-tree oil and noni-fruit – part of a travel and life-style discourse, which is due also, perhaps, to the increasingly common practice of commercial product placement in the newspapers.

---

[6] Another sign of frequency and range of coverage is headword status in learner dictionaries. The 2009 *Collins–Cobuild Advanced Dictionary* includes as headwords *antibiotic*, *anti-depressant* and *antioxidant*.

[7] Each of the papers is stored by month so that the 1993 component contains sixty texts, twelve months for each paper, three dailies and two Sunday editions. Meanwhile, the 2005 corpus contains seventy-two texts, three dailies and three Sundays, (given the inclusion of the *Observer* in the 2005 corpus).

[8] Similar collocates and clusters are found *for antibody/antibodies, anticoagulant, antiperspirant* and *anticonvulsant, antifungal* and *antivenom*) which all remain constant over the time period.

Word R1 1993	ranking 1993	ranking 2005	Word R1 2005	ranking 2005	ranking 1993
Maastricht	2	–	terrorism	5	63
racist	5	42	terror	6	51
Yeltsin	28	–	doping	7	61
ulcer	31	192	American	10	33
inflationary	22	213	globalisation	11	–
federalist	32	–	inflammatory	12	52
inflation	29	178	ageing	16	127
EC	40	–	poverty	17	101
theft	46	127	syrian	19	–
abortionists	58	183	bullying	21	104
foreigner	47	292	virus	23	74
road	67	308	capitalist	24	132
missile	54	154	Americanism	27	78
Soviet	68	115	Japanese	28	140
German	64	104	retroviral	39	–
personnel	66	150	Bush	42	–
asthma	70	250	Muslim	45	99
pollution	72	119	Blair	51	–
freeze	73	117	slavery	53	85
intellectual	76	153	Catholic	54	110
pornography	77	351	EU	57	–
Serb	79	–	spam	59	–
conservative	80	158	us	60	199
feminist	81	122	British	61	38
nafta	83	–	depressant	62	39
rejection	84	125	secession	63	–
Semites	86	114	avoidance	65	145
UN	88	468	Iraq	66	190
communism	89	174	bribery	67	–
Europe	90	153	tory	68	35
fashion	92	137	money	71	438
IRA	93	263	cellulite	73	–
white	94	320	Islamic	74	147
Europeans	95	146	Glazer	75	–

Table 1: Changes in the rank order of anti targets, that is, items in R1 (movement of more than twenty-five places in the top 100 list. A dash (–) indicates that the word is not found in the top 100 list).

Word R1 1993	ranking 1993	ranking 2005	Word R1 2005	ranking 2005	ranking 1993
poaching	96	306	mafia	76	7
socialist	97	313	labour	79	123
malarial	98	124	psychotic	80	218
			AIDS	82	34
			lock	83	18
			spyware	84	–
			wrinkle	85	–
			Israeli	86	206
			corporate	87	425
			Israel	88	258
			piracy	89	217
			bacterial	90	–
			capitalists	91	–
			dumping	92	19
			gun	95	255
			inflammatories	96	–
			HIV	97	136
			submarine	98	44
			vivisection	100	170

Table 1 (*continued*): Changes in the rank order of anti targets

Other items also show marked differences in frequency. *Anti-ulcer, anti-asthma, anti-malarial* and *anti-rejection* were discussed relatively more in 1993 compared to 2005. The question remains whether such issues are talked about less because the problem they refer to has been solved or whether it is seen as less noteworthy in terms of 'news'. The concordance lines of *anti-rejection* in 2005 represent discussions about transplant issues and new drugs. Moreover, it is not always the *anti* prefix which gives an idea of the interest in a problem, since we need to be aware of the vexed question of investigating absence – of what is not said. The relative infrequency of the term *anti-migraine* might suggest that newsmakers have little interest in migraines. However, *migraine* without the prefix occurs in many texts with relatively high frequencies, alongside the collocates *drugs, prescriptions* and *injections*; this suggests that the fight against the symptoms remains of interest even if the prefixed form is relatively rare.

The items *anti-inflammatory* and *anti-inflammatories* are more common in 2005, and the contextual discourse includes discussion of their properties, including painkilling and use for arthritis sufferers. *Antioxidants* and *antioxidant, anti-ageing* and *anti-wrinkle* are also more popular in the later time period, although the concordance lines indicate that the contexts are those of lifestyle, beauty or fashion, rather than health, and *anti-cellulite*

R1 anti collocate	pmw in 93	pmw in 05	Months 93 out of 60	Months 05 out of 72
antibiotic	0.98	1.79	40	51
antibiotics	2.61	4.64	53	66
antibacterial	0.12	1.3	4	37
anti-ulcer	0.85	0.11	31	10
anti-asthma	0.35	0.08	23	5
anti-malarial	0.22	0.17	12	14
anti rejection	0.28	0.17	15	17
anti AIDS	0.74	0.24	32	20
anti-HIV	0.15	0.21	8	10
anti-retroviral	0.000	0.64	0	37
anti-inflammatory	0.480	1.5	29	55
anti inflammatories	0.000	0.21	1	20
antioxidants	0.270	1.77	10	53
antioxidant	0.230	1.73	6	16
anti-ageing	0.160	1.3	8	56
antiwrinkle	0.030	0.26	3	22
anti-cellulite	0.030	0.33	3	15
antidepressant	0.760	1.29	31	49
antidepressants	0.79	2.52	30	51
antipsychotic	0.09	0.37	6	25

Table 2: Anti-terms relating to the medical sphere from the top 100 anti-terms

is a reflection of the same field of interest. The discourse is again, often, about the search for remedies for common problems, but also, perhaps, product placement is at work, since named products or the names of pharmaceutical companies also frequently appear in the co-text.

A similar picture of increase over time is found for *antidepressant*, *antidepressants* and *antipsychotic*, indicating an increase in the awareness of and interest in mental illness – although the contexts here concern the problem of unsuitable or wrong prescription or appear in the context of confessional material such as, 'to begin with I tried antidepressants...'

Antiretroviral, anti-AIDS and *anti-HIV* reflect an interest in HIV/AIDS[9] but as noted in relation to the decrease in *anti-malarial*, it is not the gravity of a problem that dictates the amount of space dedicated to it. The concordance lines for *anti-malarial* suggest that it is holidays abroad and preventative procedures for travellers that are the news-writers' main concern, rather than the death rate from malaria in developing countries.

[9] AIDS was among the keywords in SiBol 93. The appearance of these *anti* words in 2005 appears to reflect successes in developing treatments for it.

2.2 Hardy perennials

Leaving aside the discourse surrounding medical matters or the metaphorical fight against elements of the physical world, we find more changes. Here, it is interesting to note the differences in ranking as well as the relative frequency differences.

2.3 Ups and downs – stances, politics and protests, causes and campaigns

Rankings are not necessarily the best indicator of change over time, since they can obscure the pattern of change regarding frequency. For example, a word may go down in a top 100 ranking list between 1993 and 2005, but its raw or relative frequency could actually have increased when the two time periods are compared. To safeguard against this, only changes in rankings of twenty-five places or more have been considered, and, furthermore, the ranking information is supplemented with relative frequencies.

If we look at the list with the greatest changes in ranking, it becomes more clear what the changes in the social discourse have been and also what the categories tend to be. Some of the changes are seasonal, and, in SiBol 93, refer to events such as the Maastricht Treaty or the war in the Balkans, or, in SiBol 05, the Iraq war. The changes in ranking show the synchronic patterning of how opposition to a range of factors is covered by the broadsheets. Coverage of specific economic issues gave *anti-inflationary* and *anti-inflation* their salience in 1993 (1.0 per million words (henceforth, pmw) as opposed to 0.4 pmw in 2005), and it should be noted that the keyword list for SiBol 93 contained many more terms relating to economic and political matters in general than that of SiBol 05. In the earlier corpus, there is relatively more interest in *anti-dumping* (1.26 pmw in 1993 and 0.22 pmw for 2005). Among its collocates are *duties*, *measures*, *actions*, *tariffs*, *laws*, *actions*, *penalties* and *rules*, indicating a term which relates to politics, international relations, economics and trade. All of these are topics which are treated less, in terms of their proportions, in 2005 (see also Partington, 2010; and Duguid, 2010).

Some increases for 2005 are, as in the main keyword lists for SiBol 05, related to technology, such as the non-medical Internet meaning of *anti-virus* (1.03 pmw for 2005 as against 0.34 pmw for 1993), the non-seafaring intellectual property rights issues involved for *anti-piracy* and the Internet-related *anti-spam* and *anti-spyware*.

2.3.1 Politics

As we might expect, party-political terms appear in both lists in Table 3: *anti-conservative* and *anti-Tory* are relatively more common in 1993 when a Conservative government was in power, whilst *anti-Labour* is more common

anti+R1 collocate	pmw in 93	pmw in 05	Months 93	Months 05	Rank 93	Rank 05
anti-Conservative	0.28	0.11	16	12	80	158
anti-Labour	0.17	0.29	12	25	123	79
anti-Tory	0.73	0.35	26	24	68	35
anti-government	1.14	0.75	40	43	21	112

Table 3: Anti+ party political terms from Table 2

in 2005 – reflecting changes in government and attitudes to the party in power. *Anti-government* appears much higher in the 1993 corpus, but not all of its uses refer to the UK and its government.

Finding *anti-Yeltsin* third in the 1993 ranking and absent from the 2005 list, it might be tempting to treat it as equivalent to *anti-Bush* and *anti-Blair* in the 2005 list, signalling, merely, a change of protagonist. However, we need also to note that *anti-Yeltsin* (eighty-nine occurrences in SiBol 93) needs to be compared to *pro-Yeltsin* (161 occurrences in SiBol 93). So, on the synchronic level, while the ninety-two occurrences of *anti-Bush* in 2005 (0.62 pmw) compare with only six of *pro-Bush*, and the seventy-four occurrences of *anti-Blair* in 2005 (0.51 pmw) with eleven of *pro-Blair*, different phenomena are being denoted by the term *anti* when used with these political actors. Thus, in the case of *Bush* and *Blair*, unpopularity is denoted, but with *Yeltsin* political groupings are denoted. This must also be set against the overall number of mentions: *Blair* occurs 41,380 times (2,830 pmw) in 2005 (although all do not refer to Tony Blair, unlike the *anti-Blair* occurrences), *Bush* occurs 21,860 times (1,490 pmw) and Yeltsin, 8,109 (eighty pmw). The term *anti-Yeltsin* seems especially salient, then, in 1993, compared to similar terms in other time periods and for other leaders.

2.3.2 Political and social causes

Another category is that of political or social causes that are characterised as being *anti* something. This can be seen under Table 4. The key political causes in 1993 appear to have been anti-racism and protests about road building, which is reflected in the salience in the 1993 corpus of *anti-racist* (there are seventy occurrences in 2005) and *anti-road* (only seven occurrences in 2005). That political causes (in the sense of something that people are fighting for or against) in general are on the rise, or at least that the interest in and activism around causes has intensified, can be deduced from a group of items which share similar collocates with the last two items and which have seen a rise in the charts in 2005. They include *anti-capitalist*, *anti-corporate*, *anti-poverty* and *anti-globalisation*: the collocates they share relate to forms of opposition (*protest, protests, protesters, campaign,*

anti +R1 collocate	pmw in 93	pmw in 05	Months 93	Months 05	Rank 93	Rank 05
anti-racist	2.860	0.600	49	37	5	42
anti-road	0.380	0.000	17	7	67	308
anti-capitalist	0.150	1.010	14	44	132	24
anti-corporate	0.000	0.240	1	22	425	87
anti-poverty	0.220	1.330	46	72	101	17
anti-globalisation	0.000	1.530	0	59	–	11
anti-slavery	0.270	0.490	17	39	85	53

Table 4: Anti causes extracted from Table 2

campaigns, campaigners; *activist, activists*; *demonstration, demonstrations* and *demonstrators*). They also signal new and different forms of protest and actions in support of a cause; in 2005 *pranksters* and *hoaxers* are collocates of *anti-corporate* and *anti-globalisation*; for *anti-corporate* we also find *warriors* and *websites*; for *anti-vivisection* and for *anti-poverty* we also find the collocate *wristbands*.

The appearance of *anti-slavery* in the 2005 upwardly mobile *anti* words, though a worthy cause that is well worth campaigning for, might seem at first sight somewhat out of place. A closer qualitative examination of the collocates and the texts in which the item appears reveals that the kind of slavery under discussion is child labour (*international society, campaigner, campaigners* and *activists*). It is also part of a cultural-historiographical discourse looking back through biographies and histories published in time for a future anniversary (*publication, novel* and *writer*) celebrating the bicentenary of the Abolition of Slavery (*cause, laws, movement, pamphlet, tract* and *speeches*). This exemplifies the importance of going into the data and examining concordance lines (in CADS work, usually lines with plenty of co-text, see Partington, 2010) and even the full texts from which lines derive to see what the profile of a salient item really is. Word lists, word clouds and other means of visualising salience tell only a partial story.

2.3.3 Liminal legality

Another set of *anti* items that have increased in frequency between 1993 and 2005, as shown under Table 5, are related to the nuances of liminal legality – where laws have not caught up with events or where practices are aiming to outwit the law.

The *anti* collocates in question are *money* (almost exclusively concerning money laundering, where attempts are being made to circumvent laws) and *avoidance* (discussions of anti-tax-avoidance measures and of the best ways to formulate legislation). A discourse around *anti-gun* mixes

anti +R1 collocate	pmw in 93	pmw in 05	Months 93	Months 05	Rank 93	Rank 05
anti-money	0.02	0.32	2	26	438	71
anti-avoidance	0.13	0.37	9	27	145	65
anti-gun	0.06	0.21	5	20	255	95
anti-bullying	0.200	1.11	9	46	104	21

Table 5: Anti+ legislation issues from Table 2

concern about legislation (*lobby, lobbies, voters, crime* and *laws*) with a narrative of fighting for a cause (*campaign, campaigner(s), activist* and *poster*) but also a more polemical aspect, where an opposing faction has its own narrative (*anti-gun hype* and *anti-gun fable*). With *anti-bullying* a complex picture emerges of a cause (for concern) with a variety of reactions concerning legislation or public awareness programmes (*alliance, wristband(s), policy(ies), campaign(er(s)), organisations(s) charity, strategy, scheme, workshop, website, video, groups, project* and *drive*). These examples reveal how MD-CADS can bring to light fairly nuanced pictures of contemporary social mores.

3. Indiscriminate discrimination and prejudice

The comparison of the ranking of the top 100 *anti* terms in the SiBol corpora also reveals, in both SiBol 93 and SiBol 05, a set of collocates which concern groups or communities of either national, ethnic or religious identity. The terms in question are, for SiBol 93, *anti-racist, anti-white, anti-European, anti-German* and *anti-Serb*, and, for SiBol 05, *anti-American* (and *anti-Americanism*), *anti-Syrian, anti-Japanese, anti-Muslim, anti-Catholic, anti-British, anti-Islamic* and *anti-Israeli* (and *anti-Israel*). If we add to these the terms which have remained stable in the charts (*anti-Semitic* and *anti-Semitism*), it is clear that there is a fairly prominent and continuous discourse in the broadsheets around being *anti* national, ethnic or religious groups, although the focus on particular groups may change over time. Clearly, if diachronic comparisons are to be made, we need to have an idea of how the terms are used in general and to obtain a picture of the range of meanings used to construct the discourse around such indiscriminate discrimination and prejudice. Proceeding in the usual way by looking at collocates, concordance lines and in many cases the texts from which these derive, a pattern emerges in the way in which such discourse is constructed and the ways *anti* phenomena are reported and characterised. We can then see how the general picture can be coloured one way or another or intensified in various ways.

The diachronic data discussed in previous sections pointed to various semantic fields. Here, the analysis is intra-corpus and synchronic: rather than being a diachronic comparison it is an overall characterisation of the semantic field.

3.1 Characterising *anti* phenomena: reporting strategies and stance

Emotive or attitudinal stance can be conveyed through lexical choice on a number of structural levels, choice of adjective, verb, noun or adverb, metaphors and other fixed phrases (Biber *et al.*, 1999: Chapter 12). Opposition which can be characterised as *anti* is constructed in particular and fairly constant ways, and it is possible to classify the collocates or patterns:

(*A*) Terms which appear to the right of *anti* + target word describe the people and events involved, characterising them in terms of affect or mental processes (what might be called 'hearts and minds'), communication, actions and policy.

- For example, there are representations of the people involved in ways which can vary from the descriptive to the clearly evaluative: *allies, rioters, protesters, bigots, warlords* and *bores.*
- Similarly there are characterisations of events described as *anti* a particular group, again varying in objectivity and neutrality: *rioting, protests, war, struggle, rallies, events, attacks, backlash, pogroms* and *sectarian marches.*
- The *anti*-group phenomenon can be described in terms of strategies: *policies, line, education, segregation, campaigns, lobby, opposition, parties, campaign, trade, websites, objectives* and *legislation.*
- Another way of characterising the phenomenon is in terms of the mode of communication; again a range of evaluations can be constructed by the choice of expression: *comments, chorus, criticism, hatespeak, propaganda, squib, slogans, diatribe, gags, insults, abuse, jokes, language, songs, tirades* and *tub-thumping.*
- The range of characterisation in terms of 'hearts and minds' includes: *sentiment(s), feeling(s), opinion, stance, streak, bias, prejudice, paranoia, hysteria, blinkers, hostility, outrage, resentment, anger, hatred* and *bloodlust.*

(*B*) The left-collocates and lexical patterns, on the other hand, show choices of pre-modifying qualifications involving another set of parameters which are labelled for convenience as follows:

- **Size**: *growing, escalation in, rise in, thousands of* and *a group of.*
- **Extent**: *a note of, a wave of, sprigs of, a vision of, deeply, one of the most on the plane, one of the most in Iraq, constant diet of, tide*

of, prevailing, some, profoundly, increasingly, filled with, growing, a culture of, entrenched, a wave of and *outbreaks of.*

- **Openness**: *veiled, apparently, latent, show of, openly, perceived, shadowy* and *blatant.*
- **Time-scale factors**: *residual, periodic bouts of, recent, unprecedented, round-the clock* and *backlash.*
- **Local status**: *requisite, local, nationalist, exiled, boxed into, characteristic, controversial, unusually, global, modish, purveyor of, rash of, tide of, vehicle of, popular, populist, radical, powerful, stronghold of, at the heart of, held to be* and *institutionally.*
- **Communication**: *proclaiming, preaching, shouting, vocally, spouts, chanting* and *venting.*
- **Start-up factors**: *convert into, cobble together, fuel, fuelling, inflame, mobilise, organising, fomented, led to, whipped up, sparked, provoked* and *orchestrated.*
- **Support factors**: *boost, added to, exploiting, indulged in, intensifying of, showered favours on, cash in on, cashing in on, supports, breeding, suppress* and *tackle.*
- **Quality in terms of emotion or force**: *unjustified, facile, sneering, rabid, bloody, bloodiest, characteristic, controversial, deadly, extreme, fierce, fiery, habitually, hardcore, impeccable, intense, modish, violent, radical, simplistic, unthinking, vacuous, tireless* and *virulent.*
- **Reactions**: *condemning, play down, absolve of, prosecute for, punishes for, fears of, opposition to, legitimised, appalled by, felt victimised by, a direct response to, gripped by, accepted, adopting, fight against, going after, abhor, removed, must not become, blamed for, desire for, accused of, accuses of, showered favours on, cash in on, taking on, heckled for, deal with* and *exploiting.*

Both A and B categories can signal the stance of the writer on a cline from neutral to personally involved due to a lexical choice which can be more or less evaluative. The accumulation of marked lexical choices, either in terms of saturation, force or focus, constructs the evaluation – positive or negative – for the reader, and tells us about the representation of the opposition. Journalists appear to have a repetitive mix-and-match strategy for characterising phenomena in this way, since we find the same lexis appearing and the same moribund, if not quite dead, metaphors (e.g., *tide of* and *diet of*) in a variety of combinations in different contexts in all the papers in the corpora. Investigation of how these parameters are put together and nested in a text can reveal a general stance both to those opposing the group and, sometimes, to the group itself.

I will give some examples from the case study on anti-Americanism I mentioned earlier to show how different pictures can be built up.

Anti+R1 collocate	pmw in 93	pmw in 05	Months 93	Months 05	Rank 93	Rank 05
anti-American	0.74	1.74	42	65	33	10
anti-Americanism	0.29	0.83	20	51	78	27

Table 6: Anti-American* terms from Table 2

3.2 *Anti*+national identity: an example *anti-American* and *anti-Americanism*

Taking *anti-American(ism)* as an example of *anti* followed by a national identity, and in quantitative terms, the patterns shown under Table 6 are found. The table shows that there is an increase in relative frequency, a wider coverage in terms of months, and a change in the rankings from 1993 to 2005.

An examination of the collocates, clusters and the texts reveals that the two terms are being characterised consistently:

- In terms of qualities (adjectives and adverbs), *anti-Americanism* is described as: *wilful, visceral, trenchant, supposed, sublimated, smug, shallow, ritual, populist, latent, kneejerk, crass, compulsive, fashionable* and *increasing*.
- People *stoke* it and *combat* it; it can be *milked* or *exposed*.
- Metaphors around it included *an unprecedented wave of, an undercurrent of, a global tide of, unprecedented levels of, a poisonous cloud of, a virulent from of, bouts of* and *saturated in*.
- It is paired with *pacifism, xenophobia, paranoia* and *anti-globalisation*.
- In the case of *anti-American* (the adjective as opposed to the noun) people are described as being seen to: *inflame, deal with, tone down, counter*, or to have *fomented, indulged in*, or to be *filled with, accused of, chanting, cashing in on, overlaid with*, or to have *heckled*; a range of activities are described variously as a *backlash of, explosions of, a wave of, a constant diet of, purvey or, rash of, tide of* and *vehicle of*.
- Items which can be described in terms of the categories of hearts, minds, policy, speech, action and all labelled as anti-American are: *bias, blinkers, neuroses, nightmare, views, stance, sentiment, feelings, content, issues, line, policies, politics, position, lobby, ideology, current, chorus, criticism, comments, credentials, fixation, grandstanding, hate-comments, hate-speak, hostility, tub-thumping, tirades, statements, squib, slogans, rhetoric, rant, rantings, propaganda, poses, demonstrations, riots* and *rioting, rallies* and *protests*.

- These, in their turn, are described as: *hard-core, modish, rabid, simplistic, vacuous, sneering, bloody, deadly, tireless, growing, intense, fiery, fierce, firebrand, fuelling* and *oversimplifying.*
- And in terms of exactly how anti-American they were as: *habitually, stridently, rabidly, unreasonably, acidly, viscerally* and *passionately.*
- It is further characterised and paired with the following (*anti-American and* or *anti-american*+hyphen): *expletive filled rants, anti-Semitic, anti bourgeois, anti-Bush* and *British Muslim.*

It appears, then, that anti-American positions, along with hearts, minds, speech, policy and action, of which speech is the largest category, are represented by repeated metaphors of fire, disease, natural forces in excess, strong negative emotions and deprecating terms or expressions associated with fashion and posing; this results in an intellectual delegitimisation (*vacuous, simplistic, oversimplifying* and *unreasonably*). Most descriptions involve strong negative semantic prosody resulting in strongly negative evaluation to the terms *anti-American* and *anti-Americanism*. There was also an example – *unimpeachable/impeccable anti-American credentials* – where an apparently positive evaluation is joined with hyperbole and incongruity to give reverse evaluation irony (Partington, 2007). In the newspaper data, *anti-Americanism* is more frequently attributed than averred. It is something people say of others, and is generally constructed as a negative position. It must be noted that there are only two instances of *we're* or *we are anti* averral, as in this example:

Wiseman, however, disagrees. "We are very anti the idea we are dumbing down," he says. "These initiatives are needed because the situation is desperate."

(SiBol 05, *Sunday Times*)

We might go on to investigate how other national groups are characterised in order to see the degree to which the profile of *anti-American(ism)* is standard or deviant. In contrast, the item *anti-Syrian* (there is only one occurrence in 1993, and in 2005 a frequency of 1.14 pmw and mentioned in twenty-eight out of seventy-two months, rank position nineteen) was characterised as more political, events-led and, to some extent, legitimised ('Bush hails Beirut anti-Syria demos as key to Middle East freedom' is a headline in the *Guardian*, 9 March 2005, and the article continues, 'The American people are on your side. Millions across the Earth are on your side'). The people described as *anti-Syrian* are not characterised negatively, but, rather, in political terms, with no strong intensification in the lexical choice.

Similarly, *anti-Japanese* (0.14 pmw in SiBol 93, 0.82 pmw in SiBol 05, mentioned in ten months in 1993 and in thirty months in 2005, rank position rising from 140 to twenty-eight) was described in local and

anti +R1 collocate	pmw in 93	pmw in 05	Months 93	Months 05	Rank 93	Rank 05
anti-racism	0.55	1.12	25	50	77	20
anti-racist	2.94	0.64	49	37	5	64
anti-racists	0.28	0.06	15	16	93	241
anti-Semitism	3.700	5.21	56	66	4	4
anti-Semitic	2.32	3.23	56	69	8	8
anti-Semite	0.36	0.41	26	34	71	64
anti-Muslim	0.22	0.6	22	38	99	45
anti-Islamic	0.13	0.31	11	26	147	74
anti-Catholic	0.19	0.48	15	34	110	54

Table 7: Anti+ religious or ethnic identity terms from Table 2

seasonal event-related terms; for instance, demonstrations, and legitimised with reference to historical causes ('Tokyo remains angry about the violent anti-Japanese riots that swept several large Chinese cities earlier this year'). It is characterised with negative lexical choices (*violent*, *hysteria* and *chanting*), but less so than in the *anti-American* data.

Anti-British, on the other hand, (0.68 pmw in SiBol 93, 0.41 pmw in SiBol 05, mentioned in thirty-seven months in 1993 and in thirty-three months in 2005 in rank position of thirty-eight in 1993 and sixty-one in 2005) is dealt with in a similar fashion to *anti-American* and paired with *Shia–Sunni tensions*; *anti-Semitic* and *anti-Anti-American*, *leftwing*. Interestingly, despite this being a corpus of British papers, much less attention is paid to *anti-British*(*ness*) than to *anti-Americanism*: less intensification is used in descriptions of it, there is less intellectual disdain for it and it is less often seen as an illegitimate position to have. It is often averred as well as attributed.

3.3 *Anti-+* religious or ethnic identity

Another semantic field which is represented in the rankings and by the relative frequency data as undergoing diachronic change is that of religious or ethnic identity. It is a frequent topic in the news (*anti-racism*, *anti-racist* and *anti-racists*) and it is worth looking at the items as a set (see Table 7), divided into the various religious and ethnic identities involved.

In 2005 the Government brought its racial and religious hatred bill to the vote for the third time. In the debates, it appeared it was intended, ostensibly, to close a loophole whereby Jews and Sikhs receive protection from racial discrimination laws while Muslims and other faith groups, having a religious rather than an ethnic identity, do not.[10] Critics of the bill were afraid of the effects on freedom of speech. Many claimed that Muslim religious leaders saw the Bill as a version of the blasphemy laws which apply only to the Christian religion and would be disappointed with the reality. After the London bomb attacks in July 2005, it was reported that some Hindu and Sikh Asians claimed they exaggerated their religious identity so as not to be mistaken for Muslims.[11] Fears of a backlash after the London bombings and a rise in violent attacks against Muslim communities, and a rise in attacks on Jewish communities, also appear as part of the contexts in which *anti +* religious or ethnic identity are discussed. Uncertainties about ethnic, racial, religious, cultural and political identities mean that the targets are not always clear. Here, we are only concerned with how the broadsheets construct the *anti* discourse related to this semantic set in the two years of our corpus.

As we can see from Appendix 1, the terms *anti-Semitic, anti-Semitism, anti-Israel* and *anti-Israeli* are all high in the anti-rankings in both corpora. Further investigation of the differences between the characterisation of *anti-Semitic* and *anti-Muslim, anti-Sikh, anti-Hindu* or *anti-Asian*, would be of great interest.

Most of the occurrences of *anti-Catholic* concern historical matters either in book reviews or related to the four-hundredth anniversary of the Gunpowder Plot, which is taken up by all papers as seasonal material around Guy Fawkes Night. Other more contemporary contexts are the election of Pope Bendedict XVI, and the publication of the popular novel *The Da Vinci Code*, which was seen by some as an attack on the Catholic Church. In many cases, there are phraseologies which suggest that such discrimination is generally considered to be a thing of the past (*distaste for*, *prejudice has grown*, *emptying of significance* and *the decline in*). However, there are also items about sectarianism amongst supporters in the Scottish football league and a re-emergence of sectarian violence in Northern Ireland, which indicates regional pockets of prejudice where feelings still run high.

The issue of anti-Semitic prejudice is highly complex and contentious. A preliminary search of the concordance lines of the corpus suggests that thought and speech representation, and denial of allegations, plays a prominent part, whilst – in contrast, as we shall see with discourses

---

[10] See: http://www.homeoffice.gov.uk/about-us/news/racial-religious-hatred-bill?version=1 The bill makes it illegal to threaten people because of their religion, or to stir up hatred against a person because of their faith. It is designed to fill gaps in the current laws, which already protect people from threats based on their race or ethnic background. The final bill was altered by the Lords in two key ways:

- Only threatening words or behaviour will be classified as criminal. Generally abusive or insulting words about religion that are not actually threatening will not be illegal.

- The burden will be on the prosecution to prove the speakers intended to stir up racial hatred – the bill has strong safeguards for free expression.

[11] Found in a text in the 2005 corpus at: http://www.guardian.co.uk/world/2005/sep/05/religion.july7

around *anti-Muslim* – legislation is not an issue. It is also clear that it is seen as unacceptable. Many of the same metaphors that were found with *anti-American* are used with *anti-Semitic* (*virulent, rising tide of, worldwide upsurge of, vicious streak of, poisonous, rabid* and *visceral*). There are three occurrences of self-labelling (*our anti-Semitism*) but they are all from one article (SiBol 05 *Guardian* April). It is something against which groupings and organisations exist (*watchdog against, global forum against, fight against, battle against* and *vigilant about*). It is also clear that people can be defined as *being* anti-Semitic; that is, it is often an existential label, much more so than for any of the other *anti* terms (forms of the verb *to be* are high in the collocate lists), and the question of openness is a key one, as if the phenomenon is real but has in some way gone underground. Interestingly, in the 1993 corpus *Russian* is a key co-occurring item of *anti-Semit**, to be replaced by *Muslim(s)* in 2005, who are depicted as both fellow victims of prejudice but also as perpetrators of anti-Semitism.

The 2005 corpus deals with three seasonal issues in particular: whether a proposed boycott of Israeli academics is anti-Semitic, the Labour poster campaign depicting two Jewish Conservative MPs, Michael Howard and Oliver Letwin, in ways that are considered to be anti-Semitic (as pigs), and remarks made by the London mayor, Ken Livingstone, to a Jewish journalist, accusing him of behaving like a Nazi concentration camp guard. There are, however, more long-term concerns about rising numbers of attacks on Jews in Britain and France. There are also reviews, memoirs and historical accounts where the terms *anti-Semitism, anti-Semitic, anti-Israel* and *anti-Israeli* recur in the co-texts; there are many historical references, especially to Nazis and Europe in the early twentieth century. The following is a brief categorisation of the ways in which this set of terms is used:

A. Thought representation and existential verbs
    1. I now realise she is **anti-Semitic**
    2. I do not for one minute think he is **anti-Semitic**
    3. I don't believe he is **anti-Semitic**
    4. Does not assume those behind it to be **anti-Semitic**
B. People can be *cast as, branded* and *judged* anti-Semitic, anti-Semitism can be *alleged, complained about, condemned* and *apologised for*. It is an accusation that can be applied to a public figure and may then be denied:
    Harry they say is not **anti-Semitic** or interested in Nazism
    Vehemently denied that Pope Pius XII was **anti-Semitic**
    Denying charges of **anti-Semitism**
    Mr Howard avoided accusing labour of **anti-Semitism**
C. One of the main preoccupations is with extent, openness or intentionality – that is to say, how conscious or unconscious, hidden or overt the problem is. Anti-Semitism is described as *entrenched, casual, conscious, deliberate, deep-seated, subliminal* and *crude*:
    They either did or did not know what they were doing. If they did, they were **anti-Semitic**, if they didn't, they were stupid.

I do not believe these were **deliberately anti-Semitic**

Say he did not **intend to be anti-Semitic**

The (mass Observation) diarists are **casually anti-Semitic**

I do not think it is **deliberately anti-Semitic**

He did not believe there was any **intended anti-Semitism**

The Labour campaign is not intended to be **overtly anti-Semitic**

D. Texts and actions can be scrutinised in this way

The claim that **these posters are anti Semitic** have some credibility

The mayor who insists his **comments were not anti-Semitic**

She insisted that **certain texts were anti Semitic** and ought to be scrapped

You can rest assured **if his operas were anti-Semitic in nature** I wouldn't feel able to conduct them

Jewish leaders who said *The Passion* **was anti Semitic**

Proseutors bringing the case say at least **one of the songs was anti Semitic**

There is no evidence that this **egg-throwing was anti-Semitic**

E. Particular positions are gauged in relation to the issue

To say they were **anti-Semitic** devalues the term

Accusations that being in favour of a boycott was **anti-Semitic**

To be **anti-Semitic** belonged to the profile of the German and French nationalists

There is a case to answer that that equation is **an anti-Semitic equation**

Anti-Semitism is linked (in a list or with *and*) with a number of other stances and views – with *extremists, fascism, anti-women, anti-gay, hatred, homophobia, violence, Islamaphobia, nationalism, racism* and *xenophobia*.

A preliminary look at the characterisation of *anti*+religious grouping suggests that *anti Muslim*, on the other hand, is characterised as principally an issue of present events, imminent or recent legislation, whilst fears of being perceived as anti-Muslim and accusations of anti-Muslim stance are frequent; the most common collocates are *sentiment* and *prejudice*. Institutions are usually involved (*the government, the press, schools, the law* and *football*) and it is clear that prejudice against Muslims is taken as an issue that the administration is attempting to come to terms with and is being treated with a good deal of seriousness.

Another important topic is how *anti-Islam* and *anti-Islamic* are characterised, particularly in comparison with *anti-Muslim*. As with *anti-Muslim*, there are occurrences where anti-Islamic prejudice, violence or attempts to prevent or legislate against such acts are being recounted by the broadsheets in question. There is, however, another meaning which might be glossed as 'not in accordance with the precepts of the Islamic religion'. Stories about supposedly anti-Islamic precepts tend to enter the newspapers when they are against behaviours that are considered to be acceptable according to western cultural standards, or when their infraction results in acts of repression or violence, as in Examples 1 to 5:

(1) Tolo's nemesis is the chief justice, Fazl Hadi Shinwari, who led a government ulema, or religious council, that criticised Tolo for its "immoral and **anti-Islamic** programming".

(SiBol 05, *Guardian*)

(2) She had upset the mullahs and the conservative ways of her country, been attacked as **anti-Islamic** by the Supreme Court, and received death threats in the days after her sacking.

(SiBol 05, *Guardian*)

(3) This show, as well as many other TV programmes, is an affront to religious conservatives. They have strongly attacked films and TV music programmes as **anti-Islamic** and immoral.

(SiBol 05, *Guardian*)

(4) Shortly before Christmas a teacher was taken from his classroom in Ghazni and shot in front of his students for the **anti-Islamic** crime of teaching girls.

(SiBol 05, *Times*)

(5) This is the first attack against the film festival, but Islamic fundamentalists have often targeted cultural events. Traditional Egyptian weddings, theatre performances and even popular music are targeted by fundamentalists who consider them **anti-Islamic**.

(SiBol 93, *Guardian*)

The papers thus provide both accounts of anti-Islamic prejudice and of religious convictions which might fuel such prejudice by repressing or inciting violence against a radio station, a wedding, teaching, a female television presenter; but there are also more positive cases where negative behaviour such as violence or drug dealing are described as anti-Islamic, as in these Examples 6 and 7:

(6) Sheima and her fellow officers are also frustrated by widespread corruption within the Afghan criminal justice system. But none of this has dampened her crusading spirit. She believes fervently that drugs are **anti-Islamic** and that Afghanistan will never achieve stability until the industry is wiped out.

(SiBol 05, *Sunday Times*)

(7) He maintains he has always absolutely condemned violence as **anti-Islamic**, but insists that he should be allowed to seek to explain. "To explain is not to justify," he says.

(SiBol 05, *Guardian*)

From these qualitative analyses, then, it becomes clear that the way opposition or prejudice is represented in the broadsheets to different religious and ethnic groups, present very varied and dissimilar profiles.

4. Conclusions

This is a preliminary study which attempts to show how a diachronic corpus of this nature can provide a basis for a detailed and flexible study of socio-cultural issues and the way they are reported in the press. It is intended as an illustration of how MD-CADS enables investigation of fine shades of meaning and nuances in representation. Here, we saw how different profiles of political campaigns or legislation, and of health and medical matters, were revealed by investigation of the prefix *anti*, which also provided a number of insights into how racism and prejudice are reported in the press. One particular methodological procedure I adopted was to compare relative rankings of these items in the two SiBol corpora to see how coverage of particular issues has changed and how the reporting of a particular kind of news item helps to build up a profile of a stance. It was possible, thus, to see how the coverage of medical matters changed in the way certain forms of treatment are discussed, how antibiotics are presented as problematic in the 2005 corpus and how a discourse around self-help and complementary and alternative medical treatments has grown. The increase in travel features has also led advice about a range of preventative measures to become more prominent.

The *anti* prefix also provides a view of political and social causes which are reported in the news, and the data revealed which causes and how opposition is waged, through legislation by institutions, through protests and demonstrations, and newer forms of protest when the *anti* position is at a more grass roots level: websites, pressure groups and wristbands are part of the armoury of opposition.

Where national groupings are the target of the *anti* prefix, the patterns I found indicate distinct differences in the way in which the *anti* positions are characterised. It would appear that anti-Americanism not only receives increased coverage, a result of the news values which govern selection of events to report,[12] but is also judged more harshly than other positions and is more often characterised as an illegitimate position. The treatment of anti-British positions is more nuanced, is averred as well as attributed to others, and is not always presented with intensified negative judgments. The reporting of more distant positions is presented more neutrally and is generally related to particular events – and the evaluation is made about the events rather than the protagonists.

---

[12] Leech *et al.* (2001: 287) give data from the BNC which show that *British* (357 per million words), *European* (195 pmw), and *American* (157 pmw) are the top adjectives for regions and nations reflecting the relative importance of nations perceived to be 'close' to us or to have cultural proximity.

The corpus data also provides different profiles in the representation of prejudice against different ethnic and religious groups. Anti-Catholic prejudice is presented as being a thing of the past, and related to historical events, except in the regions of Scotland and Northern Ireland. Anti-Semitism is represented as being, worryingly, on the rise and people can *be* anti-Semitic, so it is not just a question of affect, thoughts, words or actions. Anti-Muslim and anti-Islamic sentiments and prejudice are also presented as on the rise and are linked to geopolitical events (in particular, 9/11 and the London bombings) and attempts are being made for institutions to deal with it in Britain. As with anti-Semitism, it is something that people are accused of and have to deny.

Although the corpus is limited to British broadsheets and to only two years, the study provides us with a rich set of data and a broad overview which acts as a stimulus for further research. It suggests that a limited area of investigation such as a prefix can throw open a wide number of topics for future investigation beyond the question of morphological productivity and that *anti*, while ostensibly having a clear and unequivocal meaning, is, in fact, a portmanteau prefix containing many potential nuances.

References

Baayen, H. and A. Renouf. 1996. 'Chronicling The Times: productive lexical innovations in an English newspaper', Language 72 (1), pp. 69–96.

Bauer, L. and I.S.P. Nation. 1993. 'Word families', International Journal of Lexicography 6 (4), pp. 253–79.

Biber, D., S. Johansson, G. Leech, S. Conrad and E. Finegan. 1999. The Longman Grammar of Spoken and Written English. London: Longman.

Duguid, A. 2010. 'Newspaper discourse informalisation: a diachronic comparison from keywords', Corpora 5 (2), pp. 109–38.

Gardner, D. 2007. 'Validating the construct of *Word* in applied corpus-based vocabulary research: a critical survey', Applied Linguistics 28 (2), pp. 241–65.

Hay, J. and I. Plag. 2004. 'What constrains possible suffix combinations? On the interaction of grammatical and processing restrictions in derivational morphology', Natural Language and Linguistic Theory 22 (3), pp. 565–96.

Leech, G., B. Cruickshank and R. Ivanič. 2001. An A–Z of English Grammar and Usage. London: Longman.

Lipka, L. 2002. English Lexicology. (Third edition.) Tübingen: Narr. (1992. An Outline of English Lexicology. (Second edition.) Tübingen: Max Niemeyer Verlag.)

Martin, J. and P. White. 2005. The Language of Evaluation. London: Palgrave.

Nishimoto, E. 2004. 'Defining new words in corpus data: productivity of English suffixes in the BNC' in 26th Annual Meeting of the Cognitive Science Society 2004, paper 505. Chicago.

Partington, A. 1998. Patterns and Meanings. Amsterdam: John Benjamins.

Partington, A. 2007. 'Irony and reversal of evaluation', Journal of Pragmatics 39 (9), pp. 1547–69.

Partington, A. 2010. 'Modern Diachronic Corpus-Assisted Discourse Studies (MD-CADS) on UK newspapers: an overview of the project', Corpora 5 (2), pp. 83–108.

Plag, I. 1999. Morphological Productivity: Structural Constraints in English Derivation. Berlin: Mouton de Gruyter.

Plag, I., C. Dalton-Puffer and H. Baayen. 1999. 'Productivity and register', English Language and Linguistics 3 (2), pp. 209–28.

Prcic, T. 1999. 'The treatment of affixes in the "big four" EFL dictionaries', International Journal of Lexicography 12 (4): 263–80.

Quirk, R., S. Greenbaum, G. Leech and J. Svartvik. 1985. A Comprehensive Grammar of the English Language. London: Longman.

Renouf, A. 2007. 'The chavs and the chav-nots' in J. Munat (ed.) Lexical Creativity: Texts and Contexts, pp. 61–92. Amsterdam: John Benjamins.

Scott, M. 2008. WordSmith Tools version 5. Liverpool: Lexical Analysis Software.

Stvan, L.S. 2006. 'The contingent meaning of –ex brand names in English', Corpora 1 (2), pp. 217–50.

Taylor, C. 2005. 'Electronic corpora in language study: a case study of Europe', Das Werkstatt 6, pp. 72–84.

Taylor, C. 2008. 'Metaphors of anti-Americanism in a corpus of UK, US and Italian newspapers', ESP Across Cultures 5, pp. 137–52.

Taylor, C. 2010. 'Science in the news: a diachronic perspective', Corpora 5 (2), pp. 221–50.

Tribble, C. 2006. 'What counts in current journalism: keywords in newspaper reporting' in M. Scott and C. Tribble (eds) Textual Patterns: Key Words and Corpus Analysis in Language Education, pp. 161–77. Amsterdam: John Benjamins.

Wodak, R. and M. Reisigl. 2001. Discourse and Discrimination: Rhetorics of Racism and Anti-Semitism. London and New York: Routledge.

Appendix A: The top 100 collocates of *anti* in 1993 and 2005

Word R1 93	R1 freq. 93	Word R1 05	R1 freq. 05
AIRCRAFT	425	SOCIAL	1.006
MAASTRICHT	412	WAR	938
TERRORIST	374	TERRORIST	841
SEMITISM	366	SEMITISM	761
RACIST	291	TERRORISM	751
SOCIAL	258	TERROR	639
MAFIA	247	DOPING	471
SEMITIC	229	SEMITIC	471
ABORTION	190	COMPETITIVE	258
CLIMAX	178	AMERICAN	254
COMMUNIST	174	GLOBALISATION	227
SMOKING	172	INFLAMMATORY	225
NAZI	169	SMOKING	208
APARTHEID	152	HERO	206
TRUST	152	CORRUPTION	200
COMPETITIVE	147	AGEING	198
TANK	146	POVERTY	195
LOCK	144	AIRCRAFT	180
DUMPING	125	SYRIAN	167
WAR	121	RACISM	164
GOVERNMENT	114	BULLYING	162
INFLATIONARY	102	CLIMAX	155
EUROPEAN	95	VIRUS	151
HERO	93	CAPITALIST	147
CORRUPTION	92	ABORTION	139
FASCIST	91	APARTHEID	139
YELTSIN	89	AMERICANISM	126
HUNTING	86	JAPANESE	120
INFLATION	86	NUCLEAR	120
NUCLEAR	86	ESTABLISHMENT	118
ULCER	85	TANK	116
FEDERALIST	82	WESTERN	113
AMERICAN	74	GOVERNMENT	112
AIDS	73	VIRAL	111
TORY	73	DEPRESSANTS	109
ESTABLISHMENT	72	COMMUNIST	105

Appendix A (*continued*): The top 100 collocates of *anti* in 1993 and 2005

Word R1 93	*R1 freq. 93*	*Word R1 05*	*R1 freq. 05*
DEPRESSANTS	68	TRUST	104
BRITISH	67	CANCER	95
DEPRESSANT	65	RETROVIRAL	95
EC	57	EUROPEAN	94
WESTERN	56	RACIST	94
CANCER	55	BUSH	92
RACISM	54	FRAUD	92
SUBMARINE	54	NAZI	91
DEMOCRATIC	52	MUSLIM	87
THEFT	51	IMMIGRATION	85
FOREIGNER	50	FASCIST	80
FRAUD	50	HUNTING	78
UNION	50	DRUGS	76
VIRAL	50	GAY	76
HUNT	49	BLAIR	74
INFLAMMATORY	48	DEMOCRATIC	72
CRIME	47	SLAVERY	72
MISSILE	47	CATHOLIC	71
CLOCKWISE	46	HUNT	67
DISCRIMINATION	45	DISCRIMINATION	66
GAY	45	EU	65
ABORTIONISTS	43	VIETNAM	63
IMMIGRATION	43	SPAM	62
DRUG	42	US	61
DOPING	41	BRITISH	60
IMMIGRANT	41	DEPRESSANT	59
TERRORISM	41	SECESSION	59
GERMAN	40	SEMITE	59
DRUGS	39	AVOIDANCE	58
PERSONNEL	39	IRAQ	58
ROAD	38	BRIBERY	56
SOVIET	38	TORY	53
SEMITE	36	JEWISH	51
ASTHMA	35	DRUG	50
JEWISH	35	MONEY	50
POLLUTION	35	UNION	46

Appendix A (*continued*): The top 100 collocates of *anti* in 1993 and 2005

Word R1 93	R1 freq. 93	Word R1 05	R1 freq. 05
FREEZE	34	CELLULITE	45
VIRUS	34	ISLAMIC	45
VIETNAM	33	GLAZER	43
INTELLECTUAL	30	MAFIA	43
PORNOGRAPHY	30	CLIMACTIC	42
AMERICANISM	29	IMMIGRANT	42
SERB	29	LABOUR	42
CONSERVATIVE	28	PSYCHOTIC	42
FEMINIST	28	CLOCKWISE	41
NAFTA	28	AIDS	40
RACISTS	28	LOCK	39
REJECTION	28	SPYWARE	39
SLAVERY	28	WRINKLE	38
SEMITES	27	ISRAELI	36
CLIMACTIC	26	CORPORATE	35
UN	26	ISRAEL	35
COMMUNISM	25	PIRACY	34
EUROPE	25	BACTERIAL	33
ENGLISH	24	CAPITALISTS	33
FASHION	24	DUMPING	33
IRA	24	ENGLISH	32
WHITE	24	FUR	32
EUROPEANS	23	GUN	32
POACHING	23	INFLAMMATORIES	32
SOCIALIST	23	HIV	31
MALARIAL	22	SUBMARINE	31
		CRIME	30

Science in the news: a diachronic perspective

Charlotte Taylor[1]

Abstract

In this paper, I analyse the changing rhetorical role of *science* in UK broadsheet newspapers from 1993 and 2005, and conclude that there have been noteworthy changes. First, science, and more specifically, the formulation *the science*, is increasingly employed as a model of authority, appealing to ethos rather than logos; the authority is asserted but relatively rarely justified, and this may be considered the most significant change in that it drives several others. At the same time, there has been a popularisation of *the science* in the newspapers as it becomes an 'add on' to popular stories. Furthermore, there is evidence that science is being progressively fitted into the news story format, which demands *recency* as a news value, as opposed to features-style reports. Finally, science appears to have shifted from its earlier place in opposition to art and culture, to a paradigm in which its primary *alter*, or opposition, is religion.

1. Introduction

> Unlike 'science', this new term – 'The Science' – is a deeply moralised and politicised category. Today, those who claim to wield the authority of The Science are really demanding unquestioning submission.

In an article published in *Spiked*, the online magazine, in 2008, from which the extract above was taken, Frank Furedi argued that science, or, more specifically, *the science*, is increasingly being used as a dogmatic model of authority in all spheres of life. One advantage of taking a corpus-assisted approach to discourse analysis is that such hypotheses can be tested using

[1] School of Languages and Area Studies, University of Portsmouth, Park Building, King Henry I Street, Portsmouth, P01 2DZ, United Kingdom.
Correspondence to: Charlotte Taylor,   *e-mail*: c.taylor8@lancaster.ac.uk

Corpora 2010 Vol. 5 (2): 221–250
DOI: 10.3366/E1749503210000456
© Edinburgh University Press
www.eupjournals.com/cor

large amounts of data. Therefore, the purpose of this research is to apply a rigorous investigation of the concept of science, in British newspapers. The two SiBol corpora (see Section 2.2, below) are, thus, ideally placed to test this specific hypothesis, which, in turn, has something to say about changes within our society.

It is useful to relate what Furedi has to say about the role of science to Aristotle's work on the art of rhetoric and persuasion. In *Rhetoric*, Aristotle lists ethos, pathos and logos as the three modes of persuasion, explaining that 'the first kind depends on the personal character of the speaker; the second on putting the audience into a certain frame of mind; the third on the proof, or apparent proof, provided by the words of the speech itself' (Aristotle, *Rhetoric*, Book One, Chapter Two). One of the questions posed in this paper is whether there has been a shift in the rhetorical mode to which science, as represented in the press, pertains. We might expect science to be used as part of logos, providing logical proof in support of an argument, but, in this paper, I explore evidence that it is increasingly used as part of ethos, that is, persuasion at the interpersonal level, how the speaker/writer projects their personality and stance towards the audience/readership, as an appeal to authority, making the writer's personal character appear more credible by enrolling 'science' on their side of an argument. However, it should be noted that, as presented in Aristotle, ethos is not necessarily an illogical means of persuasion, as long as 'this kind of persuasion, like the others, [...] be achieved by what the speaker says, not by what people think of his character before he begins to speak' (Aristotle, *Rhetoric*, Book One, Chapter Two).

Equally, nor is appealing to authority necessarily a fallacious form of argumentation in itself. As Kahane and Cavender (2005: 48) rather bluntly put it, 'we all have to appeal to experts for information or advice – only fools don't do so with some regularity. In this technical age we are all nonexperts in most fields'. There are many areas where accepting the opinion of authority is extremely rational and logical, but we need to be able to evaluate the validity of the authority in question. Problems arise when the authority is unspecified or unexplained, or, in the worst cases, simply unfounded. Taking the field of corpus linguistics as a salient example, statements such as 'my corpus says x', in which the corpus is projected as the authoritative source for the assertion, are meaningless unless we are also provided with essential information about the content, structure and interrogation of the corpus, what generalisation is being extended, and exactly how the corpus data supports the theory being proposed.

In brief, the aims of this paper are to test the hypothesis that references to science are increasingly being employed as part of ethos rather than logos, and to take a wider look at the changing use of *scien** (*science, scientist, scientific*, etc.) in the two diachronic corpora. A secondary aim is to provide an outline of how such a hypothesis could be tested using Modern Diachronic Corpus-Assisted Discourse Studies (MD-CADS) methods.

2. Methodology

Like all the studies in this special edition of *Corpora*, the methodology used here is MD-CADS (see Partington, 2010, for a more detailed description) and so, in this section, I will limit myself to outlining briefly how the methodology was implemented in investigating my particular research question, both with reference to the specific research processes and the more general scientific method.

The theme of appeal to science as authority is of clear relevance to the field of corpus linguistics. Recently, Stubbs (2009) recalled Sinclair's emphasis on the empirical nature of corpus research, and Partington (2009) has argued at length that corpus linguists (ideally) employ a scientific methodological paradigm. Therefore, as a corpus linguist, I was already interested in the use of science as a model of authority because it is such a salient feature of discourse in the field. For instance, in a previous study (Taylor, 2008) I noted that a comparison of a small corpus of forty-seven articles about corpus linguistics with the applied sciences section of the British National Corpus (BNC) gave the following terms as keywords for the corpus linguistics papers: *repetition*, *empirical*, *statistical*, *methodology*, *data*, *quantitative* and *qualitative*; this confirms the importance of scientific vocabulary to corpus linguistic discourse. Consequently, the choice of research question in this chapter was also subjective and there was certainly an element of synchronicity in the combination of events which led to its development.

Indeed, as the different subjects addressed in this special edition illustrate, each researcher brings his or her own primings in terms of theoretical, methodological and ideological background to the development of the research question. There is indeed 'more to seeing than meets the eyeball', as Hanson (1958: 7) put it in his seminal *Patterns of Discovery*; and, even though we are all working with a similar methodological approach, each of the contributors to this issue saw something different when looking at the two SiBol corpora and the initial keyword lists. In all science, including in the so-called hard sciences, we must recognise the role of the researcher. However, as Smith (1998: 7) illustrates, the essential conundrum for social science is that:

> Conventionally, the researcher is seen as the subject and the thing being researched is taken to be the object, but in social science we are both the subject and object of our knowledge. When we study social life we are studying ourselves.

As people living in a particular society, and, more germane to this edition, as consumers of newspapers, we are part of our own study. More generally, in corpus linguistics, too, the analyst – his or her identity, personality, tastes, theoretical and methodological choices – forms an intrinsic part of the analytical procedure, and so I would go on to argue that, within our field, research is always bound to be more 'researcher-driven' than 'corpus-driven'. That is not, of course, to reject the importance of methodological rigour – acknowledging the role of the researcher is simply part of the necessary transparency. Where we can be 'scientific' is in the presentation of the research process – the analyses and the data ensuring that findings are, at the very least, verifiable and open to replication or para-replication, which is defined by Partington (2009: 293) as 'the replication of an experiment with either a fresh set of texts of the same discourse type or of a related discourse type'.

2.1 Tools

In addition to the researcher himself or herself, another major influence on the research is, of course, the selection of tools, as Partington (2009: 296) notes:

> our knowledge of the world is driven by the technical means we have to observe it. There is a sort of indivisible hermeneutic package – the observer (including mind), observational instruments, observations, object of observation. Alterations in any of the parts will affect the entire system, a process usually known as scientific advance.

At the macro level, the computing advances which permitted corpus linguistics to develop have changed our view of language, 'the language looks rather different when you look at a lot of it at once' (Sinclair, 1991: 100), but also in more micro-terms – the choice of one set of tools, one software package over another, carries distinct methodological/theoretical implications.

This paper makes use of both WordSmith Tools 5.0 (Scott, 2008) and Xaira in a complementary way. Given that the two sets of software were created with a different view of language in mind, and a different set of assumptions about the kind of questions one might want to ask of a corpus, the combination is ideal for an 'omnivorous' approach like Corpus-Assisted Discourse Studies (CADS). Broadly speaking, for me, WordSmith Tools offers a means of access to the data through the keywords function[2] – an essential feature for CADS, which methodology is inherently comparative (Partington, 2009), while Xaira is particularly useful for initial collocation analysis and works especially well on very large corpora.

More specifically, then, in this paper WordSmith was preferred for its comparative keyword function, cluster function, and the ease with which it allows and even encourages movement from concordance to text through the 'source text' function which takes the researcher straight to the node

---

[2] Throughout this paper, the terms 'keyword' and 'keywords' are used exclusively to refer to the WordSmith-generated statistically significant items.

within the context of the whole file. (Xaira has a similar function, but rather than displaying the section of text containing the item under investigation, it displays the begining of the file, which is not very helpful when using large files.) WordSmith also facilitates closer analysis of large numbers of concordance lines by allowing the researcher to assign the concordance lines to sets. As mentioned above, Xaira was generally employed for collocation analysis, because it is much quicker at concordancing, will immediately sort collocates by z-score or frequency, and has a useful 'funnelling' structure which allows the researcher to focus and restrict the analysis without exiting the previous sets of concordances. One drawback, however, is that when searching for co-occurring items there is no way of effectively sorting these concordance lines – and so for this we need to return to WordSmith.

The range of functions mentioned briefly above, is also used as a way of achieving a kind of data triangulation. In his overview of triangulation, Bryman (2003) defines data triangulation as entailing gathering data through different sampling strategies. I would suggest that, in corpus linguistic research, the different sampling strategies may be realised at various levels of analysis. First, at a higher level, through the selection of different sets of data when compiling the corpus; for instance, the SiBol corpora contain texts from three broadsheet newspapers, rather than just one. Secondly, at a lower level, sampling may be achieved by looking at the corpus through a series of different windows – in this case, I make use of keywords, concordances, keyword concordances, collocates (calculated by simple frequency of co-occurrence), and reading selected parts of the raw text in the hope of building up a more complete picture of the differences between our two corpora.

The methodology of this paper is in part, thus, deductive, in so far as it is driven by hypothesis testing, but it is also inductive, in that, having indentified the area of research, the results continued to direct the investigation.

2.2 Corpora

Like the other papers in this issue, the principal corpora employed are SiBol 93 and SiBol 05, which contain the entire output of three UK broadsheet newspapers: *Guardian*, *Telegraph* and *Times* from the years 1993 and 2005 (see Partington, 2010, for a more detailed description). However, other corpora, which were created specifically to aid investigation of the research question in hand, were also employed. In order to check hypotheses formed from the analysis of the SiBol corpora, I compiled two additional sets of corpora using the LexisNexis database, as illustrated in Figure 1.

The first, horizontal, extension runs chronologically parallel to the SiBol corpora and consists of all articles which contained the search term *scien** from 1993 and 2005 in the other major UK broadsheet newspaper, the *Independent*, and also from the *Daily Mail*. It would also have been

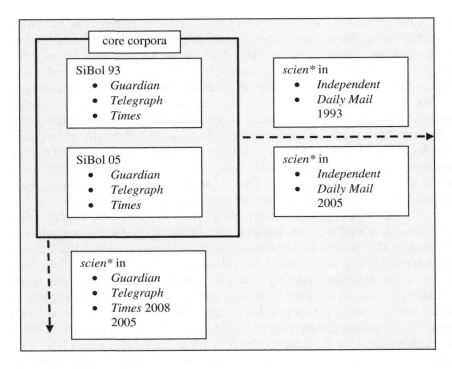

Figure 1: Diachronic and synchronic extensions to the core corpora

interesting to include other tabloids, but, unfortunately, the archives of the two biggest red-tops, the *Sun* and *Mirror* were not available for 1993 and so the essential diachronic element would have been precluded.

The second, vertical, set of additional corpora consists of articles containing the search term *scien** in the SiBol newspapers, *Guardian*, *Telegraph* and *Times*, for 2008. This group was created with the aim of corroborating or falsifying hypotheses relating to diachronic increases or decreases of a given feature. Any change – increase or decrease – observed in the 2005 data in relation to 1993 but which was not repeated in 2008 was not likely to be the result of an ongoing language transformation, but, perhaps, the result of seasonal changes or a short-lived alteration in function.

3. A little context: creating concordance-keywords

Like Marchi (2010), I employed an additional keywords list; a set of *concordance-keywords* which were created using the following process:[3]

---

[3] From a methodological viewpoint, it may be interesting to note that the process used in Marchi (2010) differs somewhat as she employs Xaira and collected whole articles.

1. To ensure optimum coverage, the search term *scien** was used. The wildcard * elicited a group of related and relevant words – *science, scientist, scientific* and *sciences*.
2. The search term was concordanced in SiBol 93 using WordSmith with 600 characters of co-text – approximately six/seven lines of text in a standard word processor.
3. The concordances of *scien** were saved in .txt format to compose a separate new 'corpus' consisting of concordance lines.
4. The process was repeated for SiBol 05.
5. WordSmith was used, first, to draw up wordlists and, subsequently, to create two sets of keywords – one for each of the two corpora of concordance lines (the wordlists from the concordance output of SiBol 93 and SiBol 05 were compared with each other, each acting as the other's reference corpus).

Given the size of the core SiBol corpora, and the popularity of the search term, *scien**, the two new corpora of concordance lines were still relatively large: the concordances from SiBol 93 amounted to a corpus 2,065,122 tokens and those from SiBol 05 to a corpus of 3,861,370 tokens.[4] This also meant that a large number of keywords were produced through the comparison, even using the most restrictive statistical settings available, and, therefore, in the results discussed below, I focus on the strongest 500 keywords for each concordance-corpus.

The calculation of concordance-keywords is particularly relevant when dealing with very large corpora since it allows us to make the amount of data for analysis more manageable and to target the comparison more closely by focussing on the key topics; it also assists in providing an overview of the semantic fields or *aboutness* (Scott, 1999) connected with each sub-corpus. On the other hand, we should be wary of over-interpreting findings from concordance-keywords, because some items will be the result of changes throughout the two original corpora, not necessarily the newly created corpora of concordance lines; for instance, among the concordance-keywords for *scien** in SiBol 93 there are various address forms, such as *Mr* and *Dr*, which are the result of changes in the use of honorifics throughout the newspapers (they tend to be used much less frequently in the more recent data) and are not connected with the specific context of reporting *science*. Therefore, the concordance-keywords need to be analysed in combination with the original keywords, and with reference to the wider co-text.

3.1 Brief overview of the *scien** concordance keywords

The keywords for the SiBol 93 *scien** concordance-corpus included a large number of items from the semantic fields of education: *courses,*

---

[4] The number given refers to the tokens used for wordlist.

subjects, curriculum, pupils and *compulsory*; jobs: *appointed, lectureship, vacancies, redundancies* and *appointments*; politics: *paper, white, minister, congress* and *ministry*; industry: *technology, industry, industrial, defence* and *manufacturing*; and finance: *wealth, recession, profits, expenditure* and *dollars*.[5]

These semantic sets were largely missing from the 2005 concordance-keywords list which was dominated by the areas in which science was being applied. Indeed, in the SiBol 05 *scien** concordance-keywords, it was much easier to identify thematic topics; for example, there was interest in climate change: *warming, global, emissions, greenhouse, Kyoto, temperatures, glaciers, carbon, renewable, energy* and *ice*; natural disasters: *earthquake, hurricane, hurricanes, Katrina, tsunamis, tsunami* and *supervolcano*; potential pandemics: *flu, pandemic, avian, birds, Tamiflu, poultry* and *SARS*; cloning: *cloning, Dolly, clones, cloned* and *clone*; and obesity: *obesity, fat* and *weight*. Other subject areas with at least two items included embryo research: *embryonic, embryos* and *embryo*; inter-planetary research: *aliens* and *alien, Beagle* (the Mars probe) and *Mars*; men's health: *Viagra* and *testosterone*; agriculture: *crops* and *rice*; fertility research: *fertility* and *reproductive*; evolution theory: *evolution* and *evolutionary*; and there were many more single items such as *autism, MRSA*, and so on.

In contrast, there were far fewer such subject terms in the 1993 concordance-keywords list, and it was less easy to identify linked areas, although the few that were found include dinosaurs: *dinosaurs, Jurassic* and *dinosaur*; whales: *whaling, whales* and *Minke*; nuclear power: *plutonium, Sellafield* and *Chernobyl*; computers: *computing, nimbus* and *cyberspace*; genetic research: *hereditary, genetic, genetics, gene* and *fingerprinting*; illnesses: *AIDS, HIV, fibrosis* and *cystic*; as well as the following single items: *ozone, chaos, motorway, homosexuality, scrapie, collider, transplant, fungus* and *volcano*.

So, from these thematic lists, despite the differences in frequency, we may observe some similarities in the interest in healthcare issues, whether it be *AIDS* and *cystic fibrosis* in 1993, or *autism* and *Parkinson's* in 2005. There was also shared interest in the effects of human activity on the environment; for example, *ozone* in 1993 and *global warming* in 2005.

Both sets also contained references to the process of doing science; from 1993 we find: *tests, equipment, laboratory, objective, equipped, instruments* and *machine*; and from 2005: *performing, researchers, treatments, study, scans, experimentation, lab* and *labs*. However, overall, a preliminary picture emerges of science in 1993 as a serious field of study and a profession, whereas in 2005 it appears to be used as a kind of adjunct to issues of current affairs.

Notable differences between the two *scien** concordance-corpora included the presence of *arts, cultures* and *culture* in the 1993 list and

---

[5] Five examples are given for each, here, for illustration.

creationism and *religious* in the 2005 list – an interesting oppositional difference to which we will return (see Section 5). Another salient difference is indicated by the appearance of the reporting verbs *says* and *said* in the 2005 list, as well as references to news-making (*stories, breaking, revealed, scare, concerns, groundbreaking* and *story*), which clearly indicate a change in the rhetorical function of science. This tendency may also be interpreted in view of the journalist Andrew Revkin's claims (cited by Kaplinsky, 2007) that 'the "study published today" model is driven by the "tyranny of the news peg"': reporters need a peg on which to hang their story and the publication or presentation of a paper plays this role'.

Having established a minimum level of context by looking at the areas in which science is discussed, we may now go on to look in more detail at *the science*.

4. Popularisation and/or trivialisation

Analysis of the 5L/5R collocates of *the science*, also highlighted a tendency towards a popularisation or tabloidisation of science over the twelve-year time period.

Two phrases which increased significantly were *the science of* (from 0.58 per million words (henceforth, pmw) to 2.75 pmw) and *the science behind* (from 0.05 pmw to 0.39 pmw).

The right collocates of *the science of* in SiBol 93 and SiBol 05 can be broadly grouped into five shared categories, as shown under Table 1.

The items marked in bold in Table 1, show the rise of health and entertainment-related sub-categories in SiBol 05 and an additional popularised set of R1 collocates relating to emotions, mental processes, sex/sexuality and belief or the supernatural.

A similar pattern of popularisation was seen with the phrase, *the science behind*. There were insufficient occurrences in SiBol 93 to identify clear patterns, but individual examples include *Nasa's* [sic] *search for extra-terrestrial intelligence, a Big Mac and a seminar on Marx, this 'bottom-gating' technique, the artefact* and *the changes*. In contrast, the phrase was much more frequent in SiBol 05, where a large proportion came from the heading of a regular section in the *Guardian* entitled, *The Science Behind the News*. However, even when these instances were removed, there was still a significant increase in occurrences over the twelve-year period. These remaining fifty-six instances fell into areas that were similar to the collocates of *the science of*. The main groups were areas of scientific research, such as: *animal research, Einstein's formula, global warming, GM crops* and *Herceptin*; health issues, particularly focussing on obesity/weight, for example: *getting fit, good health, sensible eating, the GI diet* and *the sensible drinking guidelines*; and everyday events: *a good night's sleep,*

	SiBol 93	*SiBol 05*
sciences	*aerobiology, biology, cosmology, cytology, ergonomics* (2), *palaeontology*	*biology, ecology, electromyography, evolution, forensic entomology, genetic engineering, genetics* (3), *geology, kinesiology, nanotechnology, modern medicine, molecular biology*
areas of traditional scientific endeavour	*artificial intelligence, classification, genetic engineering, genetics, heat, matter, medicine, metals, moving bodies, the make up of the earth's crust, optics, Parkinson's, the greenhouse effect, vaccination*	*anaesthesia, cancer, cell death, conservation, hurricanes* (2), *hydration, cartography, life* (5), *nuclear re-processing, nuclear weapons, weather forecasting, flying, friction and lubrification, information technology, language patterns, mind, plants*
social issues	*complexity, finance, herbalism, investments, locust control, marketing, music, national economic planning, Numerology, offender profiling, paper-making, perspective, prediction, racism, the future, rainmaking, restoration, selection, society, sound, statistics, Summitology, testing latex strength*	*crime, human behaviour, journalism, logistics, management* (2), *risk measurement, war, getting shoppers through the door, psephology, Kremlinology* ***ageing, obesity*** (2), ***nutrition, GI, sunburn, wellbeing, calorie counting***
everyday activity	*cooking* (2), *fitting the tool to the work, food preferences, romantic detection, scalp and hair, watching life pass you by, the examination syllabus*	*Christmas, clothes shopping, coffee, cookery, food* (6), *footwear, home lighting, ice-cream making, rock, scrummaging, snobbery, sports, brewing, central heating, mobile phones,* ***showmanship, singing, stand up, car chase cinematography, getting a laugh***

Table 1: R1 collocates of *the science of* (frequency of occurrence = 1, unless otherwise indicated)

	SiBol 93	SiBol 05
book titles	*Dress*, *Love*	*Aliens* (16), *Cooking* (8), *Discworld II* (5), *Feelings* (3), *Middle Earth* (4), *Seduction* (3), *Finding True Fulfilment* (2)
emotions		**emotions**, **fun**, **happiness**
mental processes		**decision making**, **deduction**,
sex/sexuality		**desire**, **female sexuality**, **seduction**, **sexuality**
supernatural		**belief**, **intelligent design**, **harnessing divine providence**, **the supernatural**, **monsters**

Table 1 (*continued*): R1 collocates of *the science of*

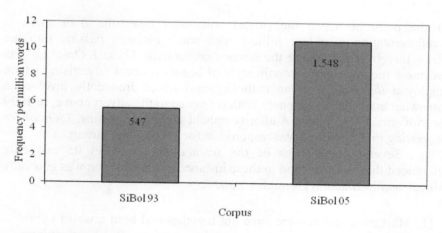

Figure 2: Occurrences of *the science* per million words

cooking, league tables, emotional responses to films, shoes, shopper's rush and *the smile*.

There is little doubt that science then has become popularised over the twelve-year period that was under investigation, being addressed to many more areas of life. The shift can either be seen unfavourably as representing the trivialisation and 'dumbing down' of science reporting, or more favourably as evidence of the widening appeal of science. As *the science* has gained weight as an authority, it is perhaps inevitable that the authority will be 'borrowed' by new fields; a clear example of this is the *L'Oréal Effect*.

A prominent R1 collocate of *the science* in SiBol 05 was *bit*, which was distributed across all three newspapers, and many UK-based readers will recognise the phrase *the science bit* from adverts for a large cosmetics and beauty company, *L'Oréal*. Essentially, the adverts employ the twin authorities of a guarantor, a well-groomed celebrity, and *the science*, as illustrated in the following transcript which used the actress Jennifer Aniston:

Aniston:	I've just fallen in love – with a shampoo. New L'Oréal Elvive, now even fine hair can have more body. Here comes the science bit – concentrate.
Male voice over:	L'Oréal has duplicated Ceramide one of the hair's natural strengtheners creating Ceramide R which penetrates the hair rebuilding its strength from within.
Aniston:	For stronger thicker fuller hair, wash the strength back in.
Male voice over:	L'Oréal Elvive shampoo with Ceramide R.
Aniston:	Because it's L'Oréal and I'm worth it.

At the point at which the (male) voice-over takes the floor there is a representation of a hair follicle with small globules passing into the pores, thereby emphasising the science credentials. These *L'Oréal* adverts became a metonym for a certain style of beauty product advertising which employed *the science* as an authority, and which frequently involved a somewhat questionable science. With reference to the advert above, in 1999 the Advertising Standards Authority upheld complains against *L'Oréal* for suggesting that Ceramide was responsible for making hair strong.

Several occurrences of *the science bit* in SiBol 05 explicitly referenced these adverts, and in these instances the evaluation was generally critical, as illustrated in Examples 1 and 2:

(1) Marketing and science have got together and bred a weird hybrid form of sales-experiments that have taken over our advertising culture. The next time they get to **"*the science bit*"**, don't forget to add a pinch of salt. As L'Oréal's customers have discovered, much of what we are told might just as easily be science fiction.

(SiBol 05, *Guardian*)

(2) potential buyers were assured that the high price was justified because of the sophisticated "engineering" techniques required to develop the "miraculous" cream. Here, as Jennifer Aniston might say in a L'Oral [sic] advert, is **the science bit**: "Through the wonders of engineering, water molecules are declustered, virtually split in two" [...] The Advertising Standards Authority found that the research was unpublished, non-peer reviewed and dependent on uncontrolled product trials.

(SiBol 05, *Sunday Telegraph*)

However, the majority of the examples (in a ratio of 5:1, or 7:2 if multiple examples from the same article are excluded) use the phrase uncritically, in a very similar way to the adverts, employing it as a discourse marker indicating that what follows will, (*a*) provide an explanation, involving scientific vocabulary, for the preceding assertion, and, usually, (*b*) explain why the entity under discussion is to be evaluated positively. For example:

(3) Smoothies are quick, nourishing, easy to eat (useful if your headache is so bad that chewing hurts) and completely delicious. That, a couple of aspirin and the rest of the morning snoozing in bed should speed recovery. ***The science bit.*** Fruit smoothies are full of fructose, a fruit sugar that speeds up the rate your body gets rid of the hangover-inducing toxins

(SiBol 05, *Telegraph*)

(4) Despite its long relationship with Nasa, [sic] as well as a multitude of other uses for its products, from bagpipes to dental floss, the company is probably most well-known for Gore-Tex, its breathable, water-resistant fabric that blesses a host of outdoors wear. At the core of all products (**here comes** ***the science bit***) is a versatile polymer, the sexily named polytetrafluoroethylene (PTFE).

(SiBol 05, *Times*)

As Examples 3 and 4 illustrate, *the science bit* does not appear to be the only language borrowed from advertising discourse (see Duguid, 2010, for analysis of the increase in evaluative and promotional lexis). In Example 3, the highly favourable evaluation serves to justify the selection of that recipe for the cookery section, while in Example 4, the article justifies or explains why the company was rated as number one in the paper's Top 100 Companies.

5. Science and authority

5.1 *the science*

In the article mentioned under Section 1, Furedi comments on how the use of the definite article as a pre-modifier to *science* contributes to the aura of authority. In order to investigate whether there had been a quantitative increase, I concordanced the phrase *the science* in each SiBol corpus and compared the relative frequencies. This ability to work on relative frequencies and relative percentage changes is one of the great advantages of working with a discourse-complete corpus – that is, a corpus which contains the entire output of a given discourse type over a specified period (as compared with working on topical corpora which have been collected by keyword). While such topical corpora are extremely useful for analysing changes in functions, or collocational frequencies and patterns relating to the topic under analysis, they cannot give reliable data regarding frequency changes. As we have seen with the SiBol corpora, the size of the broadsheet newspapers has changed enormously over the period in question (from approximately 100 million words in SiBol 93 to 145 million in SiBol 05) and, therefore, any results based on raw frequencies alone would be skewed.

As Figure 2 illustrates, there was a marked increase in references per million words to *the science* from 1993 (5.5 pmw) to 2005 (10.6 pmw), although it should be noted that the relative increase was far greater in the *Guardian* (174 percent) than the *Telegraph* (16 percent) or *Times* (31 percent).

5.2 *the science* as an autonomous entity

A detailed reading of the concordance lines showed that there were no instances of *the science* being used as an autonomous entity in SiBol 93, compared to eighteen unambiguous instances where it is used as an *actor* or *sayer* in systemic functional grammar terms in SiBol 05. For instance:

> (5) **Scientific studies show** this female reluctance to take risks is there from as young as one year old. Place a noisy, wind-up toy six feet from a child and a boy will approach it, while a girl will stay where she is and watch. It's called "inhibitory control". ***The science*** also **shows** that the difference is amplified by the way we rase [sic] our children.
>
> (SiBol 05, *Telegraph*)

This particular example also serves to illustrate a similar structure in 'scientific studies show'. Moving briefly from the concordance back to the corpus showed that the rather generic *scientific studies* increased by almost 120 percent from SiBol 93 to SiBol 05, compared to an increase of just 7 percent for the rather more precise, less vague, phrase *scientific study*.

Returning to Example 5, and this time moving from concordance to text, a key phase in CADS methodology – actually reading the article – showed that neither the *scientific studies* nor *the science* were given any more detail; there was no reference to the scientists involved, institutions where the research was carried out, publications where it was reported, or, indeed, any information that would allow for the facts to be verified or contested.[6] The reader is expected to trust or believe in *the science* without knowing *what* science. In other words, *the science* is being used to invoke an unspecified authority, augmenting the ethos rather than logos of the argument, as I hypothesised in the introduction.

---

[6] The full article is available online at: http://www.telegraph.co.uk/education/3352497/When-not-to-play-it-safe.html

guao05	he stereotypes. But does	*the science*	**stand up** to the theory? Do men and
gua05	ne TB experts setting out	*the science*	which, <u>they argue</u>, **proves a link** between
gua05	ne of which is anastrozole.	*The science*	**shows** that these drugs work - but many of
gua05	of cardiovascular disease.	*The science*	**suggests** that the walnut is one festive food
tim05	d hope to live to 150. But	*the science*	**suggests** that if you restrict calories a bit,
gua05	ding those for children. Yet	*the science*	that **supported** its approval was "biased,
tim05	w-risk area of medicine.	*The science*	effectively **relies on** replacing compounds
tel05	at atened with extinction. "	*The science*	which **produced** these beautiful kittens is
gua05	The dream is that, as	*the science*	**develops**, paraplegics might walk again,
tels05	pro-life campaigners fear	*the science*	**could make it easier** to clone babies,
gua05	e said: "Make no mistake,	*the science*	already **justifies** reversing - not merely
guao05	y objective is to see	*the science*	**trickle down** to the person on the street. I'd
gua05	to Tony Blair, sums it up: "	*The science*	**speaks clearly**: climate change is
tims05	. en a few years later when	*the science*	**changes** - as it always does: that is the
gua05	was a shame, because when	*the science*	**was allowed to speak for itself**, it was g.

Figure 3: *The science* as *actor/sayer*, shown in KWIC format

Further examples of *the science* as *actor/sayer* are shown in the KWIC format shown under Figure 3. The lines also illustrate the way in which *the science* is predominately used to affirm some proposition.

As we can see from the line-initial abbreviations, there were more instances in the *Guardian* than the other newspapers; but we should remember that it also contains more occurrences of the phrase *the science* overall (803 mentions in the *Guardian*, 245 in the *Telegraph* and 500 in the *Times*) so this is not necessarily indicative of a markedly different usage. We might also note that four of the above instances mark attribution, rather than averral, and another, the second concordance line above, contains the distancing *they argue*.

From the concordances analysed, the shift in usage from 1993 to 2005 seems clear. However, since the numbers are quite low, we might want to look for further corroboration or falsification. In this case, we move from concordance back to corpus building and, as described in the methodology section, an ad hoc plain-text corpus was compiled of articles containing the search term *scien** from the other main UK broadsheet, the *Independent*, and the mid-market tabloid, the *Daily Mail*.

This procedure retrieved 176 articles for 1993 and 248 for 2005 from the *Independent*. Again, there were no examples of *the science* as an autonomous personified entity in 1993 and a small number of examples (four) from 2005, including Example 6:

(6) 'In short, we have here a classic example of the problem or paradox of co-operation [. . .] ***the science* tells us clearly** we need to act now to reduce inputs of greenhouse gases

(SiBol 05, *Independent*)

In the *Daily Mail* there were seventy-two instances of *the science* in 1993 and 130 in 2005. As with the *Independent*, these results could suggest an increase but must be interpreted with caution, since we do not have information about the relative frequency in these ad hoc corpora. However, we can be more certain about our hypothesis that *the science* is increasingly used to refer to some unspecified, autonomous, authoritative entity. Once again, looking in more detail at the concordance lines confirmed that there were no examples in 1993 and a small number, eight, in 2005, for example:

> (7) Dr Julian Little, of the Crop Protection Association, which speaks for the pesticide industry, said: 'All ***the science* suggests** there is no risk when pesticides are applied properly.
>
> > (*Daily Mail 2005*)

These numbers are still very small, less than ten instances for each newspaper, but the findings are certainly consistent across the five different newspapers.

We could also test the hypothesis by looking at more recent data, for example, from 2008 – the most recent complete calendar year at the time of writing, using the second set of ad hoc corpora described under Section 2, which contain all articles containing *scien** from the three SiBol newspapers in that year. This supplementary dataset was found to contain 453 instances of *the science* in the *Guardian/Observer*, 196 in the *Telegraph* and 433 in *Times*. Examples of *the science* as *actor/sayer* were found in all three new corpora, and in greater numbers; while there were just nineteen instances in SiBol 05, there were fifty-two examples in the 2008 corpora. As we found previously, a large proportion of the examples were within quotations (eighteen out of the fifty-two), which could be an indication that, while the media is propagating the usage, it originated in other fields. There were also differences in usage among the three newspapers. For instance, of the twenty-eight examples in the *Guardian*, *the science* was followed in five by a reporting verb (*says* (2), *tells* (2) and *is saying*), and this is not a common usage in the other papers. This use of *the science* as *sayer* of a verbal process is illustrated in Example 8:

> (8) Tony Juniper, executive director of Friends of the Earth, said governments needed to improve all aspects of carbon markets, including setting more ambitious targets for emissions cuts, clearer standards and better monitoring of claimed credits. "There are big holes that need to be closed. That's not to say market mechanisms won't play a role – they probably will – but we need a much tighter framework to make the emissions reductions ***the science* says** we need to make."
>
> > (*Guardian* 2008)[7]

---

[7] The full article is available online at: http://www.guardian.co.uk/environment/2008/jun/25/carbonemissions.fossilfuels

As can be seen, *the science* is part of a quote by the executive director of Friends of the Earth, (which describes itself as, 'a national environmental organization dedicated to preserving the health and diversity of the planet for future generations').[8] As per Example 1, in Example 4 there is no specific reference to the source of *the science* and, indeed, it is largely incidental to the article, which focusses on carbon credit schemes.

It is also interesting to note that Example 8 forms the concluding paragraph of the article, and from reading all the instances, an interesting pattern of textual colligation emerged. This use of *the science* seems to be textually primed, in Hoey's (2005) sense, to occur in the final paragraph. Hoey's (2005: 129) third textual claim for the theory of Lexical Priming is that 'every lexical item (or combination of lexical items) is capable of being primed (positively or negatively) to occur at the beginning or end of an independently recognised "chunk" of text'. The apparent textual priming of *the science* is further illustrated in Example 9:

(9) Friends of the Earth executive director Andy Atkins said: "We are absolutely delighted that Ed Miliband has committed the UK to cutting its emissions by 80% by 2050 – this is what *the science* **demands**." But he added: "Miliband's admission that pollution from international aviation and shipping will be dealt with outside the bill is a sign that these industries are being picked out for special treatment yet again."

(*Guardian* 2008)

This paragraph concluded an article by the newspaper's political editor which was headlined 'Minister pledges UK will make 80 percent cut by 2050' and, as previously, *the science* mentioned in the quote is not discussed anywhere in the article, nor is it central to the topic of the article.

In SiBol 05, two examples out of the eighteen occurred in the final paragraph, compared to thirteen out of fifty-two in the 2008 instances (approximately 10 percent and 34 percent. respectively, although percentages on such small numbers should be treated with caution). This positioning is particularly interesting given that Murphy and Morley (2006: 213), who analysed the distribution of adverbials of stance, modals and the phraseology '*it is* + evaluative expression + *that/to*' in UK and US broadsheets and tabloids, found that 'several parameters which contribute to the characterisation of editorials and op-eds as persuasive discourse become more frequent in the last paragraph of the articles'. They liken this effect to the peroration of a speech – that is, 'the concluding part of an oration, speech, or written discourse, in which the speaker or writer sums up and commends to his audience with force or earnestness the matter which he has placed before them; hence, any rhetorical conclusion to a speech' (OED definition,

---

[8] See: www.foe.org/

cited in Murphy and Morley, 2006). Therefore, we may conclude, tentatively, that the increasing textual colligation of *the science* as *actor/sayer* for use in the last paragraph, the most strongly persuasive section of the article, offers some further evidence of its changing rhetorical role in the broadsheet newspapers.

An additional means of testing the hypothesis was through the investigation of the expressions *the research* and *the evidence* in the SiBol corpora. Regarding the former, an increase in frequency of 55 percent was observed, although the rise was consistent across the three newspapers. Cluster analysis showed an increase in the use of *the research* as *sayer* and, therefore, literally as the voice of authority; there was also an increase in references to *published*; these, together, indicate how research is being progressively made to fit the news formula, reflecting claims made in several areas for the growing influence of the press release in modern-day news reporting (see, for instance, Davies, 2008, and Gardner, 2008). In contrast to *the science* and *the research*, there was a decrease of 12 percent in references to *the evidence*, which seems to counter the overall trend. However, it may be that in the general shift towards raising *the science* as an unquestionable authority, *the evidence* itself becomes superfluous. Obviously, such interpretations of the data are always subjective, but it seems to be one plausible explanation and it is supported by the qualitative research of Taylor and Nathan (2002).

5.3 *Scientists* and *experts*

Expanding the focus of the analysis once again, we might look at those involved in science, for example, *scientists*, and the closely associated *experts*. The relative frequency of both plural forms *the scientists* and *the experts* increased from SiBol 93 to SiBol 05, by 36 percent and 103 percent, respectively, which suggests, once again, an increasing interest in reporting authoritative opinion.

The analysis was initially widened to look at all occurrences of *scientists*, and, subsequently, narrowed to analyse what *scientists* are portrayed as doing in the two corpora by examining the R1 collocates of the node, and then focussing only on those terms which would be classified as processes in Hallidayan terms. In the results which follow, I concentrate on the fifty most frequent processes in each list.

The first difference, in line with previous findings reported in this paper, was an increase in verbal processes in the R1 position, from eight in SiBol 93 to eighteen in SiBol 05. The two corpora shared *say, said, claim, announced, report* and *concluded*. While *told* only occurred in the fifty most frequent R1 collocates for the 1993 corpus, the 2005 corpus included *warn, predict, reported, warned, call, argue, revealed, suggest, confirmed, tell, insist* and *admit*.

First of all, we may note that the rise in verbal processes offers some support to the hypothesis that science is increasingly used as an authority; the expert opinion of *scientists* being employed to support a particular point or point of view. Secondly, the presence of *scientists warn* (thirty-one instances) and *scientists warned* (seventeen) in SiBol 05 compared to just one instance of each in the 1993 corpus (both from the *Times*) indicate a shift towards a more sensationalist way of reporting *scien**. This co-occurrence is of particular interest given that, overall, WARN decreased significantly from SiBol 93 to SiBol 05 (as reported in Clark, 2010). Once again, it should be noted that this increase was not equally distributed across the three papers; forty-four of the forty-eight occurrences in SiBol 05 were from the *Guardian*, as illustrated in Example 10:

(10) CO2 emissions turn oceans to acid
Soaring carbon dioxide levels have begun to make the oceans more acidic, **Britain's most senior *scientists* warn**. Exhausts from fossil fuels have already increased the acidity to a level that cannot be reversed in a human lifetime. Only swift and drastic cuts in emissions could begin to stabilise the oceans by 2100.

A Royal Society report published yesterday **warns** that many of the biological and chemical processes in the ocean have yet to be understood. But after a preliminary survey, ***scientists* fear** that: [...]
(SiBol 05, *Guardian*)

This pattern was particularly characteristic of the *Guardian* and, revealingly, the only newspaper with a comparable number was the *Daily Mail* for 2008 (sixty-two instances of *scientists warn/ed*). Example 10 was typical in that many of the occurrences in the *Guardian* related to climate change, and it has been quoted at some length to show how the alarm is built up. The somewhat sensationalist nature of the reporting starts with the headline 'CO2 emissions turn oceans to acid' which exaggerates a report on increasing acidity to the oceans actually turning to acid. The authority of the sources is then emphasised with *Britain's most senior scientists*, and the specification that it was a Royal Society report, while the danger is intensified by the repetitions of *warn*, *warns* and, finally, by *scientists fear* before the list of potential problems.

Furthermore, moving from the text back to the collocates and looking at the mental processes in the R1 position, we find that *scientists fear* occurs twenty-five times in SiBol 05 compared to just four times in SiBol 93, and the two most common contexts again relate to climate change (six instances, of which five occur in the *Guardian*) and also to bird flu / the H5N1 virus (seven instances, of which five occur in the *Guardian*).

This sensationalisation may also be seen in the use of the rather dramatic *scientists revealed* in SiBol 05 (eleven instances, compared to three in SiBol 93), which is illustrated in Example 11:

(11) Only last week, *scientists revealed* that colour influences performance in sport and teams with a bright red strip have a distinct competitive advantage over their rivals.

(SiBol 05, *Guardian*)

As we can see, in Example 11 the use of *revealed* appears somewhat hyperbolic given the context. This use of REVEAL appears to be part of a more general pattern of change in all the broadsheets: Clark (2010), in her analysis of evidentiality, notes an increase of 30 percent from SiBol 93 to SiBol 05, going on to add that, '[t]he revealing source is generally the offices of political figures, government authorities and institutions, and the surveys, analyses, reports and statistics they issue, whereby the exact identity of the "revealer" remains unknown, and the proposition cannot, therefore, be verified' (Clark, 2010: 148).

Returning to Example 11, it is also of interest to note the reference to *when* the science was carried out, namely, *last week*, which is premodified by an intensifier, *only*. In Example 10 we saw a similar temporal emphasis with the phrase *A Royal Society report published yesterday*. This proved to be a common feature of the reports, as illustrated in the following sentence concordances of *scientists revealed* (one from each paper):

(12) WHALES sing to each other across thousands of miles of ocean and use sound to create their own mental 'A to Z' of the sea floor, *scientists revealed* **yesterday**.

(SiBol 05, *Guardian*)

(13) *Scientists revealed* **last night** that at least one parrot that died last week had a strain of the H5N1 virus they had not seen before.

(SiBol 05, *Telegraph*)

(14) **Last week** *scientists revealed* that 20 per cent of Britain's wildflower species face extinction, probably as a direct result of modern farming techniques.

(SiBol 05, *Times*)

As I noted under Section 5.2, the references to the time of the 'revelation' act as a kind of justification for fitting the science reporting into the news-story format, which is typified by such temporal references.

Interestingly, while looking at these extended concordances, an article analysing the very phenomenon discussed in this section was found, highlighting the importance of looking for what news practitioners themselves have to say about their own trade. Ben Goldacre writes a weekly column for the *Guardian* called Bad Science (a collection of which have been published as a book, see Goldacre, 2008). In a column which analyses not a specific story, but how science is reported more generally, he writes the following:

> So how do the media work around their inability to deliver scientific evidence? They use authority figures, the very antithesis of what science is about, as if they were priests, or politicians, or parent figures. "Scientists today said... scientists revealed... scientists warned." And if they want balance, you'll get two scientists disagreeing, although with no explanation of why [...]

> The danger of authority figure coverage, in the absence of real evidence, is that it leaves the field wide open for questionable authority figures to waltz in.

(SiBol 05, Guardian)

So, as we have seen it is not just *the science* which is increasingly treated as an absolutist authority in the press, but also *the* (frequently unidentified) *scientists*.

A final observation on the R1 process collocates of *the scientists* concerns the presence of the modal *must* in the 1993 collocate list (eight occurrences, 0.08 pmw) and its absence from the 2005 list (seven occurrences, 0.047 pmw). While it is true that *must* was, proportionately, much more frequent in SiBol 93 overall, Xaira also shows that the strength of collocation with *scientists* was also somewhat greater in SiBol 93 (z-score 5.0) than SiBol 05 (z-score 2.4). Although the numbers are, clearly, too small for generalisations to be drawn, it is revealing to contrast for the two periods the instances of deontic modality where the obligation is portrayed as coming from the author: compare Examples 15 to 18 with Examples 19 to 21:

(15) Issues of ethics, politics, funding, are part of the coversation [sic] that **scientists must** have with the rest of us

(SiBol 93, Guardian)

(16) **scientists themselves must** acknowledge that not all, or even the most important, questions can yield to the methods of science

(SiBol 93, Guardian)

(17) **Scientists must** always try to spell out the implications and possible side-effects of their work. But decisions on how to apply new knowledge shouldn't be left to specialists – they should involve everyone.

(SiBol 93, Telegraph)

(18) Science can never provide the answers to everything; even when there is a unified theory that might explain almost everything, there must always be something the justification for the theory, the basic postulates that remains unexplained, unaccounted for, and **scientists must** accept this.

(SiBol 93, Times)

(19) **Scientists must** take the lead in casting aside the myths about ourselves, especially those who say we are rational and can live, or have ever lived, in harmony with nature.

(SiBol 05, *Guardian*)

(20) Educators should take more time to find out about the real prospects before condemning the sciences and encouraging students to take other career paths. **Scientists** and engineers **must** make a greater effort to extol the virtues of that career path.

(SiBol 05, *Telegraph*)

(21) **Scientists must** point out how many lives they save and improve, how many jobs they create and how much they contribute to our balance of trade. But they **must** make the message interesting and accessible, and ensure the communication is effective.

(SiBol 05, *Telegraph*)

In Examples 15 to 18 from SiBol 93, it is the very authority of the scientists which is being challenged. This is in stark contrast to the extracts from SiBol 05, Examples 19 to 21, where there is very little sense of criticism of the scientists in the *must* concordances – they are, mainly, being asked to improve their communication of the positive qualities of science. In Example 16, we may note that the force of the statement is strengthened by the emphatic *themselves*. There were just three instances of *scientists themselves* in SiBol 05 (0.02 pmw) compared to sixteen (0.16 pmw) in the smaller SiBol 93, of which at least seven carried a degree of unambiguous criticism, as, for instance, in Example 22:

(22) As illustrations of the ways in which **scientists themselves** sometimes encourage the belief that science is deeply dehumanising, one might quote an article in the New Statesman last year by Richard Dawkins, describing religion as a virus infection on mankind

(SiBol 93, *Guardian*)

The other figure which has become more frequent, as noted at the beginning of this section, is *the experts*, the relative frequency of which doubled from SiBol 93 to SiBol 05. Looking briefly at the R1 verbal process collocates (listed in order of frequency, and with a minimum of two occurrences), we can also see how the persuasive role of *the experts* has changed:

SiBol 93: *say* (18), *said* (8), *tell* (5), *predicted* (3), *assure* (2), *predict* (2), *insist* (2) and *describe* (2)

SiBol 05: *say* (192), *said* (74), *predict* (32), **advised** (11), *tell* (19), **advise** (9), **recommended** (7), **suggested** (7), **recommend** (5), *warned* (5), *commended* (5), *warn* (3), *admit* (3), *claim* (3), *told* (3), *concluded* (2), *describe* (2) and **suggest** (2)

As well as the more sensationalist *warn* and *warned*, *the experts* are not merely providing information in SiBol 05 but are accompanied by a range of verbal processes of admonition – recommending, suggesting and advising on a range of topics (highlighted in bold above); so, *the* (largely unidentified) *experts* advise on how we should live in Example 23:

(23) People who skip breakfast regularly are more likely to be overweight. If you must forgo a meal, it should be dinner. Of course, few of us live as **the experts recommend**.

(SiBol 05, *Times*)

Another potential sign of the increasing use of the authority model in science which was indicated in the R1 collocates, was the presence of the term *writer*, and so the concordance search was extended to *science writer*. Excluding references to writing awards, there were eighteen instances in SiBol 93, compared to forty-four in SiBol 05 (approximately twice as many instances, proportionately). In some cases, the term appeared in a description at the end of the column or article, which, presumably, serve as justifications of the author's authority to comment on the subject, while in other cases it appeared in book reviews, and in a third group it accompanied quotations. Of this last group, which is perhaps the most interesting, it is unclear in several instances exactly how the authority of the *science writer* impacts on the argument – indeed, it appears to be used fallaciously, where the authority of being a science writer is somehow transferred to another area, as, for instance, in Example 24, to education:

(24) Henry Gee, a palaeontologist and **a science writer** at Nature magazine, agrees that the way science is taught in many schools – with an emphasis on facts and formulae and very few whizzy experiments – leaves kids cold.

(SiBol 05, *Times*)

In such cases, the use of authority can only involve recourse to ethos and not logos, as I outlined in my introduction.

6. *Science and ?*

As noted under Section 3, among the *scien** concordance-keywords in SiBol 93 were the words *arts*, *culture* and *cultures*, while the keywords for SiBol 05 included *creationism* and *religious*. A similar pattern emerged from the collocates of *the science*. An analysis of the phraseologies of * *and*

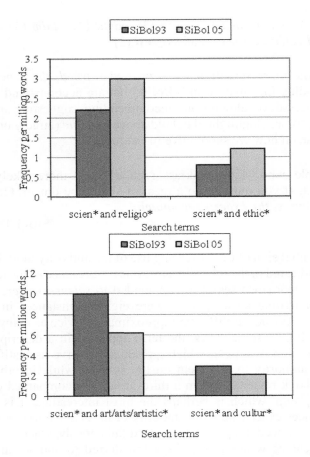

Figure 4: Relative change in references to science and religion, ethics, art and culture in SiBol

science, and *science and* * also showed a stronger collocation with *religion* in SiBol 05 than SiBol 93, while, conversely, the collocation with *culture* was weaker in the more recent corpus. Another interesting difference was the rise in occurrences of *ethics* in SiBol 05 in the pattern *science and* *. These findings seem to indicate that, while in 1993 the dominant paradigm was still centred on the Two Cultures debate (Snow, 1959; and Leavis, 1962) with literary intellectuals and scientists being depicted as being in an antithetical relationship, in 2005 the principal antagonist of science is seen to be religion. In order to investigate this further, WordSmith Tools was used to calculate the number of co-occurrences of *scien** within a twenty word span (20L–20R) of *art/arts/artistic**, *cultur**, *religio** and *ethic**, and the results are displayed under Figure 4. The wider span was used as it was hypothesised that the terms might not co-occur in the same phrase but the co-occurrence of the topics in relatively close proximity seemed relevant in the construction of science.

As the two charts under Figure 4 show, there was a decrease, in terms of relative frequency, in the co-occurrence of science and art (–38 percent) and science and culture (–30 percent), which contrasts with a diachronic increase in the co-occurrence of science and religion (+35 percent) and science and ethics (+50 percent). We may conjecture that the increase in co-references to *scien** and *religio** is driven by the creationist attacks on the central tenet of biology – evolution, and possibly by the new atheist attacks on religion from a supposedly scientific perspective. This hypothesis remains intuitive at this stage, but it is lent some support by comparing the relative frequency of *religio** in the two corpora, which increased by 26 percent overall and is, therefore, lower than that of the increase in the co-occurring *scien** and *religio**.[9]

Looking at the extended concordances of *scien** and *ethic** it immediately becomes clear that many of the occurrences are the result of the increased professionalisation of ethics – that is, the item appears as part of a job title. For example, out of the 181 instances, thirty co-occurrences accompany quotes or letters to the editor by the British Medical Association's Head of Science and Ethics, although in most cases the relevance of ethics to what was being discussed was unclear; this is true of Example 25:

(25) The medical establishment, however, is sceptical. Dr Vivienne Nathanson, the **head of science and ethics** at the British Medical Association, said that moderate exercise **should not** be set aside in favour of lazing around.

(SiBol 05, *Telegraph*)

A further six instances refer to *ethicists*, the professionals of ethics, and another sixteen refer to committees or groups, for example, the *Board of Ethics and Medicine*, or the *European Group on Ethics in Science*. In total, then, these account for approximately 29 percent of the co-occurrences. In terms of ethical topics in the context of *scien**, a preoccupation with genetics links the corpora. In SiBol 93 ethics and science came together over fertility treatment, and the supposed identification of a gene claimed to be associated with homosexuality; in SiBol 05 concerns were voiced about the overlapping areas of cloning, the use of human embryos, stem cell research and transplants, as well as genetically modified crops and animal testing.

With reference to the co-occurrences of *scien** and *religio**, in both corpora, as expected, there were instances where science and religion were opposed:

(26) **Religion** and **science** are more sharply opposed today that at any time since the enlightenment

(SiBol 93, *Guardian*)

---

[9] My thanks go to an anonymous reviewer for suggesting this test.

(27) I find it ironic that it is the **scientists** who seem most open to the unfolding mysteries of the Universe, while it is the **religious** who are stuck with a single, dogmatic viewpoint

(SiBol 05, *Times*)

... as well as instances in which they were seen as complementary:

(28) Many of the greatest scientists say they have had no difficulty in reconciling **religion** and **science**

(SiBol 93, *Times*)

(29) 'What is **science**?' he asks. '**Science** is an attempt to understand how our universe works, including humans. What is **religion**? It is an attempt to understand the purpose, the meaning of this universe, including humans.

(SiBol 05, *Guardian*)

... or even, in a small number of cases, instances in which they are equated in some way – frequently in contrast with another option:

(30) people have lost faith in official **science** and **religion**

(SiBol 93, *Times*)

(31) Alongside the **religious** and **scientific** responses to natural disaster lies another, humanist tradition

(SiBol 05, *Times*)

The most noticeable, but not unexpected, difference in the co-occurrences of *scien** and *religio** in SiBol 05 is the increase in references to *intelligent design* (overall, two occurrences in SiBol 93, neither with the current meaning, compared to 355 in SiBol 05), in which science appears to be invoked in support of religious argument. This rise in literal interpretations of the Bible was also illustrated by references to *creationism* which, as we saw under Section 3, also appeared in the SiBol 05 *scien** concordance-keywords list. Through expanding the search term we find that *creationis** occurs 0.21 pmw in SiBol 93 compared to 2.24 pmw in SiBol 05, although even this did not capture all instances, as per Example 32:

(32) In 1987 the Supreme Court ruled that "**creation science**" is **religious** and it is unconstitutional to teach it in public schools.

(SiBol 05, *Telegraph*)

Interestingly, in the co-occurrences from SiBol 93, where religious lexis was being used to describe science, it almost always involved an unfavourable evaluation as shown in Example 33 – a tendency that was approximately twice as frequent in SiBol 93 compared to SiBol 05.

(33) The environmentalism that has possessed the government of the United States has little to do with **science**. It is **religious** millenarianism

(SiBol 93, *Telegraph*)

Another salient development witnessed in SiBol 05 regards references to science *replacing* religion, both in the past and the present; this feature appears to be approximately twice as frequent in the 2005 corpus, as, for instance, in:

(34) more than a century ago the Victorians were beset by angst over what was seen as the retreat of **religion** in the face of **scientific** discovery or material progress

(SiBol 05, *Times*)

(35) [Peter Atkins] denounced his co-speakers for peddling "incomprehensible nonsense" and said it was **science's** duty to "stamp out the scourge of **religion**".

(SiBol 05, *Times*)

Finally, as noted under Section 5.4 with reference to the modal *must*, from reading the concordance lines, it appeared that 'science' in SiBol 93 was treated somewhat more critically, and where it was criticised from a religious/ethical viewpoint, the criticism was more likely to be on religious/ethical grounds, as opposed to the pseudoscientific grounds of creation science.

7. Conclusions

To summarise, then, the frequency of references to science, and more specifically, *the science*, increase notably in the period studied; but, of more significance, there are also clear changes in the rhetorical functions in the newspapers between 1993 and 2005.

In the corpora analysed here, *the science*, and similarly *the research*, *the scientists* and *the experts*, is seen to be used increasingly as an authority, as illustrated by the analysis of the processes attributed to *the science*, through the innovation of the verbal processes, in particular. In these instances, *the science* is used to function as ethos to indicate a simple, favourable evaluation of the argument. Furthermore, the collocation analysis, as focussed on the modal verb *must*, indicated a less critical attitude towards *the science* – although that is certainly not to deny the concern with pseudoscience and bad science which is evident in the 2005 corpus.

In part, the preoccupation with pseudoscience may be seen as a result of the popularisation/trivialisation of science in which it becomes employed as an absolute, unspecified authority in many areas. When conducting initial research for this paper, it seemed that the increased interest in *scien** in 2005 was a counter-instance to the general trend of popularisation and sensationalisation (as discussed in Duguid, 2010); however, closer analysis showed that, rather than reflecting a greater interest in traditional scientific issues, it is science terms which have shifted field – and this has been illustrated through the collocates of *the science of* and *the science behind*. Moreover, science is seen to be somewhat sensationalised with increasing co-occurrence with the more dramatic processes of WARN and FEAR, as well as references to *scare/s*, *concerns*, and so on, particularly with reference to climate change in the *Guardian*.

Furthermore, the analysis has highlighted how *scien** has become adapted to fit the structure of the news story, increasingly co-occurring with references to news-making such as *stories*, *breaking*, *revealed*, *groundbreaking*, *story* and time references.

Finally, we have noted how the principle antithesis to science, as created in the UK broadsheets, seems to have shifted from 1993 to 2005, from a focus on arts and culture in 1993 to religion in 2005.

In future research, it would be interesting to test these findings against a comparable corpus containing the entire output of the same newspapers from a more recent year. Conversely, as well as looking at greater quantities of data, it would be equally fruitful to focus on detailed comparative case studies from the two years – for example, to explore the relationship between *scien** and *ethic**, we might compare reporting on issues which feature in both SiBol corpora, such as research into genetics. Alternatively, to explore *scien** and *religio** we might compare the reporting on an issue which has traditionally been debated and challenged from a religious viewpoint, such as abortion, and on an issue which has traditionally 'belonged' to science, like evolution, and investigate how science and religion appear to have crossed over in these topics. Finally, in terms of a topical extension of this paper, it would be interesting to explore the two co-existing, but apparently incompatible, newspaper discourses of science as absolute authority and science as object of suspicion.

References

Aristotle. Rhetoric. Translation by W. Rhys Roberts. Available online at: http://www.public.iastate.edu/~honeyl/Rhetoric/

Bryman, A. 2003. 'Triangulation' in M.S. Lewis-Beck, A. Bryman and F.T. Liao (eds) Encyclopedia of Social Science Research Methods, pp. 1142–3. London: Sage.

Clark, C. 2010. 'Evidence of evidentiality in the quality press 1993 and 2005', Corpora 5 (2), pp. 139–60.

Davies, N. 2008. Flat Earth News. London: Random House.

Duguid, A. 2010. 'Newspaper discourse informalisation: a diachronic comparison from keywords', Corpora 5 (2), pp. 109–38.

Furedi, F. 2008. 'The tyranny of science', Spiked. Available online at: http://www.spiked-online.com/index.php?/site/article/4275/

Gardner, D. 2008. Risk: The Science and Politics of Fear. London: Virgin Books.

Goldacre, B. 2008. Bad Science. London: Harper Collins.

Hanson, N.R. 1958. Patterns of Discovery. Cambridge: Cambridge University Press.

Hoey, M. 2005. Lexical Priming. London: Routledge.

Kahane, H. and N. Cavender. 2005. Logic and Contemporary Rhetoric: The Use of Reason in Everyday Life. Belmont: Wadsworth Publishing.

Kaplinsky, J. 2007. 'The dangers of lazy science reporting' Spiked. Available online at: http://www.spiked-online.com/index.php?/site/article/3911/

Leavis, F.R. 1962. Two Cultures? The Significance of C.P. Snow. London: Chatto and Windus.

Marchi, A. 2010. ' "The moral in the story": a diachronic investigation of lexicalised morality in the UK press', Corpora 5 (2), pp. 161–89.

Murphy, A. and J. Morley. 2006. 'The peroration revisited' in V.K. Bhatia and M. Gotti (eds) Explorations in Specialized Genres, pp. 201–15. Bern: Peter Lang.

Partington, A. 2009. 'Evaluating evaluation and some concluding thoughts on CADS' in J. Morley and P. Bayley (eds) Wordings of War: Corpus-Assisted Discourse Studies on the Iraq War Conflict, pp. 261–303. London and New York: Routledge.

Partington, A. 2010. 'Modern Diachronic Corpus-Assisted Discourse Studies (MD-CADS) on UK newspapers: an overview of the project', Corpora 5 (2), pp. 83–108.

Scott, M. 1999. WordSmith Tools Help Manual. Oxford: Oxford University Press.

Scott, M. 2008. WordSmith Tools version 5. Liverpool: Lexical Analysis Software.

Sinclair, J.M. 1991. Corpus, Concordance, Collocation. Oxford: Oxford University Press.

Smith, M.J. 1998. Social Science in Question. London: Sage Publications.

Snow, C.P. 1959. The Two Cultures and the Scientific Revolution. Cambridge: Cambridge University Press.

Stubbs, M. 2009. 'The search for units of meaning: Sinclair on empirical semantics', Applied Linguistics 30 (1), pp. 115–37.

Taylor, C. 2008. 'What is corpus linguistics? What the data says', ICAME Journal 32, pp. 143–64.

Taylor, N. and S. Nathan. 2002. 'How science contributes to environmental reporting in British newspapers: a case study of the reporting of global warming and climate change', The Environmentalist 22 (4), pp. 325–31.

Printed and bound by CPI Group (UK) Ltd, Croydon, CR0 4YY

14/03/2025

01833348-0001